Rational Commitment

RATIONAL COMMITMENT

A Foundation for Macroeconomics

BRENDAN O'FLAHERTY

Duke University Press Durham, 1985

Printed in the United States of America on acid-free paper
∞
Library of Congress Cataloging in Publication Data
O'Flaherty, Brendan. Rational Commitment.
Bibliography: p. Includes Index.
1. Rational expectation (Economic theory) I. Title.
HB172.5.035 1985 339 85-13161 ISBN 0-8223-0454-6

To Charles O'Flaherty and Harry L. Wheeler

Contents

Acknowledgments

Without the encouragement and assistance of many people this book would not have been completed, or even started. My debts are so large and widespread that they are difficult even to catalogue.

My primary debt is to my parents, Annette and Charles O'Flaherty. Neither my father, nor my "political father," Harry L. Wheeler, lived to see the book completed, and it is dedicated to them.

I want to thank the people who actually produced the manuscript: Martha Hayward Sanders, who did most of the typing, Bobbi Norman, Eleanor Martins, Maggie Pinckney, Angenell Jackson, and LaVerne Craddock. Tom Banker and Richard Hillman are responsible for some of the artwork. Without the indulgence of the staffs of the Seton Hall University Library, the Newark Public Library, and the South Orange Public Library, there would have been nowhere to write the book.

By far the largest category of helpers were those whose moral support kept a three-year journey moving: Dan Akwei, in whose office the manuscript usually stayed, Mayor Kenneth A. Gibson, Zinnerford Smith, State Senators John P. Caufield and Wynona Lipman, Raymond Durkin, Elton Hill, Ed Segraves, Pearl Beatty, Stephen Adubato, John Alati, Adrianne Davis, Bill Werner, the late Mother Nellie Grier, Hubert Williams, Sonia Haddad, Joyce Moore, Essie Richardson, Mary Willis, Remay and Emory Pearce, and all my former colleagues at the Mayor's Office of Employment and Training and the New Jersey Institute of Technology.

The West Ward Democratic Committee deserves special recognition: its 78 members not only encouraged me, but they also reelected me each year and thus kept me in touch with reality. So too does Yvonne Still, whose forbearance, knowledge, help, and zeal for the enterprise did much to make it possible.

My intellectual debts are to my teachers at Harvard, particularly Richard Freeman, Jerry Green, Richard Zeckhauser, and Thomas Schelling. More directly, the comments of several anonymous reviewers improved the book considerably, and probably would have improved it more had I followed all of them.

I also want to thank Richard Rowson and Duke University Press. Their patience and faith have been exemplary.

Finally, I must beg one more indulgence from all those whose contributions I have inadvertently failed to acknowledge.

Newark, New Jersey
November 1984

I ▪ Why Read This Book

I sometimes feel inclined to apply the historical method to the multiplication table. I should make a statistical inquiry among school children, before their pristine wisdom had been biased by teachers. I should put down their answers as to what 6 times 9 amounts to, I should work out the average of their answers to six places of decimals, and should then decide that, at the present stage of human development, this average is the value of 6 times 9.

P. E. B. JOURDAIN, *The Philosophy of Mr B*rtr*nd R*ss*ll.*

The people that economists write about do not use historical-method multiplication tables; they do arithmetic right. They are, it is said, rational. Economists write about such people because of what Arrow (1951, p. 406) identified as "the general tradition of economics, which tends to regard rational behavior as a first approximation to actual."

Why, then, do economists so frequently disagree in their predictions of what rational people will do? The reason is simply, as von Neumann and Morgenstern (1944, p. 9) have stated, "that there exists, . . . no satisfactory treatment of the question of rational behavior." And a little reflection will show that treating this question satisfactorily is no small problem.

There are, to be sure, occasions when the problem of rationality is not difficult. For a Robinson Crusoe alone in a world of certainty there is an unambiguous correspondence between actions and outcomes; every action by Crusoe is associated with an outcome that it brings about. If we define "outcome" broadly enough to include everything Crusoe cares about (including the exhilaration or exhaustion needed to bring it about), then all economists would predict that Crusoe would take the action associated with the outcome he most desires. Everyone would call such behavior rational.

The one-person world with certainty is a world in which we can talk about rationality without trepidation. For every action by Crusoe, there is only one outcome; and so the rational Crusoe will choose the action with the best outcome. This idea is the basic principle of rationality.

When Mother Nature or Friday enters the picture, however, outcomes will depend on their actions as well as Crusoe's. Crusoe's actions will no longer be linked uniquely to outcomes. Whether Crusoe wants to go swimming will depend not only on his preferences for aquatic exercise, but also on whether Mother Nature has placed man-eating sharks nearby; whether he wants to make marmalade will depend on whether Friday has made toast. "The action with the best outcome" will no longer be clear for Crusoe; how Crusoe will act and what action is rational will no longer be clear for us observers. Generalizing rationality from the one-person world is not easy.

The tradition of economics has been to treat a many-person world as a collection of simultaneous one-person worlds. Economists would study poker as a collection of simultaneous games of a suitably defined variant of solitaire. This tradition is a reasonable response to the complexity of the many-person world. Just as the best place to search for a lost dime on a dark street is under a street light (to mangle Tobin's simile) so the best place from which to investigate rationality in a many-person world is under the relatively bright light of what we know (and we know quite a bit) about rationality in a one-person world.

Using this light is what has made economics different from other social sciences such as psychology and sociology, which tend to wander around in the dark. Many worthwhile results have been found beneath the street light of one-person world rationality, and it is the goal of this book to find a few more pieces of change—some change people did not expect to be there—under that street light. We look there because we are, quite frankly, afraid to venture into the dark.

But while economists are agreed about using the light of one-person world rationality to discuss rationality in many-person worlds, they are not agreed on how to use it. A many-person world should be treated as a collection of one-person worlds, but what collection? This is the question that divides economists.

Nash (1950, 1951), for instance, asks us to imagine that each person in a many-person world acts as if the actions of all other people are fixed. Then outcomes are uniquely linked to the person's action, and each, we may assume, takes the action with the best outcome. Similarly von Neumann and Morgenstern (1944) ask us to imagine that each person acts as if, whatever action he or she chooses, everyone else will get together and choose a set of actions that will make him or her as bad off as possible. Since this paranoia makes everyone else's action depend on the action of the person we are concerned about, it makes outcomes solely dependent on that person's actions, and thus creates (for each person) a one-person world in which rationality is well defined. (Extending this analysis to some of the cooperative game theory solution concepts is more difficult, but is done in chapter 2.)

The best known trick for turning many-person worlds into collections of simultaneous one-person worlds is due neither to Nash nor to von Neumann and Morgenstern, but to Walras. Each Walrasian agent acts as if all other agents were vending machines, giving out goods and services in amounts exactly proportional to the amounts of goods and services that the agent gives them. Theories of monopolistic competition use the Walrasian trick, but do not require that vending machines maintain exact proportionality between receipts and disbursals. Microeconomics has come to be almost synonymous with the Walrasian tradition.

Keynes and his followers used still another method to decompose many-person worlds into collections of one-person worlds. Unfortunately, though, Keynes did not explicitly state his theory of rationality and dealt instead only with its consequences, which at the time were of the utmost importance. The result of this lacuna has been the emergence of a distinct division of economics, macroeconomics, whose existence without a theory of rationality has remained an embarrassment to the profession:

> Mathematical general equilibrium theorists have at their command an impressive array of proven techniques for modelling systems that "always work well." Keynesian economists have experience with modelling systems that "never work." But, as yet, no one has the recipe for modelling systems that function pretty well most of the time but sometimes work very badly to coordinate activities. And the analytical devices and routines of neo-Walrasian general equilibrium theory and Keynesian theory will not "mix." (Leijonhufvud, 1976, p. 103)

This embarrassment has intensified in recent years because the success of macroeconomics in providing useful policy advice—the record that could be used to silence its theoretically inclined detractors—has diminished. Fisher (1976, p. 4) expresses a common sentiment: "I yield to few economists in my ignorance of the causes or cures for the situation of combined recession and inflation which has troubled our economies in recent years, but I cannot help suspecting that the apparent partial failure of macroeconomic analysis to cope with it may stem from the attempt to go on dealing at an aggregate level with general equilibrium questions involving relatively detailed microconsiderations."

This book tries to solve the problem of macroeconomics' embarrassing lack of a foundation in explicit rationality. It uses a new concept of rationality—a new way of decomposing many-person games into collections of one-person games—to do so. This concept turns out to include all the other types of rationality that have been used heretofore as special cases. To illustrate the power of the methods we propose, we develop a macroeconomic model from first principles.

Of course, the problem of reconciling macroeconomics with a theory of rationality has by no means been neglected by other writers. In particular, the contributions of Clower (1965), Leijonhufvud (1968), Barro and Grossman (1971), Drèze (1975), Boehm and Lévine (1976), and Malinvaud (1977), inter alia, have shown how some Keynesian results can be obtained by modifying Walrasian rationality to allow for quantity constraints (vending machines with depletable stocks). My debt to these writers is immense. Most of the macroeconomic results in this book will be similar to those of the quantity constraint school, but will be placed in the broader context, and acquire the firmer foundation, of a more general and explicit view of rationality.

Why bother? Because macroeconomic problems are serious ones and economists have no good ways of attacking any kind of problems, except in the light of rationality. Over the last decade macroeconomics has not enjoyed the same degree of success that microeconomics—a theory firmly based in rationality—has. This disparity strongly suggests that reconciling macroeconomic theory to explicit rationality will improve macroeconomic policy. Good theories make good practices—that is our hope at any rate.

I

But what makes theories good? Surely this question must be answered if we are to try to improve on existing theories.

The first desideratum is simplicity:

> All scientific activity amounts to the invention of and the choice among systems of hypotheses. One of the primary considerations guiding this process is that of simplicity. Nothing could be much more mistaken than the traditional idea that we first seek a true system, and then, for the sake of elegance, seek a simple one. We are inevitably concerned with simplicity as soon as we are concerned with system at all; for system is achieved just to the extent that the basic vocabulary and set of first principles used in dealing with the given subject matter are simplified. (Goodman, 1958, p. 1064)

Theories that are as complicated as their subject matter do nothing to explain or elucidate that subject matter; they merely substitute one complex morass for another. "Frustra fit per plura quod potest fieri per pauciora."[1]

Consideration of the following two very short "theories" provides a startling example of the potency of simplicity:

Theory A. Humans shot in the heart always die.

Theory B. Humans shot in the heart always die, except for you tomorrow.

The two theories are observationally equivalent today; the only difference between them is that theory A is simpler than theory B. Many philosophers therefore take the strong willingness of almost everyone to act on the precepts of theory A rather than theory B as evidence of the compelling power of simplicity.[2]

There is no consensus on what simplicity is.[3] Just counting axioms, for instance, will get us nowhere. Rudner (1966, p. 45) points out that "the number of axioms (assuming it is finite) of any formulation can be trivially reduced to one by the simple operation of conjunction. By the criterion of number of axioms every formulation would thus be equivalent to one that was maximally simple. . . . Nor would it be possible to ameliorate this unwelcome result by any stipulation regarding the number of conjuncts in a set of axioms. For, any pair of conjuncts may be trivially reduced to a corresponding unconjoined statement by appropriate definitions involving the predicates originally contained in those conjuncts."

Intuitively, though, we may speak about two aspects of simplicity. The first is scope. The wider a theory's scope, the fewer theories are needed to explain the subject matter within its scope. Thus a single theory—a single concept of rationality—for both macro- and microeconomics is ipso facto desirable, as long as it is more simple than the conjunction of the prevailing macro- and microtheories. The second aspect of simplicity is ontological parsimony: "Pluralitas non est ponenda sine necessitate," as William of Occam put it. Primitive terms should be as few as possible.

The second major desideratum for a theory is empirical accuracy. Not all propositions in a theory need to be empirically testable, but there should be some that are, and these should be true. This requirement distinguishes our quest from pure logic or mathematics.

1. This is a form of the Razor that Occam himself used. The commonly quoted version, "Non sunt multiplicanda entia praeter necessitatem," is an eighteenth-century paraphrase. See Thorburn (1918).

2. For a dissenting view, see, e.g., Reichenbach (1968).

3. For attempts to answer this question, see, e.g., Goodman (1958), Rudner (1961), Ackermann (1960), Kemeny (1955), Putnam (1975), Boyd (1973), and Sober (1975).

It also means that when we choose among concepts of rationality, it will be equilibria we are concerned with. By equilibrium we mean a state where all people are acting rationally (for a particular definition of rationality). Postulating a definition of rationality is thus equivalent to predicting that only equilibria under this definition will occur. Approaches to rationality that cannot give rise to equilibria are thus clearly defective. Similarly we may say, e.g., that the existence of unemployment argues against Walras's definition of rationality, since no Walrasian equilibrium has unemployment, and that the existence of trade argues against Nash's definition of rationality, since all Nash equilibria are autarkic.

Notice, then, that we do not judge rationality definitions by how satisfying they are to introspection, or by how plausible the accompanying stories of out-of-equilibrium adjustment appear, especially when that out-of-equilibrium adjustment is not governed by the rationality definition itself. Most definitions are radical failures on both these counts anyway (does anyone really do calculus in the grocery store?).

Our goal, therefore, is to find a simple definition of rationality that has as equilibria the kinds of things we observe happening in the world.

II

The way we try to do this is through game theory. Essentially, the approach follows Shubik's (1975) suggestion that macroeconomics be analyzed with the tools of noncooperative game theory. There are two reasons, closely related to each other: the first is that game theory has a concept, that of a strategy, that makes questions of time tractable; the second is that game theory was explicitly designed for talking about rationality in cases where agents are mutually interdependent and conscious of their mutual interdependence. Such phenomena abound in macroeconomics. Consider, for instance, Keynes's stock market (1936, pp. 155–156):

> Nor is it necessary that anyone should keep his simple faith in the conventional basis of valuation having any genuine long-term validity. For it is, so to speak, a game of Snap, of Old Maid, of Musical Chairs —a pastime in which he is victor who says *Snap* neither too soon nor too late, who passes the Old Maid to his neighbour before the game is over, who secures a chair for himself when the music stops . . .
>
> Or, to change the metaphor slightly, professional investment may be likened to those newspaper competitions in which the competitors have to pick out the six prettiest faces from a hundred photographs,

> the prize being awarded to the competitor whose choice most nearly corresponds to the average preferences of the competitors as a whole; so that each competitor has to pick, not those faces which he himself finds prettiest, but those which he thinks likeliest to catch the fancy of the other competitors, all of whom are looking at the problem from the same point of view. It is not a case of choosing those which, to the best of one's judgment, are really the prettiest, nor those which average opinion genuinely thinks the prettiest. We have reached the third degree where we devote our intelligence to anticipating what average opinion expects average opinion to be. And there are some, I believe, who practice the fourth, fifth and higher degrees.

Infinite regress—I believe that you believe that I believe that you believe, etc.—is a problem at the heart of game theory, and game theory's techniques have been deliberately designed to describe rationality in its presence. Indeed, game theorists were the first to raise the fundamental question of what rationality really is, and have supplied most of the answers to this question.

This book, then, is about game theory in the wide sense that it attempts to describe rationality in non-Walrasian ways in situations involving mutually interdependent conscious actors.

The book incorporates from game theory a distrust of the concept of "expectations," an idea that has played a major role in macroeconomics, but has never played such a role in game theory. This distrust is not of the literary use of the term—changing any specification of rationality from "agents act as if" to "agents act as if they expect" changes nothing. What is objected to, and what is missing from game theory, is the view that agents act as if the actions of other agents were determined by chance, with probabilities somehow related to some set of external objective events. "Expectations" here are used to relate the objective events to unobservable probability distributions in agents' heads, and these unobservables in turn determine how each agent associates his or her actions with outcomes. Occam's Razor argues against such a two-step process, and the issue is examined in more detail in chapter 5.

III

Such is the approach around which the book is built. We begin our discussion, then, in the next chapter with a broad view of the rudiments of game theory. This is a necessary preliminary. Particular attention is paid to the various definitions of rationality—or, as they are more usually known, solution concepts—that have been used and how they have difficulty in coming to grips with macroeconomic problems.

The third chapter introduces and develops the solution concept we will be using, which we call "commitment equilibrium." It also relates this solution concept to the von Neumann-Morgenstern and Nash concepts, and shows how any equilibrium of a system built on any imaginable version of individual rationality must be a commitment equilibrium. Appendix B extends the idea of commitment equilibrium to games where some commitments may be impossible.

The fourth chapter extends our results in chapters 2 and 3 to games involving time, ignorance, and uncertainty.

In the fifth chapter we consider in detail the various ways people have proposed to relate objective events to internal expectational numerical probabilities, and demonstrate the pitfalls of this approach.

In chapter 6 and its sequelae (including Appendix A, on social contracts and crime) we turn to the consideration of particular games and particular equilibria these games may possess. In the sixth chapter we use some very simple examples to show how commitment equilibrium works in economic games. We also develop a method for dealing with more complex games; this method, moreover, permits us to see easily how Walrasian equilibrium is related to commitment equilibrium.

Building on chapter 6, chapter 7 introduces time into the analysis of economic games, and studies a series of increasingly more complicated problems. We see here for the first time how commitment equilibria with involuntary unemployment can occur. In chapter 8 we first show how large numbers of agents need not obliterate non-Walrasian results, and then go on to examine the workings of trade unions and the economics of discrimination.

Chapters 9 and 10 present a macroeconomic model that is complicated enough to include such things as money, banks, stocks and bonds, capital, and embodied technological progress. It is, though, *a* model, not *the* model. Our goal, after all, is primarily methodological: we are building foundations, not houses. But methods are justified only by their uses, and something would be seriously wrong with a foundation if no house could be built upon it. The easiest and most convincing way to show that a house can be built is to build one, and that is what we do in these chapters. The house we happen to build for illustrative purposes, then, is not the only type of house that can be built on these foundations; the construction will have succeeded if it convinces more expert builders that their laboring to erect a better house on these foundations is not likely to be in vain.

Chapter 10, because it deals with macroeconomic policy, also investigates the sort of advice that economists can give, both to well-meaning governments and to well-meaning citizens. The latter question, while not novel, has not received much attention recently.

Just-wage and just-price theories have been in disrepute in economics ever since Adam Smith argued for the optimality of an equilibrium based on unrestrained greed, but there would seem to be no a priori reason for such obloquy to carry over into situations where the "invisible hand" does not seem to work properly. Biology and medicine have not been diminished in scientific stature by giving advice to individuals on matters both private ("Wash your hands before eating") and social ("Don't urinate on your neighbor's lawn"); why should economics shy away from such activities? Indeed, it is often easier to find well-meaning citizens to advise than benevolent governments.

The conclusion comes at the end, which is a very good place for it.

Some sections of the book are quite technical; others are chiefly literary. Little mathematical knowledge is assumed beyond standard optimization theory, and no knowledge of game theory, but for the technical sections a bit of mathematical sophistication and, unfortunately, a generous dose of patience are needed. For those who are willing to take their results on faith, however, the proofs and technical derivations can be omitted costlessly. Model construction, especially in chapters 2, 4, 7, and 9 is also sometimes time-consuming, but omitting it is likely to be somewhat more expensive than omitting proofs.

Chapter 3, the discussion of commitment equilibrium, and chapter 11, the conclusion, contain the book's central results; even the most impatient readers should look at these, although chapter 3's proofs can of course be omitted. Readers whose primary interests are in game theory and philosophy will find the first five chapters more valuable than the remainder, although chapter 6 and Appendix B will also appeal to game theorists, and chapter 10 and Appendix C to those with a philosophical inclination. Impatient macroeconomists can concentrate on chapters 7, 9, and 10, while impatient microeconomists can look at chapters 6 and 8 and Appendix A.

There is, though, a certain logic, however slight, to the way the book has been put together, and a certain unity, however mystical, to its results; reading the chapters in sequence, therefore, has certain advantages.

PART ONE ▪ GENERAL

2 ▪ Game Theory

For some minutes Alice stood without speaking, looking out in all directions over the country—and a most curious country it was. . . . "I declare it's marked out just like a large chess-board!" Alice said at last. "There ought to be some men moving about somewhere—and so there are!" she added in a tone of delight, and her heart began to beat quick with excitement as she went on. "It's a great huge game of chess that's being played—all over the world—if this *is* the world at all, you know."
LEWIS CARROLL, *Through the Looking Glass*

Game theory is not the frivolous study that sometimes comes to people's minds when they hear the name for the first time. Parlor games present situations in which the rewards to each agent depend on the actions of other agents, as well as on the actions of the agent himself or herself. This property is not unique to parlor games. What is learned about the formal structure of parlor games can be applied in situations that share this interdependence property. We call serious activities like war, diplomacy, crime, and markets "games" not to trivialize them or imply that they are fun, but rather to point out that there are general results from the mathematical theory of mutual interdependence that may be useful.

This chapter will provide the reader with the smattering of knowledge about game theory that is needed to follow the argument in later chapters. We will also state explicitly what we mean by rationality, and show how game theory has evolved as an exercise in rationality. Finally, we will note why much that has already developed under the rubric of game theory is inadequate for the problems we are seeking to address, and why we will have to create (in chapter 3) a more general solution concept.

I

By a *game* we will mean here a set of rules. "The game is simply the totality of the rules which describe it" (von Neumann and Morgenstern,

1944, p. 49). Those rules describe how the actions taken by the persons participating in the game—the *players*—determine the utility they will enjoy. The simplest way to summarize a game Γ and its rules is by a triplet, $\Gamma = \langle I, S, f \rangle$, where I is the index set of players, S is called the *strategy space*, and f is called the *payoff function*. I tells who plays the game, S tells what they can do, and f says what happens when they do it. Games described in this manner are usually referred to as "normal form games," and will be our concern in this chapter.

Let us be more precise about the constituents of a normal form game. The strategy space S contains all the sets of possible actions by the players in I. Specifically, a possible action by player i will be called a *strategy*, and the set of all strategies for player i will be called S_i, player i's strategy set. In a simple game like Matching Pennies, each player's strategy set may consist of only two simple possible actions—choosing heads and choosing tails—while in complex games like those we discuss in chapter 4, strategy sets can be enormous and complicated.

The strategy space S, then, is the Cartesian product of all the players' strategy sets

$$S = \mathop{\mathsf{X}}_{i \in I} S_i$$

and its elements are n-tuples of strategies, where n is the number of players. Such n-tuples of strategies (i.e., the elements of S) are called *situations*. A situation thus represents a combination of actions that the players in Γ can take.

The payoff function f tells what happens to each of the players as a result of their choosing a particular situation. Specifically, the payoff function f assigns to every situation s in S an n-vector of utilities:

$$f : S \to \mathbf{R}^n.$$

Thus $f_i(s)$ is the scalar that gives player i's utility when the players in the game have chosen the n-tuple of strategies s. What player i gets depends not only on his own action, but on the actions of the other players as well —and what the other players get depends on what player i does, as well as what they themselves do.

While quite general, the normal form characterization of a game appears to neglect the effects of time, uncertainty, ignorance, and information. However, we will see in chapter 4, that such appearances are deceiving: appropriate definitions of "strategy," "player," and "payoff function" are all that is needed.

II

We want to think about what it might mean for a player to act rationally in a game. We noted in the first chapter that disagreement prevails on this matter. Nevertheless it is possible to identify certain elements that all attempted definitions have, and that anything that somebody wanted to call rationality would have to have. To do this, we will have to invent a nomenclature for the general problem of rationality, and relate this nomenclature from time to time with nomenclature that has grown up around specific approaches to rationality.

Rationality in games is a problem, it will be recalled, because players can choose only their own strategies, while utility is ascribed only to situations. For a player to decide on an action, he should know its consequences for him, and to know those consequences he needs to know what the other players will do. Every definition of rationality, therefore, must establish for each player a set of what we will call *response correspondences* that reflect what he is supposed to believe about what the other players will do. A player may have more than one response correspondence. Since a set of response correspondences is sufficient to determine a definition of rationality, most controversies in economics are about what the proper set of response correspondences is.

Specifically, for each player i we will define S_{-i} as the strategy space of all the other players:

$$S_{-i} = \underset{k \neq i}{\mathsf{X}} S_k.$$

Since player i may have several response correspondences, we will index the different response correspondences by j; thus $q_{ij}(\cdot)$ will denote the *j-th* response correspondence of player i. (When a definition of rationality specifies only one response correspondence for a player we will omit the second subscript.) Each response correspondence is a mapping from S_i to S_{-i}:

$$q_{ij} : S_i \rightarrow S_{-i} ;$$

it assigns to every strategy for i a set of plausible responses by the other players.

Sometimes it will be more convenient to talk about response correspondences in a slightly different way. Associated with each one $q_{ij}(\cdot)$ of player i's response correspondences is a set T_{ij} called the *interesting set* for player i and response correspondence j. $T_{ij} \subseteq S$ consists of all situations of the form (s_i, s_{-i}) where $s_{-i} \in q_{ij}(s_i)$. These are the situations that are plausible to i under response correspondence j.

A situation $s \in T_{ij}$ is *worthy for i at response correspondence j* if no other situation in T_{ij} is better for i. Thus s is worthy for i at response correspondence j iff: $s \in T_{ij}$ and $f_i(s) \geq f_i(\hat{s})$ for all $\hat{s} \in T_{ij}$. Worthy situations are the best that are plausible for i, and we would expect that he would act to achieve them.

A situation will be called *worthy for i* if it is worthy for i at some response correspondence.

A situation is an *equilibrium* if it is worthy for all players.

We are interested in equilibria because we expect that people will act rationally—that is, they will try to bring about worthy situations. If a player finds himself at a situation that is not worthy, he will do better for himself by changing strategies, since there is an interesting situation where he can do better. (Note also that all equilibria are in some sense "rational expectations equilibria": each player must find all the other players acting exactly as he expects them to act under some response correspondence, for if he did not the situation would not be interesting to him, and situations that are not interesting cannot be worthy.)

If people act rationally, then, the situation we observe will be an equilibrium. We want our definitions of rationality to have equilibria, at least in the games we are most concerned about, because if they do not it is inconceivable that people could ever act rationally. We also want the situations our rationality definitions point up as equilibria to resemble the situations that actually occur in "the real world"; for if they do not we cannot maintain that people in "the real world" are acting rationally.

In the remainder of this chapter we will look at some types of games and some proposed rationality definitions in this light.

III

One-person games are easy to analyze because there is no need for response correspondences. All situations are interesting; the situations that maximize the player's utility are worthy; those situations are equilibria; and the strategies that are identical to those situations are rational. We expect that the player will act to maximize utility. If the payoff function does not achieve a maximum over S no equilibrium will exist; if it does, but f and S are sufficiently complicated, the task of computing an equilibrium can be tedious; but otherwise one-person games present no problems.

IV

There are no problems in defining rationality in another class of games as well: two-person constant-sum games. These are games with two players, 1 and 2, which have the property that for every $s \in S$,

$$f_1(s) + f_2(s) = K$$

for some constant K. Without loss of generality we take $K = 0$:

$$f_1(s) + f_2(s) = 0. \tag{1}$$

In the next chapter we will see precisely why there is agreement about this class of games. Often the agreement is attributed to the overwhelming elegance of von Neumann and Morgenstern's pioneering treatment of the subject, which had a considerable effect, but we will see that there are more objective forces at work as well.

Von Neumann and Morgenstern used only one response correspondence for each player:

$$q_1^{NM}(s_1) = \arg \min_{\hat{s}_2 \in S_2} f_1(s_1, \hat{s}_2)$$
$$q_2^{NM}(s_2) = \arg \min_{\hat{s}_1 \in S_1} f_2(\hat{s}_1, s_2).$$

Thus

$$T_1^{NM} = \{(s_1, s_2) \mid s_2 = \arg \min_{\hat{s}_2 \in S_2} f_1(s_1, \hat{s}_2)\}$$
$$T_2^{NM} = \{(s_1, s_2) \mid s_1 = \arg \min_{\hat{s}_1 \in S_1} f_2(\hat{s}_1, s_2)\}.$$

Players who are rational in von Neumann-Morgenstern's sense act as if their opponents will do everything in their power to harm them. Since harming one's opponent is synonymous with helping oneself in constant-sum two-person games, such a definition has considerable intuitive appeal.

Is it conceivable, though, that both players could act rationally? This is the question of whether an equilibrium exists with this type of rationality. Suppose, then, that s is an equilibrium. Then it is worthy (maximal in T_i^{NM}) for both players:

$$f_1(s) = \max_{\hat{s}_1 \in S_1} \min_{\hat{s}_2 \in S_2} f_1(\hat{s}_1, \hat{s}_2)$$
$$f_2(s) = \max_{\hat{s}_2 \in S_2} \min_{\hat{s}_1 \in S_1} f_2(\hat{s}_1, \hat{s}_2).$$

From (1), $f_2(s) = -f_1(s)$, so

$$f_2(s) = \max_{\hat{s}_2 \in S_2} \min_{\hat{s}_1 \in S_1} (-f_1(\hat{s}_1, \hat{s}_2))$$

$$= -\min_{\hat{s}_2 \in S_2} \max_{\hat{s}_1 \in S_1} f_1(\hat{s}_1, \hat{s}_2)$$
$$= -f_1(s).$$

Thus an equilibrium exists iff $f_1(\cdot)$ is such that there is some s with

$$f_1(s) = \min_{\hat{s}_2 \in S_2} \max_{\hat{s}_1 \in S_1} f_1(\hat{s}_1, \hat{s}_2) = \max_{\hat{s}_1 \in S_1} \min_{\hat{s}_2 \in S_2} f_1(\hat{s}_1, \hat{s}_2). \tag{2}$$

If (2) holds, s is said to be a *saddle-point* of f_1, and is an equilibrium. That f_1 have a saddle-point is a necessary and sufficient condition for an equilibrium.

Since we have placed no restrictions on f_1, other than that it map from S to **R**, it should not be surprising to learn that for some games f_1 has a saddle-point, and for some games it does not. The former are called *strictly determined* games; an example of such a game is

		Player 2	
		s_2^1	s_2^2
Player 1	s_1^1	2 −2	−1 1
	s_1^2	1 −1	−2 2

(Player 1 may be imagined as choosing a row and player 2 as choosing a column. The number in the lower left-hand corner of a cell is player 1's payoff when he chooses the row and player 2 chooses the column intersecting at that cell; the number in the upper right-hand corner is player 2's payoff.) In this game, the equilibrium is (s_1^2, s_2^1).

There are, however, large classes of games that are not strictly determined and hence would appear to lack equilibria. Consider, for instance, the game of Matching Pennies:

		Player 2	
		Heads	Tails
Player 1	Heads	−1 1	1 −1
	Tails	1 −1	−1 1

(Each player chooses heads or tails. If the players' choices match, player 1 wins; if they differ, player 2 wins.) Von Neumann-Morgenstern rationality would seem to be useless for these games, since it is not conceivable that both players could act rationally.

Von Neumann and Morgenstern showed, however, in essence that all games whose strategy spaces and payoff functions met certain convexity and continuity requirements had equilibria, and most importantly, that every finite game that did not have an equilibrium could be easily associated with a game that did. (A *finite* game is a game where $|S|$ is finite.)

The game that von Neumann and Morgenstern associated with every finite game is called its *mixed strategy extension*. This is a game where players choose, instead of actions *simpliciter* (*pure strategies*), only probability distributions (*mixed strategies*) for choosing pure strategies; their payoffs are then the expected payoffs that result from the mixed strategies they have chosen. Specifically, if $\langle I, D, h\rangle$ is a finite game in pure strategies, then $\langle I, S, f\rangle$ is its mixed strategy extension where:

$$S_i = \{p_i \geq 0 \mid \sum_{j \in D_i} p_i^j = 1\},$$

the $|D_i|$-dimensional unit simplex, and

$$f_i(p_1,\ldots,p_n) = \sum_{j_1 \in D_1} \sum_{j_2 \in D_2} \cdots \sum_{j_n \in D_n} \left[\prod_{k=1}^{n} p_k^{j_k}\right] h(j_1,\ldots,j_n).$$

Von Neumann and Morgenstern's famous "Minimax Theorem" states that every mixed-strategy game has an equilibrium. Thus their concept of rationality is applicable for all zero-sum two-person finite games. This result was first stated and proved in von Neumann (1928) and was extended to classes of games with infinite strategy sets by Ville (1938). Von Neumann (1953) saw this theorem as the fundamental result of game theory. We will not present a proof here; the interested reader may consult virtually any standard work on game theory, e.g., von Neumann and Morgenstern (1944, pp. 128–158), Luce and Raiffa (1957, pp. 385–393), Owen (1968, pp. 17–24), and Vorob'ev (1977, pp. 21–23).

V

An alternative type of rationality for two-person constant-sum games is that of Nash (1950). A player who is rational in Nash's sense acts, not as if his opponent is out to hurt him, but as if his opponent will never change. Nash equilibria and von Neumann-Morgenstern equilibria, however, are identical for two-person zero-sum games.

Formally, Nash's rationality uses a system of multiple response correspondences. In fact, player 1 has a response correspondence for every one of player 2's strategies, and player 2 has a response correspondence for every one of player 1's strategies. These response correspondences, however, are very simple: player 1's response correspondence associated with a particular strategy of player 2 has player 2 choosing that strategy no matter what player 1 does. Since each response correspondence is associated with a unique strategy of the other player we can index the response correspondences by those strategies. Thus suppose that $s_2^1, s_2^2, s_2^3, \ldots, s_2^j, \ldots$ are player 2's strategies. Then we will call player 1's response correspondences $q^N_{1s_2^1}(\cdot)$, $q^N_{1s_2^2}(\cdot)$, $q^N_{1s_2^3}(\cdot), \ldots q^N_{1s_2^j}(\cdot), \ldots$; similarly for player 2.

Nash rationality, then, uses the following response correspondences:

$$q^N_{1s_2}(s_1) \equiv s_2 \qquad \text{for all } s_2 \in S_2$$

for player 1; and

$$q^N_{2s_1}(s_2) \equiv s_1 \qquad \text{for all } s_1 \in S_1$$

for player 2.

A situation s is worthy for player 1 at response correspondence s_2, then, iff:

$$f_1(s) \geq f_1(\tilde{s}_1, s_2) \qquad \text{for all } \tilde{s}_1 \in S_1. \tag{3}$$

A situation is worthy for player 1 if (3) holds; similarly for player 2. There is a special word for situations that has been used for situations that are worthy in Nash's sense: *acceptable.* From (3) we see that if a situation is acceptable to a player he is doing as well as he can, given what the other player is doing.

A Nash equilibrium (sometimes abbreviated NE) is, of course, a situation that is acceptable (i.e., worthy) for both players. If (s_1, s_2) is an NE, s_1 must be a best strategy for player 1 given that player 2 is choosing s_2 and s_2 must be a best strategy for player 2 given that player 1 is choosing s_1. Neither will change unless the other does also.

It is easy to show that Nash and von Neumann-Morgenstern equilibria coincide for all constant-sum two-person games.

First we will show that all Nash equilibria are von Neumann-Morgenstern equilibria. That is, we will show that if (s_1, s_2) is a Nash equilibrium it must be worthy for both players in the von Neumann-Morgenstern sense. Since (s_1, s_2) is an NE, it is acceptable to player 2, and hence

$$f_1(s_1, s_2) = -f_2(s_1, s_2) = -\max_{\tilde{s}_2 \in S_2} f_2(s_1, \tilde{s}_2) = \min_{\tilde{s}_2 \in S_2} f_1(s_1, \tilde{s}_2).$$

Hence $s_2 \in q_1^{NM}(s_1)$ and $(s_1, s_2) \in T_1^{NM}$. For any $(\tilde{s}_1, q_1^{NM}(\tilde{s}_1))$ in T_1^{NM}, it follows from the definition of $q_1^{NM}(\cdot)$ as a minimizer that

$$f_1(\tilde{s}_1, q_1^{NM}(\tilde{s}_1)) \leq f_1(\tilde{s}_1, s_2) \qquad \text{for all } \tilde{s}_1 \in S_1. \tag{4}$$

Since (s_1, s_2) is acceptable to player 1,

$$f_1(s_1, s_2) \geq f_1(\tilde{s}_1, s_2) \qquad \text{for all } \tilde{s}_1 \in S_1.$$

Combining this with (4) we obtain:

$$f_1(s_1, s_2) \geq f_1(\tilde{s}_1, q_1^{NM}(\tilde{s}_1)) \qquad \text{for all } \tilde{s}_1 \in S_1$$

and so (s_1, s_2) maximizes $f_1(\cdot)$ in T_1^{NM}. This means it is worthy for player 1. A symmetrical argument will establish von Neumann-Morgenstern worthiness for player 2. Thus (s_1, s_2) is a von Neumann-Morgenstern equilibrium.

Now suppose (s_1, s_2) is a von Neumann-Morgenstern equilibrium; we will show it is a Nash equilibrium. For

$$f_1(s_1, s_2) = \min_{\tilde{s}_2 \in S_2} \max_{\tilde{s}_1 \in S_1} f_1(\tilde{s}_1, \tilde{s}_2),$$

and so

$$f_1(s_1, s_2) \geq f_1(\tilde{s}_1, s_2) \qquad \text{for all } \tilde{s}_1 \in S_1$$

by definition of a maximum. Thus (s_1, s_2) is Nash-worthy for player 1 at response correspondence s_2 and is acceptable for player 1. From a similar argument, (s_1, s_2) is acceptable for player 2. Thus (s_1, s_2) is a Nash equilibrium.

The equivalence between von Neumann and Nash rationality for constant-sum two-person games should not be terribly surprising. In these games, a gain for one player is automatically an equal loss for the other. Maximizing one's own utility is equivalent to minimizing one's opponent's, and so the requirement that one do as well as possible given what the opponent is doing is identical to the requirement that one do as well as possible given that the opponent will hurt one as much as possible, since with a rational opponent "what the opponent is doing" and "what hurts one as much as possible" are the same thing.

VI

In two-person constant-sum games, helping oneself is equivalent to hurting one's opponent, but few if any other many-person games share this property. In all other games there are advantages to cooperation as well as antagonism. No consensus has emerged as to what rationality is in the presence of such phenomena; Shubik (1968) estimated that 20 to 30 different "solution concepts" for general games had been proposed.

Both the von Neumann-Morgenstern and Nash definitions of rationality can be generalized simply, but so far no one has shown any serious interest in the simple generalization of the von Neumann-Morgenstern definition. One reason is that paranoia—which is what psychologists would call the simple generalization—has had little appeal for economists or game theorists as a rule for behavior; another reason is that for many games general paranoia may not lead to any equilibria at all.

The Nash definition has received much more attention. The generalization is simple: instead of indexing response correspondences on the other player's strategy, index them instead (since there is no simple "other player") on $(n - 1)$-tuples of other players' strategies. Thus for player i

$$q_{is_{-i}}(s_i) \equiv s_{-i} \qquad \text{for all } s_{-i} \in S_{-i}$$

and a situation s is Nash-worthy or acceptable iff:

$$f_i(s) \geq f_i(\tilde{s}_i, s_{-i}) \qquad \text{for all } \tilde{s}_i \in S_i.$$

An NE is a situation acceptable to all players; at an NE all players are acting rationally.

Nash (1950, 1951) proved that every finite game has an NE in mixed strategies. Glicksberg (1952) extended this result to games with compact strategy spaces and continuous payoff functions, while Nikaidô and Isoda (1955) showed that all games with convex, continuous payoff functions have NEs in pure strategies.

Nash's view of rationality is perhaps the simplest that has been proposed, and we will be using it as the foundation for the remainder of the book. Serious objections have been raised to it, however. Since NEs do exist for most games, these objections are necessarily empirical, if only casually so. It is conceivable that people could act in the manner described by Nash, but, the objectors insist, they do not, or, more weakly, do not always. Consider, for instance, the game of prisoners' dilemma:

		Player 2	
		Don't Confess	Confess
Player 1	Don't Confess	1, 1	0, 6
	Confess	6, 0	5, 5

(The players are prisoners being held for interrogation on a minor crime. If neither confesses to a major crime, they will both receive light penalties for the minor crime. If one confesses to a major crime and implicates the other in it, while the other confesses to nothing, then the player confessing will go free and the player not confessing will receive a very harsh sentence. If they both confess to a major crime, they will both receive harsh sentences.) The only NE is dual confession, but both players would be better off if neither confessed. If people act rationally à la Nash they will always confess and never cooperate. But there is, at times, honor among thieves, and cooperation for mutual advantage among individuals who are neither saints nor inmates of lunatic asylums. Situations that are not NEs sometimes occur. Cooperation is, in fact, pervasive in modern economic life. Thus Nash's definition of rationality does not seem to be the best one for describing how people act.

VII

In contrast to Nash's so-called "noncooperative" approach to rationality are the "cooperative" approaches. Most of these involve sophisticated—not simple—generalizations of the von Neumann-Morgenstern rationality definition. The original discussions of cooperation used transferable utility. Aumann (1961), however, showed how they could be extended to games with nontransferable utility, and since games with transferable utility are in fact a special subclass of games with nontransferable utility, we will for the most part follow his discussion. (There will be two exceptions, for the sake of simplification: we will ignore correlation of mixed strategies across players, and β-effectiveness.)

Coalition is a fundamental notion in cooperative game theory. By this is meant simply a subset (possibly improper) of the set of players I. Rationality in cooperative game theory requires that players try to form coalitions to act together to advance their interests.

Core-rationality, introduced by Gillies (1953), is probably the best known and easiest to use form of cooperative rationality. For any player i let $\Psi(i)$ denote the set of all coalitions of which i is a member: $\Psi(i) = \{J \subset I \mid i \in J\}$. For any coalition J let $I - J$ denote (the coalition that is) J's complement in I, and let

$$s^J = (s_i),\ i \in J$$

denote a $|J|$-tuple of strategies chosen by the members of J. The set of all the s^J available to the members of J will be denoted S^J; thus

$$S^J = \mathop{\times}_{i \in J} S_i.$$

Define $v(J)$ as the set of all situations for which coalition J is *effective*:

$$v(J) = \{s \in S \mid (\exists \bar{s}^J \in S^J)(\forall \tilde{s}^{I-J} \in S^{I-J})(\forall j \in J) f_j(\bar{s}^J, \tilde{s}^{I-J}) \geq f_j(s)\}.$$

Coalition J is effective for situation s if it has a joint strategy that can guarantee all its members at least as much as they receive with s, no matter what the remaining players do. (This is Aumann's "α-effectiveness"; "β-effectiveness" reverses the existential and first universal quantifiers.)

Define $v(J, s_i)$ where $J \in \Psi(i)$ as the set of all $(n-1)$-tuples of strategies for the players other than i which when concatenated with s_i result in situations for which J is effective:

$$v(J,s_i) = \{s_{-i} \in S_{-i} \mid (s_i, s_{-i}) \in v(J)\}, \; J \in \Psi(i).$$

Then the response correspondence assigns to each strategy s_i of player i all the $(n-1)$-tuples in $v(J, s_i)$ for all $J \in \Psi(i)$:

$$q_i^c(s_i) = \bigcup_{J \in \Psi(i)} v(J,s_i).$$

Thus the interesting set is

$$T_i^c = \bigcup_{J \in \Psi(i)} v(J)$$

and a situation is core-worthy for player i iff it maximizes his payoff in T_i^c. That is, at a core-worthy situation a player can find no coalition that can guarantee him an increase in payoff. A core-equilibrium, of course, is a situation that is worthy for all players.

A situation s is said to be *dominated* if for some J, $s \in v(J)$ and for some $j \in J, f_j(\bar{s}^J, \tilde{s}^{I-J}) > f_j(s)$. It is easy to show that s is a core-equilibrium iff it is undominated. If s is undominated, then there is no $\hat{s} \in \bigcup_J v(J)$ with $f_i(\hat{s}) > f_i(s)$ for any i, and so in particular there is no $\hat{s} \in \bigcup_{J \in \Psi(i)} v(J)$ with that inequality. Thus s is worthy for all i. On the other hand, suppose s were dominated. Then $f_i(\bar{s}^J, \tilde{s}^{I-J}) > f_i(s)$. By definition $(\bar{s}^J, \tilde{s}^{I-J}) \in v(J)$ and hence interesting for i. Thus s is not worthy for i.

Note that all core-equilibria are Pareto-optimal, because a situation that was not Pareto-optimal would be dominated by the coalition of the whole, I.

For many games, core-equilibria do not exist; for instance, there are none in any many-person constant-sum games where cooperation matters (see, e.g., Luce and Raiffa, 1957, pp. 194–195). This would be a serious defect of core-rationality for us if we were primarily concerned with such games; but it is not, as our primary concern in the second part of this book is with economic games for which it has been shown that core-equilibria exist.

The general von Neumann-Morgenstern rationality approach is similar to the core, but it considers coalition-forming rationality not universally, as the core does, but only relative to some prevailing "standard of behavior." We will represent such a standard of behavior by V, a subset of S; we will explain later what requirements we place on V for it to be acceptable as a standard of behavior. V is a restriction on each player's interesting set; the new interesting set is:

$$T_i^V = \bigcup_{J \in \Psi(i)} v(J) \cap V$$

and worthiness and equilibria are defined as before. We denote by $V^* \subset V$ the set of V-equilibria. The requirement that we place on V for it to be acceptable as a standard of behavior is that if s is not in V, then for some player i and some $s^* \in V^*$, situations s^* and s are both core-interesting, but $f_i(s^*) > f_i(s)$. Thus for any V, the set V^* of V-equilibria is internally stable in the sense that no coalition wants to move from any situation in it to any other; if V is a workable standard of behavior, then V^* is also externally stable in the sense that for every situation not in V^* there is a situation in V^* that some coalition wants to move toward.

V-equilibria are much more plentiful than core-equilibria. For almost every game there is a set V that has V-equilibria, and many games have many sets. In the constant-sum three-person game with transferable utility, for instance, every situation is a V-equilibrium for some V or another. It was once believed that every game had at least one V-equilibrium, but Lucas (1968) and others have found a few that do not.

No situation that is Pareto-inferior to another situation in V can be in V^*, but V-equilibria in games without transferable utility do not have to be Pareto-optimal. V may be a workable standard of behavior even if some of its equilibria are Pareto-inferior to situations outside V, because there may be other V-equilibria that coalitions can and will enforce against these outside situations. If utility is transferable or close to it, however—e.g., if players have available to them strategies like paying each other money or some other good—V-equilibria must be Pareto-optimal. The games we will be most concerned about—games where people can transfer goods and services between each other—are of this type.

VIII

One cooperative "solution concept" that does not fit our scheme is "value." Shapley (1953) formulated value for games with transferable utility; Aumann and Shapley (1974) and Aumann and Kurz (1977) extended the concept to games without transferable utility. Value is a way of assigning a utility to the prospect of having to play a game. Given that one is playing the game, value gives no advice about how to play it. It is not necessarily even the payoff from a situation in the game, and has nothing to do with rationality (once the game has started) or equilibrium. Value will not concern us in this book.

IX

There are several other cooperative approaches to rationality as well, including the Walrasian one, which we will discuss in detail in chapter 6. What most of these approaches have in common is a requirement that equilibria be Pareto-optimal. Just as the empirical observation of cooperation was a serious empirical objection to Nash's rationality approach, so the empirical observation of Pareto-inferior outcomes is a serious objection to the use of these cooperative concepts.

Requiring Pareto optimality is a defect, for our study in particular, because we wish to study phenomena—unemployment being the prime example—where Pareto optimality is violated. We suspect we will make little progress if we rule out a priori the existence of the phenomena we are supposed to be studying.

The question we are interested in, then, is why Pareto-inferior results can occur in worlds where there is sometimes cooperation—why the coalition of the whole can't get together and have somebody say, "Gee, guys, if we did so-and-so, everybody would be better off." To be sure, there are two cooperative solution concepts that do not require Pareto optimality: Luce's (1955) "Ψ-stability" and Aumann and Maschler's (1964) "bargaining set." Both concepts, however, beg the question we are interested in by essentially ruling out the formation of certain coalitions a priori. For both of them, for instance, the existence of involuntary unemployment among telephone users would cause a problem. For it is clear (and was more clear before the recent antitrust decision) that the set of American Telephone and Telegraph's employees, shareholders, and customers is a coalition that has in fact formed, that is cooperating, and that encompasses virtually the entire U.S. population. How such a coalition could allow Pareto-inferior situations is a mystery, as long as cooperation is of the all-or-nothing type that characterizes the core and V-equilibria.

In the next chapter, therefore, we go on to a new type of rationality that allows us to examine the *mechanics* of cooperation—as well as the possibility of noncooperation. The type of rationality needed to deal with the cooperative but not perfect world familiar to macroeconomics will, moreover, turn out to be a generalization of the types of rationality we have been discussing here.

3 ▪ Commitment Equilibrium

It is not those who can inflict the most but those who endure the most who will conquer. TERENCE MACSWINEY, Lord Mayor of Cork, August 1920, at the beginning of his hunger strike in Brixton Prison

Schelling (1960, pp. 120–121) describes the situation:

> . . . of twenty men held up for robbery and ransom by a single man who has a gun and six bullets. They can overwhelm him if they are willing to lose six of themselves, if they have a means of deciding which six to lose. They can defeat him without loss if they can visibly commit themselves to a threat to do so, if they can simultaneously commit themselves to a promise to abstain from capital punishment, once they have caught him. He can deter their threat if he can visibly commit himself to shoot in disregard of any subsequent threat they might make, or if he can show that he could not believe their promise. If they cannot deliver their threat—if, say, he understands only a foreign language—they cannot disarm him verbally. Nor can they make a threat unless they agree on it themselves; so if he can threaten to shoot any two who talk together, he can deter agreement. . . . If fourteen of the twenty can over-power the remaining six and force them to advance, they can demonstrate that they could overwhelm the man; if so, the threat succeeds and the gunman surrenders, and even the six "expendables" gain through their own inability to avoid jeopardy.

Coalition formation, indeed any departure in the direction of cooperation from the thoroughly noncooperative Nash equilibrium, requires commitments, promises, or threats—the sort of thing Schelling calls *strategic moves*. Strategic moves are the mechanism through which cooperation occurs. This chapter will be about strategic moves, or more specifically, about rationality with strategic moves.

The first section of this chapter will show in an example how strategic moves work; the second will formalize our procedure for dealing with strategic moves. It turns out to be more convenient to start with a definition of equilibrium and derive a definition of rationality from it, and this is the procedure we will follow. The second section therefore defines "commitment equilibrium," and derives some basic results. The third section uses these results in a series of examples, while sections four and five provide more results for use later in the book. In section IV we show the existence of commitment equilibria—i.e., that it is conceivable that people could act in the way we are talking about. Finally, in the last section, we tie these results in to the discussion of the last two chapters by displaying explicitly the definition of rationality that underlies commitment equilibrium, and show that all the equilibria we discussed in chapter 2 were special kinds of commitment equilibria, and indeed any kind of rationality is commitment-rationality.

I

If a situation that is not a Nash equilibrium occurs, some player is choosing a strategy that is disadvantageous to himself, given what the other players are doing. What is there about commitments, promises, and threats that allow them to induce contrary behavior? They cannot make inherently unattractive situations more attractive, because that is magic: even if such magic existed it would be used to make all situations more attractive, and the NE would not be changed. On the contrary, as Schelling (p. 150) argues, strategic moves are selective *subtractions* by a player from his own payoff function.

Suppose, for instance, that I can either play tennis or break your legs, and that you can either pay me a hundred dollars or pay me nothing. I prefer playing tennis to breaking your legs and you prefer not paying me to paying me. This game can be illustrated as

		You: Don't pay	You: Pay
Me	Tennis	3 (Me), 3 (You)	4 (Me), 2 (You)
	Breaking	2 (Me), 1 (You)	3 (Me), 0 (You)

The only NE of this game is the upper left situation where I play tennis and you don't pay me. In the absence of two-way communication of some sort, there is no reason for either of us to deviate from this happy state.

But suppose—just suppose—that I threaten to break your legs unless you pay me a hundred dollars. How do I make this threat, since I in fact prefer playing tennis to breaking your legs, even if you don't pay me? What I must do is to subtract 2 or more units from my payoff in the upper left situation; then it will be true that I would rather break your legs than play tennis if you don't pay me. The mechanism for carrying out this subtraction will not concern us—perhaps my concern for my reputation is such that my announcing the threat is sufficient to subtract 2 units from my payoff function if I "chicken out," or perhaps I must engage some sort of external enforcer to do me 2 units of harm if I fail. (If there is no mechanism, then I can make no threat, for you will merely laugh at me and call my bluff, and I will play tennis.)

After I threaten, then, there is a new payoff matrix:

		You	
		Don't pay	Pay
Me	Tennis	1, 3	4, 2
	Breaking	2, 1	3, 0

The new NE is the lower left situation where I break your legs and you don't pay me. Notice that I am worse off here (my payoff is 2) than I was before making the threat (my payoff was 3). Given your lack of commitment of any kind, I was better off not making any threat at all. In this sense, the original circumstance of no threats, no paying and no breaking was stable.

But, however foolish my threat may have been, suppose I have made it. If nothing else happens, you will find your legs broken, something you find quite distasteful, even if you keep your money. What can you do to prevent this? You can promise to pay me if I don't break your legs. How do you make this promise? You make it by subtracting 2 or more units from your payoff in the upper left situation where I play tennis and you don't pay. Again, the mechanism for this subtraction will not concern us. After my threat and your promise the new payoff matrix is:

		You	
		Don't pay	Pay
Me	Tennis	1, 1	4, 2
	Breaking	2, 1	3, 0

The NE is the upper right situation where I play tennis and you pay me.

Notice now that since you promised to pay me if I don't break your legs, my threat to break your legs if you don't pay me is no longer foolish. For suppose you promised but I didn't threaten. The payoff matrix would be:

		You	
		Don't pay	Pay
Me	Tennis	3, 1	4, 2
	Breaking	2, 1	3, 0

The NE is still the upper right situation where I play and you pay, so my threat no longer hurts me. Note, however, that if I don't make my threat, you are better off not promising, because if you promise your payoff will be 2 at play and pay, and if you don't promise your payoff will be 3 at play and don't pay. In the absence of my threat, your promise is foolish.

Thus we have identified two occasions where neither of us is acting foolishly:

No commitments, I play tennis, you don't pay.
I threaten and play tennis, you promise and pay.

Soon we will learn to call these occasions "commitment equilibria." What makes these occasions special is that no player would want to change his commitment, given what the other player's commitment is, nor would any player want to change his strategy, given his own commitment and the other player's strategy. Commitment equilibrium will represent our basic approach to rationality.

II

Now we want to incorporate strategic moves into our formal description of games. It will be simpler here and throughout to insist that payoffs be nonnegative; this can be done without loss of generality. Thus let $\Gamma = \langle I, S, f \rangle$ be a game in normal form, where S contains no strategic moves and the range of f is in the nonnegative orthant of $\mathbf{R}^n$. (We will take S and its generic element s to include mixed as well as pure strategies whenever appropriate; for more detailed discussion see Appendix B.)

One way we could accomplish this incorporation would be to expand S to include all possible strategic moves. Schelling (pp. 150–158) used this procedure. By giving a special status to strategic moves, however, we can obtain more interesting results.

First we must decide, though, what strategic moves to consider. As Schelling illustrates in his discussion of the six bullets and twenty men, a player cannot always effect any desired reduction in his payoff matrix. We will ignore this difficulty in the sequel, however, and proceed under the principle that one can always make oneself thoroughly miserable. This will be called the "free disposal of utility" axiom. The reason for this axiom is simply to keep our task of manageable size. Systems without free disposal are no doubt of great concern, but we will reserve our consideration of them to Appendix B. Fortunately we will find there that limitations on utility disposal do not necessitate great changes in our basic theory.

We denote by $\Gamma^* = \langle I, S, f \rangle^*$ the game that obtains from Γ by allowing strategic moves under the free disposal axiom.

In Γ^*, the players first choose amounts to subtract from their own payoff functions in Γ, and then the new game after these subtractions is played. Precisely, Γ^* differs from Γ in that each player i first chooses a function

$$g_i : S \to \mathbf{R}_+,\ g_i(s) \leq f_i(s), \qquad \forall s \in S$$

and then the game $\langle I, S, f-g \rangle$ is played, where $g = (g_i)$, $i \in I$. The amounts that player i subtracts from his payoff function, that is, the function g_i, will be called *i's commitment*; the n-tuple of commitments, that is, the function g, will be called the *commitment pattern*.

We will be concerned whether any player can improve his payoff by changing his commitment. A commitment pattern-situation pair will be called *beaten* if some player, by changing only his own commitment, can create a game with an NE more favorable to him than the game with the original commitment pattern.

Specifically let g and g' be commitment patterns for $\langle I, S, f\rangle^*$ and let s and s' be situations. Then:

(g', s') *beats* (g, s) *through player i* if

(a) s is an NE of $\langle I, S, f-g\rangle$ and s' is an NE of $\langle I, S, f-g'\rangle$
(b) $(f_i - g_i')(s') > (f_i - g_i)(s)$ and
(c) $g_j' = g_j$ for all $j \in I, j \neq i$.

(g',s') *beats* (g, s) if there is some player i through whom (g',s') beats (g,s).

We will define a commitment equilibrium as a commitment pattern-situation pair where no player has any reason to change either his commitment or his strategy. Thus:

(g,s) is a *commitment equilibrium* for $\langle I, S, f\rangle^*$ if

(a) s is an NE of $\langle I, S, f-g\rangle$and
(b) no $(g' s')$ beats (g, s).

In a commitment equilibrium, as we discussed in the last section, no player may change strategies without hurting himself (with other players' strategies and his own commitment held constant), and no player can change commitments (with other players' commitments held constant, but all strategies adjusted). Each player's strategy is his best response to the other players' strategies, and each player's commitment is his best response to the other players' commitments, when NEs are compared.

III

Now that we know what they are, we will talk about what commitment equilibria are like, and how we can find them. It will shorten presentation if we denote by $A(i, g)$ the set of situations that are acceptable to player i in $\langle I, S, f-g\rangle$ and by $N(g)$ the set of situations that are Nash equilibria of $\langle I, S, f-g\rangle$. Clearly

$$N(g) = \bigcap_{i \in I} A(i,g).$$

We will also call a situation *possible for i in* $\langle I, S, f-g\rangle$ if it is acceptable for all players but i in $\langle I, S, f-g\rangle$. $P(i, g)$ will denote the set of situations that are possible for i in $\langle I, S, f-g\rangle$; i.e.:

$$P(i,g) = \bigcap_{\substack{j \neq i \\ j \in I}} A(j,g).$$

Since $N(g) = P(i, g) \cap A(i, g)$ for any player i, if $N(g)$ is nonempty,

$P(i, g)$ must be nonempty for all i, and if $N(g)$ is empty, g is not a commitment pattern in which we have any interest.

Our first theorem tells us that a commitment pattern-situation pair is beaten if and only if there is a better situation (in terms of the original game) in some player's possible set.

Theorem 1. (Possible Point Theorem). *Suppose $s \in N(g)$ and $g_i(s) = 0$. Then (g, s) is beaten through i iff $f_i(s) < f_i(\hat{s})$ for some $\hat{s} \in P(i, g)$.*

Proof. Sufficiency. Suppose $f_i(\hat{s}) > f_i(s)$ and $\hat{s} \in P(i, g)$.

We will show that there is a $\hat{g}$ such that $(\hat{g}, \hat{s})$ beats (g, s) through i. Construct $\hat{g}$ in the following manner:

$$\begin{aligned} &\hat{g}_j = g_j && \text{for } j \neq i \\ &\hat{g}_i(\hat{s}) = 0 && \\ &\hat{g}_i(\bar{s}) = f_i(\bar{s}) && \text{for } \bar{s} \neq \hat{s}. \end{aligned}$$

We need to show that (a) $\hat{s} \in N(\hat{g})$, and (b) $(f_i - \hat{g}_i)(\hat{s}) > (f_i - g_i)(s)$.

Ad (a). Since $\hat{s} \in P(i, g)$, $\hat{s} \in A(j, g)$ for all $j \neq i$. But for all these players $\hat{g}_j$ is the same as g_j and so $A(j, \hat{g}) = A(j, g)$ and $\hat{s} \in A(j, \hat{g})$. By construction, $\hat{s} \in A(i, \hat{g})$. Hence s is acceptable for all players in $\langle I, S, f - \hat{g} \rangle$ and $\hat{s} \in N(\hat{g})$.

Ad (b). Since $\hat{g}_i(\hat{s}) = 0$ we have

$$(f_i - \hat{g}_i)(\hat{s}) = f_i(\hat{s}) > f_i(s) = (f_i - g_i)(s)$$

since $g_i(s) = 0$ by hypothesis. Thus we have shown that $(\hat{g}, \hat{s})$ beats (g, s) through player i.

Necessity. Suppose (g', s') beats (g, s) through i, but that $f_i(s) \geq f_i(\hat{s})$ for all $\hat{s} \in P(i, g)$. Then $(f_i - g_i')(s') > (f_i - g_i)(s) = f_i(s) \geq f_i(\hat{s})$ for all $\hat{s} \in P(i, g)$. Thus $s' \notin P(i, g)$. If $s' \notin P(i, g)$, there must be some $j \neq i$, such that $s' \notin A(j, g)$. But by definition of beating through i, $g_j = g_j'$ and $A(j, g') = A(j, g)$. Thus $s' \notin A(j, g')$. Hence $s' \notin N(g')$ and (g', s') does not beat (g, s) through i. Since this is a contradiction, we have proved necessity. ∎

The condition $g(s) = 0$ in the Possible Point Theorem will be no hindrance to us, as the next theorem shows. It states that players never use strategic moves to hurt themselves at commitment equilibria. At equilibrium, no one's bluff ever gets called.

Theorem 2. (No Real Suffering). *If (g, s) is a commitment equilibrium, then $g(s) = 0$.*

Proof. Suppose (g, s) is a commitment equilibrium, and $g_i(s) > 0$ for some i. Construct g' in the following manner:

$$\begin{aligned} g'_j &= g_j && \text{for } j \neq \text{i} \\ g'_i(\hat{s}) &= g_i(\hat{s}) && \text{for } \hat{s} \neq s \\ g'_i(s) &= 0. \end{aligned}$$

We assert that (g', s) beats (g, s) through i, contrary to hypothesis. To prove the assertion we must show:

(a) $s \in N(g')$.

Since $s \in A(j,g)$, $s \in A(j,g')$ for $j \neq i$ by the usual reasoning. It is also easy to see that $s \in A(i,g)$ implies $s \in A(i,g')$, since

$$\begin{aligned} (f_i - g'_i)(s) = f_i(s) > (f_i - g_i)(s) &\geq (f_i - g_i)(\hat{s}_i, s_{-i}) \\ &= (f_i - g'_i)(\hat{s}_i, s_{-i}) \end{aligned}$$

for all $\hat{s}_i \neq s_i$ in S_i.

(b) $(f_i - g'_i)(s) > (f_i - g_i)(s)$.

This is true because $g'_i(s) = 0 < g_i(s)$.

(c) $g'_j = g_j$, $j \neq i$.

This is true by construction of g'. Therefore (g', s) beats (g, s) and (g, s) is not a commitment equilibrium. ∎

The next result provides our basic tool for finding commitment equilibria. We will call a situation *good for player i* if it maximizes his payoff in his possible set. The next theorem states that a situation is associated with a commitment equilibrium if and only if the situation is good for all players.

Specifically, we will denote the set of situations that are good for player i by $B(i, g)$:

$$B(i,g) = \{s \in P(i,g) \mid (\forall \tilde{s} \in P(i,g))\ f_i(s) \geq f_i(\tilde{s})\}.$$

Then we have the following theorem:

Theorem 3. (Goodness). *(g,s) is a commitment equilibrium of $\langle I, S, f \rangle^*$ iff $s \in \bigcap_{i \in I} B(i, g)$.*

Proof. Sufficiency. Suppose $s \in \bigcap_{i \in I} B(i,g)$. We need to show (a) $s \in N(g)$, and (b) (g, s) is not beaten.

Ad (a). $s \in B(i, g)$ for all i and thus $s \in P(i, g)$ for all i a fortiori. Hence

$$s \in \bigcap_i P(i, g) = \bigcap_i \left(\bigcap_{j \neq i} A(j, g)\right) = \bigcap_i A(i, g) = N(g)$$

where the penultimate equality follows from commutative properties and the fact that the intersection of any set with itself is itself.

Ad (b). Suppose (g', s') beats (g, s) through i. Then by the Possible Point Theorem $s' \in P(i, g)$ and $f_i(s') > f_i(s)$. Then $s \notin B(i, g)$ and $s \notin \cap_i B(i, g)$. Since this is a contradiction, the supposition that (g, s) is beaten cannot be maintained.

Necessity. Suppose (g, s) is a commitment equilibrium but that $s \notin \cap_i B(i, g)$. Then there is some player, say j, for whom $s \notin B(j, g)$. Either $s \in P(j, g)$ or not.

Suppose $s \in P(j, g)$. Then there must be some $s' \in P(j, g)$ with $f_j(s') > f_j(s)$. But then by the Possible Point Theorem (g, s) is beaten through j and cannot be a commitment equilibrium.

Thus we must suppose $s \notin P(j, g)$. This means there is a player $k \neq j$ for whom $s \notin A(k, g)$. Thus $s \notin N(g)$ and (g, s) cannot be a commitment equilibrium. This contradiction proves necessity. ■

With the Goodness Theorem, we can show some properties of commitment equilibria easily. The first property that we want to show is what we call individual improvement: no player in a finite game is ever worse off at a commitment equilibrium than at the best point he could assure himself of on his own.

Theorem 4. (Individual Improvement). *If (g, s) is a commitment equilibrium of the finite game $\langle I, S, f\rangle^*$, then for every player i:*

$$(f_i - g_i)(s) = f_i(s) \geq \max_{\hat{s}_i \in S_i} \min_{\hat{s}_{-i} \in S_{-i}} f_i(\hat{s}_i, \hat{s}_{-i}).$$

Proof. The first equality, of course, follows from the No Real Suffering Theorem. For the inequality, we need to show first that for every $\tilde{s}_i \in S_i$ there is some $\tilde{s}_{-i} \in S_{-i}$ such that $(\tilde{s}_i, \tilde{s}_{-i}) \in P(i, g)$.

To show this for an arbitrary $\tilde{s}_i \in S_i$, consider the game

$$\Gamma(\tilde{s}_i) = \langle I - \{i\}, S_{-i}, (f - g)(\tilde{s}_i, \cdot)\rangle,$$

i.e., the game played among the other players given that player i has chosen $\tilde{s}_i$. Since S is finite, S_{-i} is also and $\Gamma(\tilde{s}_i)$ is a finite game. Hence by Nash's theorem (1951), $\Gamma(\tilde{s}_i)$ has an NE; call one of these NEs $\tilde{s}_{-i}$.

We claim $(\tilde{s}_i, \tilde{s}_{-i}) \in P(i, g)$. Consider a player $j \neq i$. Since $\tilde{s}_{-i}$ is an NE of $\Gamma(\tilde{s}_i)$ it is acceptable to j in that game:

$$(f_j - g_j)(\tilde{s}_i, \tilde{s}_{-i}) \geq (f_j - g_j)(\tilde{s}_i, \bar{s}_j, \tilde{s}_{-i,-j})$$

for all $\bar{s}_j \in S_j$. ($\tilde{s}_{-i,-j}$ is $\tilde{s}_{-i}$ without its *j-th* component). But this means that

$(\tilde{s}_i, \tilde{s}_{-i})$ is acceptable to j in $\langle I, S, f-g\rangle$. Since j is arbitrary, $(\tilde{s}_i, \tilde{s}_{-i}) \in P(i, g)$. This completes our first claim.

Now we will show that for every $\tilde{s}_i \in S_i$

$$f_i(s) \geq \min_{\hat{s}_{-i} \in S_{-i}} f_i(\tilde{s}_i, \hat{s}_{-i}). \tag{1}$$

Since $(\tilde{s}_i, \tilde{s}_{-i}) \in P(i,g)$, Goodness tells us

$$f_i(s) \geq f_i(\tilde{s}_i, \tilde{s}_{-i})$$

and the definition of a minimum tells us

$$f_i(\tilde{s}_i, \tilde{s}_{-i}) \geq \min_{\hat{s}_{-i} \in S_{-i}} f_i(\tilde{s}_i, \tilde{s}_{-i}).$$

Inequality (1) follows immediately.

Since $\tilde{s}_i$ is arbitrary in (1), the theorem is just an instance of (1). ■

The Individual Improvement results cannot be extended to infinite games unless restrictions are placed on f and g to assure that the appropriate auxiliary games $\Gamma(s_i)$ have NEs. Consider the following game as a counter-example: Let $I = \{1, 2\}$, $S_1 = \{1, 2\}$, $S_2 = \{x \in \mathbf{R} \mid x \geq 1\}$, and

$$\begin{aligned} &f_1(1,1) = f_2(1,1) = 10 \\ &f_1(1,x) = f_2(1,x) = 0 \quad \text{for } x > 1 \\ &\left.\begin{aligned} f_1(2,x) &= 15 \\ f_2(2,x) &= 2 - (1/x) \end{aligned}\right\} \quad \text{for } x \geq 1. \end{aligned}$$

Let $g_1(2, x) = 15$ for $x \geq 1$ and $g(\cdot) = 0$ otherwise. Then it can be verified that $(g, (1, 1))$ is a commitment equilibrium even though it is not individually improving for player 1.

The phenomenon of multiple NEs would seem to present problems for the definition of commitment equilibrium. When a game has multiple NEs, which one counts for the comparison for which player? The next theorem shows that this problem is not a problem at all. If g is a commitment pattern that can give rise to a commitment equilibrium, then there is one NE of $\langle I, S, f-g\rangle$ that is better than all others for every player, and it is this NE that is relevant:

Theorem 5. (Unquestioned Superiority). *(g, s) is a commitment equilibrium only if $(f_i - g_i)(s) \geq (f_i - g_i)(\hat{s})$ for all $i \in I$ and $\hat{s} \in N(g)$.*

Proof. Suppose that for some $i \in I$ and $\hat{s} \in N(g)$,

$$(f_i - g_i)(s) < (f_i - g_i)(\hat{s}).$$

Then $(g, \hat{s})$ beats (g, s) through i. Hence (g, s) is not a commitment equilibrium. ■

A consequence of Unquestioned Superiority is that payoffs are uniquely determined by commitment patterns: if two commitment equilibria have the same commitment patterns, then payoffs are the same for every player at both equilibria.

Theorem 6. (Same Commitment, Same Payoff). *If (g, s') and (g, s'') are both commitment equilibria of $\langle I, S, f\rangle^*$, then $f(s') = f(s'')$.*

Proof. Suppose that for some $i \in I$,

$$f_i(s') > f_i(s'').$$

From the No Real Suffering Theorem, we have

$$g_i(s') = g_i(s'') = 0.$$

Hence

$$(f_i - g_i)(s') > (f_i - g_i)(s'')$$

and by Unquestioned Superiority, (g, s'') is not a commitment equilibrium. ■

A final result for this section deals with constant-sum two-person games. We have already seen that von Neumann-Morgenstern and Nash equilibria are the same for these games; now we will see that commitment equilibria are also.

Theorem 7. (Saddle Points). *Let $\langle I, S, f\rangle$ be a finite constant-sum two-person game. Then for $\langle I, S, f\rangle^*$:*

(a) *(g, s) is a commitment equilibrium only if $s \in N(o)$, i.e., only if s is a saddle point.*
(b) *If $s \in N(o)$, then (o, s) is a commitment equilibrium.*

Proof. Ad (a). Suppose (g, s) is an equilibrium. Then by Individual Improvement we have for player 1

$$f_1(s) \geq \max_{s_1' \in S_1} \min_{s_2' \in S_2} f_1(s_1', s_2')$$

and for player 2

$$f_2(s) \geq \max_{s_2' \in S_2} \min_{s_1' \in S_1} f_2(s_1', s_2'),$$

or, from the constant-sum property,

$$f_1(s) \leq \min_{s_2' \in S_2} \max_{s_1' \in S_1} f_1(s_1', s_2').$$

Thus

$$\min_{s_2' \in S_2} \max_{s_1' \in S_1} f_1(s_1', s_2') \geq f_1(s) \geq \max_{s_1' \in S_1} \min_{s_2' \in S_2} f_1(s_1', s_2').$$

But by the Minimax Theorem of von Neumann and Morgenstern (1944)

$$\min_{s_2' \in S_2} \max_{s_1' \in S_1} f_1(s_1', s_2') = \max_{s_1' \in S_1} \min_{s_2' \in S_2} f_1(s_1', s_2').$$

Hence

$$f_1(s) = \min_{s_2' \in S_2} \max_{s_1' \in S_1} f_1(s_1', s_2') = \max_{s_1' \in S_1} \min_{s_2' \in S_2} f_1(s_1', s_2')$$

and s is a saddle point and von Neumann-Morgenstern solution of $\langle I, S, f \rangle$. By Nash (1951), moreover, $s \in N(o)$.

Ad (b). Assume s is a saddle point. We must show that s is good for both players. Consider player 1. Since he has only one opponent, $P(1, 0) = A(2, 0)$. A situation

$$(s_1', \bar{s}_2) \in A(2, 0) \quad \text{if}$$

$$f_2(s_1', \bar{s}_2) \geq f_2(s_1', s_2'), \qquad \forall s_2' \in S_2,$$

that is, using the constant-sum property, if

$$f_1(s_1', \bar{s}_2) = \min_{s_2' \in S_2} f_1(s_1', s_2').$$

A situation, $s \in A(2, 0)$, then, is good for player 1, if

$$f_1(s) = \max_{s' \in A(2,0)} f_1(s') = \max_{s_1' \in S_1} \min_{s_2' \in S_2} f_1(s_1', s_2').$$

Since this is true by hypothesis, we see that s is good for player 1. By a symmetrical argument, s is good for player 2 also. ■

IV

It is appropriate now to show that commitment equilibria exist for large categories of games. In practicality, we will have no difficulty finding such equilibria for the games we look at, so the existence theorem will not need to be used afterward. For this reason, it is not as strong as it could be. We prove existence by first showing that every NE has a commitment pattern that yields a commitment equilibrium.

Lemma 1. (NEs Have Equilibria). *Let f be strictly positive. If s is an NE of $\langle I, S, f \rangle$, then there exists a g such that (g, s) is a commitment equilibrium of $\langle I, S, f \rangle^*$.*

Proof. Let g be given by:

$$\text{For all } i\text{: } g_i(\hat{s}) = f_i(\hat{s}) \qquad \text{if } \hat{s}_i \neq s_i$$
$$= 0 \qquad \text{if } \hat{s}_i = s_i.$$

We must show that (g, s) is a commitment equilibrium. Since $f(\cdot)$ is strictly positive, it is clear that s is an NE of $\langle I, S, f-g\rangle$. We must show that (g, s) is not beaten.

Consider any $i \in I$. In $\langle I, S, f-g\rangle$, player $j \neq i$ is always better off choosing s_j than any other strategy no matter what the other players do. Hence every element of $P(i, g)$, i's set of possible points, is of the form $(s_{-i}, \bar{s}_i)$. Because s is an NE of $\langle I, S, f\rangle$,

$$f_i(s) \geq f_i(s_{-i}, \bar{s}_i) \quad \text{for all } \bar{s}_i \in S_i.$$

Hence by the Possible Point Theorem, (g, s) is not beaten. Therefore (g, s) is a commitment equilibrium. ■

Theorem 8. (Existence). *Let f be strictly positive and let $\langle I, S, f\rangle$ be finite or satisfy the Glicksberg conditions. Then $\langle I, S, f\rangle^*$ has a commitment equilibrium.*

Proof. By Nash (1951) or Glicksberg (1952), $\langle I, S, f\rangle$ has an NE. Let s denote one such NE. By lemma 1, there is a g such that (g, s) is a commitment equilibrium of *QED.* ■

V

Commitment equilibrium, we mentioned before, lets us study the mechanism of cooperation. Cooperative behavior is possible only when players make promises and threats by selectively reducing their payoff functions. Game theory's *pons asinorum*, prisoners' dilemma, illustrates what commitments can—and cannot—do.

We repeat the payoff matrix:

		Player 2: Don't Confess	Player 2: Confess
Player 1	Don't Confess	5 (Player 1), 5 (Player 2)	0 (Player 1), 6 (Player 2)
Player 1	Confess	6 (Player 1), 0 (Player 2)	1 (Player 1), 1 (Player 2)

Since either player can assure himself of 1 by confessing, Individual Improvement prevents the single confession situations from supporting commitment equilibria.

One commitment equilibrium occurs when nobody promises and both confess. With no commitments, each player's possible set consists of the situations where:

He doesn't confess, the other player confesses, and his payoff is zero.
Both confess, and his payoff is one.

Clearly the dual confession situation is good for both, and thus is an equilibrium. It makes no sense for a player to make a commitment in this game if his partner has not made a commitment; a lonely commitment can result only in a long and lonely jail term.

The only stable cooperative pattern is a dual promise: the commitment pattern where each promises not to confess if the other does not, and the situation of no confessions is also a commitment equilibrium. To make the promises, each player must subtract an amount greater than one from his payoff in the situation where he alone confesses. The situations in each player's possible set are then:

Neither confesses, and his payoff is five.
Both confess, and his payoff is one.

Neither confessing, then, is good for both, and the equilibrium. It makes no sense for a player not to promise if his partner has already promised: given his partner's promise the NEs are at dual confession, if he makes no promise, and at no confessions, if he promises not to confess alone.

VI

Now we will show how the concept of commitment equilibrium fits in with what we were saying about rationality in the first two chapters.

First, it should be clear that commitment equilibrium is a type of rationality. The goodness theorem does all the work for us here. "Possibility" is a type of interesting-ness, as we used that term in chapter 2, and "goodness" is a type of worthiness. A situation must be rational in this sense for every player in order for it to be associated with a commitment equilibrium.

Much more interesting is the fact that any situation that is an equilibrium for any type of rationality is also a commitment equilibrium with some commitment pattern. We have already shown this to be the case for von Neumann-Morgenstern two-person constant-sum game rationality (theorem 7, part b) and for Nash rationality (lemma 1). Our claim in chapter 2 that for any type of rationality saddle-points are the only equilibria in two-person constant-sum games follows from this relationship and theorem 7, part a.

Why this relationship should hold is also something that can be demonstrated through the goodness theorem. Consider any arbitrary type of rationality—call it R-rationality—that has at least one R-equilibrium, situation s. Since s is R-worthy for all i, it must be R-interesting for all i a fortiori. Thus there must be some collection of interesting sets, one for each player, such that s is in the intersection of these sets. Let T_i denote the interesting set for player i that is in this collection.

Consider the following commitment pattern:

$$\begin{aligned} g_i(s) &= f_i(s) \quad \text{if } s \notin \bigcap_{j \in I} T_j \quad \text{for all } i \in I \\ &= 0 \qquad\quad \text{otherwise.} \end{aligned}$$

For a situation to be acceptable to some player j it must be in T_i, and for a situation to be possible for player i, it must be acceptable to player j. Thus for a situation to be possible for player i it must be in T_i:

$$P(i, g) \subset T_i \qquad \text{for all } i \in I. \tag{2}$$

We claim that the R-equilibrium s is in $P(i, g)$. Suppose it is not. Then there is some player $j \neq i$ for whom $s \notin A(j, g)$; that is, there is some $\tilde{s}_j \in S_j$ with

$$(f_j - g_j)(\tilde{s}_j, s_{-j}) > (f_j - g_j)(s). \tag{3}$$

Since s is interesting for all players, $g_j(s) = 0$. Either $(\tilde{s}_j, s_{-j})$ is interesting for all players or it is not. If it is not, the left-hand side of (3) equals zero and (3) does not hold. Thus if (3) holds, $(\tilde{s}_j, s_{-j})$ must be interesting for all players, and in particular it must be interesting for player j. But then from (3), s is not worthy for player j and is therefore not an R-equilibrium. Since this is a contradiction, s is in $P(i, g)$ for every player i.

Therefore since s is maximal for every player in his interesting set and is in his possible set, it follows from (2) that s is maximal for every player in his possible set. Thus it is good for all players and (g, s) is a commitment equilibrium. This is the relationship we wanted to show.

Commitment equilibrium, therefore, is the most general "solution concept" there is, and includes all other definitions of rationality as special cases. Studying commitment equilibrium lets us find out whether more particular approaches to rationality and particular sets of institutions (commitment patterns) are viable and capable of producing the situations we actually observe as equilibria. It does all this by a "micro-microanalysis" of promises and threats, the mechanics of cooperation.

4 ▪ Time

. . . And indeed there will be time
For the yellow smoke that slides along the street,
Rubbing its back upon the window-panes;
There will be time, there will be time
To prepare a face to meet the faces you meet;
There will be time to murder and create,
And time for all the works and days of hands
That lift and drop a question on your plate;
Time for you and time for me,
And time yet for a hundred indecisions
And for a hundred visions and revisions
Before the taking of a toast and tea. . . .
T. S. ELIOT, "The Love Song of J. Alfred Prufrock"

Not everything happens simultaneously. Because of this, people know different things at different points in their lives. This changing of knowledge is the game-theoretic function of time.

For the last two chapters time did not concern us. At the beginning of chapter 2, however, we promised that time, ignorance and uncertainty could be easily incorporated into the atemporal normal form framework we were using. Here we will make good on that promise. Doing so is easy because von Neumann-Morgenstern (1944), Kuhn (1953), and Selten (1975) provide all the results we need. (Readers familiar with those papers may omit this chapter virtually costlessly.)

In this chapter, then, some players will be able to receive new information—information they did not have at the beginning of the game—before they have made all their decisions. Time for us, as for Prufrock, is time for indecisions, visions, and revisions; if the passage of time does not mean that a later decision can use some additional piece of information, then it is really of no interest to us. Clocks and calendars do not concern us:

In a minute there is time
For decisions and revisions which a minute will reverse.

I

Games in which time figures explicitly are called *extensive games*. Following Selten (1975) we can describe any extensive game as a sextuple:

$$\Gamma = (K, P, U, C, p, h)$$

where the six constituents provide a summary of the rules of the game.

The first constituent is the *game tree* K. This is simply a tree with a distinguished vertex o, called the *origin* of K. The sequence of vertices and edges that connects o with a vertex x is called the *path* to x. Vertex y *comes after* vertex x if x is different from y and the path to y contains the path to x. An *endpoint* is a vertex that has no vertices coming after it. A path from the origin to an endpoint is called a *play*. The set of all endpoints is denoted by Z, and the set of all vertices that are not endpoints is denoted by X. An edge that connects vertex x with a vertex after x is called an *alternative* at x.

Roughly speaking, the game tree provides a summary of the various ways that a game can be played. Every vertex represents some choice a player (or Chance) can make in the course of playing the game, with the edges at the vertex corresponding to the alternatives of the choice. Every path from the origin to an endpoint represents a particular way that the game can be played from beginning to end; that is why we called it a play.

The second constituent of an extensive game is the *player partition* $P = (P_0, P_1, \ldots, P_n)$, which partitions X, the set of vertices of K that are not endpoints. Each element P_i of P is called player i's *player set*; roughly speaking, it contains all the vertices where player i is the decision-maker. Player 0 represents Chance, or Mother Nature, or the Umpire, or whatever it is that decides the things no player in the game decides. A player set may be empty.

The next constituent is the *information partition* U. For $i = 1, \ldots, n$ a subset u of P_i is called *information-eligible* if u is not empty, if no play intersects u more than once, and if the number of alternatives at every vertex in u is the same. A subset $u \in P_0$ is *information-eligible* if it contains exactly one vertex. The information partition U is a refinement of the player partition P into *information-eligible* subsets u of the player sets. These sets u are called *information sets*. The set of all information sets in P_i is denoted by U_i.

Roughly speaking, again, all the vertices in an information set u are indistinguishable for the decision-maker. He knows that play has progressed to a point where one of the choices is the one he has to make, but he has no idea of which one. Perfect information is when every information set is a singleton; then every decision-maker knows precisely what has gone on before.

The fourth constituent of an extensive game is the *choice partition C*. For $u \in U$ let A_u be the set of all alternatives at vertices $x \in u$. A subset c of A_u is *choice-eligible* if it contains exactly one alternative at x for every vertex $x \in u$. The choice partition C partitions the set of all edges of K into choice-eligible subsets c of the A_u with $u \in U$. These sets c are called *choices*. The choices c that are subsets of A_u are called choices at u, and the set of all choices at u is called C_u. If $u \in U$, and $i > 0$, then the choices are called personal choices (i.e., if Chance is not the decision-maker). A vertex x *comes after* a choice c if one of the edges in c is on the path to x.

Thus, all the edges in a choice c are indistinguishable to the decision-maker, just as all the vertices in an information set u are indistinguishable. A plurality of elements in an information set reflects the decision-maker's ignorance of what has gone on; the consequent plurality of elements in his choice sets reflects the consequent ignorance of what it is that he is doing.

A game has *perfect recall* if every player's information partition U_i, $i = 1, \ldots, n$ has the following property: if u and v are both in U_i and if one vertex $y \in v$ comes after a choice c at u, then every $x \in v$ comes after this choice. In a game with perfect recall a player who has to make a decision at one of his information sets knows which of his other information sets have been reached in the previous course of the play and which choices he made there. We will consider only games with perfect recall.

The fifth constituent of an extensive game is the probability assignment p that specifies the probabilities of the random choices that we leave to Chance or Mother Nature. Precisely, the probability assignment p is a function that assigns a probability distribution p_u over C_u to every $u \in U_0$; we require that $p_u(c)$ be strictly positive for every $c \in C_u$ (otherwise the possibility would not be a possibility at all).

Finally, the *payoff function h* assigns a vector $h(z) = (h_1(z), h_2(z), \ldots, h_n(z))$ with nonnegative real numbers as components to every endpoint z. The vector $h(z)$ is the *payoff vector* at z and the component $h_i(z)$ is player i's *payoff* at z.

II

People play extensive games by choosing alternatives at whatever information sets present themselves; they play normal form games by choosing strategies. These two processes can be reconciled by analyzing decision-making in extensive games a bit more deeply.

The way to do this is to consider von Neumann and Morgenstern's definition of a "strategy." For each player, a strategy is "a plan which specifies what choices he will make in every possible situation, for every possible actual information which he may possess at that moment in conformity with the pattern of information which the rules of the game provide for him for that case" (1944, p. 79). An extensive game strategy, then, provides a player with a choice at every one of his information sets. Playing an extensive game is then a process of choosing strategies, just like a normal form game.

As von Neumann and Morgenstern argue, "Observe that if we require each player to start the game with a complete plan of this kind, i.e., with a strategy, we by no means restrict his freedom of action. In particular, we do not thereby force him to make decisions on the basis of less information than there would be available for him in each practical instance in an actual play. This is because the strategy is supposed to specify every particular decision only as a function of just that amount of actual information which would be available for this purpose in an actual play. The only extra burden our assumption puts on the player is the intellectual one to be prepared with a rule of behavior for all eventualities—although he is to go through one play only. But this is an innocuous assumption within the confines of a mathematical analysis." (ibid.)

One may imagine a strategy as a complete, detailed instruction book, covering all eventualities, that a player could give to a trusted surrogate if he was unable to attend an actual play of the game; the surrogate would then serve as a perfect substitute for the player himself. All players, in fact, could send surrogates like this; there is no need for their actual attendance. There is no need, in fact, for the surrogates, either, once every player has compiled his instruction book: some central authority could gather all these instruction books, painstakingly compare them, construct from them the course of the play that would have eventuated if these instruction books had been followed, and assign each player the payoff associated with that play. One can thus consider the payoffs as functions of the instruction books, or strategies, alone, since once the instruction books have been compiled, all else follows.

Kuhn and Selten show how this argument can be formalized and extended to varieties of mixed strategies.

A *local strategy* b_{iu} at the information set $u \in U_i$ is a probability distribution over the set C_u of the choices at u; it assigns a probability $b_{iu}(c)$ to every choice c at u. A *pure local strategy* assigns a probability of one to one choice at u and zero to the other choices.

A *behavior strategy* b_i is a function that assigns a local strategy b_{iu} to every $u \in U_i$. The set of all of player i's behavior strategies is denoted by B_i. The behavior strategy that is formed from b_i by changing the local strategy at u from b_{iu} to $\hat{b}_{iu}$ is denoted by $b_i/\hat{b}_{iu}$. A behavior strategy that assigns a pure local strategy to every information set u is called a *pure strategy*. The set of all player i's pure strategies is denoted by π_i. A *mixed strategy* is a probability distribution over π_i; it assigns a probability to every pure strategy.

Most generally, a behavior strategy mixture m_i for player i is a probability distribution over B_i. The set of all behavior strategy mixtures is denoted by M_i. Note that behavior strategies, pure strategies, and mixed strategies are all particular kinds of behavior strategy mixtures: behavior strategies are behavior strategy mixtures where all the probability is assigned to one behavior strategy, pure strategies are behavior strategy mixtures where all the probability is assigned to one behavior strategy that is pure, and mixed strategies are behavior strategy mixtures that assign positive probability only to pure strategies.

A situation $m = (m_1, m_2, \ldots, m_n)$ in behavior strategy mixtures is an n-tuple of behavior strategy mixtures. Given such a situation m, we can compute a *realization probability* $\rho(x, m)$ for every vertex $x \in K$; this is the probability that the play will reach vertex x if the players use the behavior strategy mixtures of m. From the realization probabilities for the endpoints of K, we can compute an *expected payoff vector* $H(m) = (H_1(m), H_2(m), \ldots, H_n(m))$ for every behavior strategy mixture situation m:

$$H(m) = \sum_{z \in Z} \rho(z, m)\, h(z).$$

(Obviously this definition applies to situations in pure, mixed, and behavior strategies as well.)

Thus we have shown how an extensive game can be considered a normal-form game $\langle I, M, H \rangle$.

There is, moreover, an even simpler normal-form game we can use: $\langle I, B, H \rangle$. This is because Kuhn proved that one need consider only behavior strategies; anything that can be done with behavior strategy mixtures in games with perfect recall can also be done with behavior strategies.

To be precise, we say that two of player i's behavior strategy mixtures m_i' and m_i'' are *realization equivalent* if they make the realization probabilities of every vertex identical no matter what the other players do:

$$\rho(x, (m_{-i}, m_i')) = \rho(x, (m_{-i}, m_i''))$$

for all $x \in K$ and all $m_{-i} \in X_{j \neq i} M_j$. Selten's statement of Kuhn's theorem is that "in every extensive game with perfect recall a realization equivalent behavior strategy b_i can be found for every behavior strategy mixture m_i of a personal player" (1975, p. 30). Thus we can restrict our attention to behavior strategies.

III

Since we can describe every extensive game with perfect recall as a normal form game $\langle I, B, H \rangle$, all of our results in chapters 2 and 3 about rationality for normal form games carry over without any problems. Strategies are somewhat more complicated objects than we may have imagined in those two chapters, and the associated optimization problems are correspondingly more tedious, but these difficulties are, in principle at least, entirely inconsequential. In particular, we know that because of the generality of commitment equilibrium, we can simulate any form of rationality we want to by making appropriate subtractions from payoff functions and then finding Nash equilibria. All we need to be concerned about, then, are Nash equilibria, and since the definition and basic results for NEs carry over there appears to be no cause for concern.

There is, however, one problem with NEs in extensive games. It centers on unreached information sets. Suppose b is an NE and that with b the realization probability of every vertex in some information set u of player i is zero. Information set u "never happens." Then what player i plans to do at information set u cannot affect his (or any other player's) payoff. Player i can change his local strategy at u to anything at all, no matter how silly, without disturbing the NE. Clearly, such frivolity at irrelevant parts of the game should not affect the NEs, and if only one player is acting frivolously it will not; but when several players do so together, joint frivolity in never-never land can impinge on the real world and create NEs that owe their existence to frivolity. Selten calls such NEs *imperfect*; he calls other NEs *perfect*.

Before being more precise about these matters, we will be more concrete and present Selten's numerical example. This is the extensive game pictured in figure 1. Player sets are identical with information sets (each player has only one information set), and are indicated by dashed lines. Payoff vectors

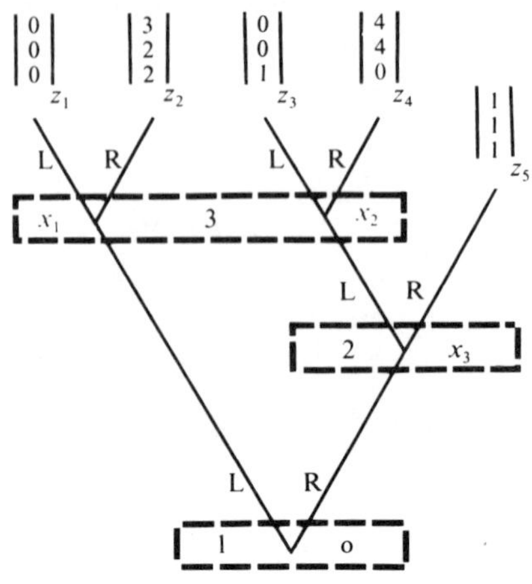

Figure 1

are indicated by column vectors above the corresponding endpoints. In this game player 1 moves first and chooses either left or right. If player 1 chooses left, player 3 moves next and chooses either left or right and the game ends. If player 1 chooses right, player 2 moves next and chooses either left or right. If player 2 chooses right, the game ends. If player 2 chooses left, player 3 gets to complete the game by choosing either left or right. When player 3 gets to move, however, he does not know whether or not player 2's move has intervened between his move and player 1's.

Since every player has only one information set and only two choices available at that information set, every player's behavior strategy can be described completely by the probability with which he selects right. A behavior strategy situation is a triplet (p_1, p_2, p_3).

This game has two types of NEs:

Type 1: $p_1 = 1, p_2 = 1, 0 \leq p_3 \leq 1/4$
Type 2: $p_1 = 0, 1/3 \leq p_2 \leq 1, p_3 = 1.$

Type 2 NEs are imperfect. Player 2's information set is never reached, and so what he does does not affect his payoff. His local strategy there is frivolous in this sense: Suppose that for some reason player 2's information set is reached. Then since at type 2 NEs player 3 is certainly choosing right, the outcome of the game will be at z_4 if player 2 chooses left and at z_5 if he chooses right. Since player 2 receives 4 at z_4 and 1 at z_5, it would be entirely irrational under these circumstances for him to do anything but choose left with certainty—but at type 2 equilibria he is choosing right with a probability of at least one-third.

Nor is such frivolity inconsequential, even if it occurs in make-believe. Player 2's frivolity makes it rational for player 1 to choose left rather than right, and this in turn makes it rational for player 3 to choose right instead of left. Type I NEs end up (with certainty) at z_5 with payoff vector (1, 1, 1); type 2 NEs end up (with certainty) at z_2 with payoff vector (3, 2, 2).

What Selten uses to formalize the difference between frivolous and non-frivolous behavior strategies on which the definition of perfect equilibrium must rest is the notion of slight mistakes. *A perturbed game* $\hat{\Gamma}$ is a pair (Γ, η) where Γ is a finite extensive game with perfect recall, and η is a function that assigns a positive probability η_c to every personal choice c in Γ such that

$$\sum_{c \text{ at } u} \eta_c < 1$$

and requires every local strategy at u to satisfy $b_{iu}(c) \geq \eta_c$ for all c. In a perturbed game, the behavior strategies available to the players are restricted—by the irreducible possibility of a slight mistake, so to speak—to those where every choice is possible; pure strategies are not available in $\hat{\Gamma}$. If $\hat{B}$ denotes the set of behavioral strategies available in $\hat{\Gamma}$, then $\hat{\Gamma}$ can be represented as $\langle I, \hat{B}, H \rangle$, and there is no problem defining NEs in $\hat{\Gamma}$.

Every information set in U has some positive probability of being reached in $\hat{\Gamma}$, no matter what behavior strategy situation applies. Thus at an NE in $\hat{\Gamma}$ there is no room for frivolous behavior, because there is no never-never land. This is why Selten uses perturbed games to define perfect equilibria.

Specifically, consider a sequence $\hat{\Gamma}^1, \hat{\Gamma}^2, \ldots, \hat{\Gamma}^k, \ldots$ of perturbed games $\hat{\Gamma}^k = (\Gamma, \eta^k)$ of Γ. If for every personal choice c, the minimum probability η_c^k converges to 0 for $k \rightarrow \infty$, the sequence is called a *test sequence*. A behavior strategy situation b is called a *limit equilibrium* of a test sequence $\hat{\Gamma}^1, \hat{\Gamma}^2, \ldots, \hat{\Gamma}^k, \ldots$ if for every k an NE $\hat{b}^k$ can be found such that for $k \rightarrow \infty$ the sequence of the $\hat{b}^k$ converges to b. A behavior strategy situation b^* is a *perfect equilibrium* for Γ if there is at least one test sequence, $\hat{\Gamma}^1, \hat{\Gamma}^2, \ldots, \hat{\Gamma}^k, \ldots$ for which b^* is a limit equilibrium. Selten proves that every perfect equilibrium of Γ is an NE of Γ (p. 37, lemma 3), and that every finite game with perfect recall has at least one perfect equilibrium (p. 48, theorem 6). Most importantly, he also shows that at a perfect equilibrium every player plans to behave Nash-rationally from every one of his information sets on to the end of the game, even if that information set will never be reached (pp. 45–46, theorem 3).

We will, therefore, for the remainder of the book, be concerned for the most part with perfect NEs, their continuous game analogues, and the notion of acceptability implied by perfection. Players should act rationally no matter what information set they find themselves at. For continuous games, moreover, and for many finite ones as well, perfect equilibria are often easier to compute than imperfect ones. Computational ease and theoretical correctness are not always consonant with each other, but when they are the effect is compelling.

IV

Finally, let us note that the perfectness concept simplifies our definition of commitment equilibrium: A commitment equilibrium is a perfect equilibrium of a two-stage game in which players make commitments at the first stage and play the modified game at the second.

5 ▪ Expectations

Blessed is he who expects nothing, for he shall never be disappointed.

ALEXANDER POPE

Modelling expectations is an accepted part of macroeconomics. What people do now depends on what they think will happen in the future, and what they think will happen in the future depends in some way on what happened in the past. Thus, it is commonly believed that it is impossible to do macroeconomics without some probability theory mechanism that links people's subjective views about the future to objective events in the past. Many of the major macroeconomic controversies of the last fifteen years have centered on different mechanisms for doing so.

In this chapter we will argue that the search for such a mechanism is not consonant with the tradition of rationality that defines economics. There are, to be sure, times when these mechanisms are not inappropriate: games against nature. But games with other players differ fundamentally from games against nature, and it is a misleading analogy that leads economists to seek some parallel process that allows external events to imprint probabilities of other players' actions onto players' psyches. Rationality is not a method for attaching numbers to conjectures.

Our arguments in this chapter may appear somewhat diffuse because the views we are arguing against have rarely been stated explicitly. Indeed I have been unable to find an explicit argument *for* the use of expectations anywhere in the literature. This lack of an explicit argument is even more surprising in light of the substantial volume of writing that questions the use of expectations, probability theory, and analogies with games against nature. This literature is surveyed in the first section of this chapter.

The next section analyzes games against nature, the mechanisms proposed for linking external events to probability assessments in these games, and the justifications for these mechanisms. The third section asks whether these mechanisms and their justifications can be extended to games with other players and concludes that they cannot. The fourth section shows that even if some justifiable method were found to link external events to internal probabilities, it could not be considered rational if it did not coincide with commitment equilibrium—thus there is no advantage to searching for better methods. The fifth section is about "temporary equilibrium."

(Appendix C, on Newcomb's problem, may also be read in conjunction with this chapter. There we show that this philosophical problem arises from a mistaken application of games-against-nature methods to a game with other players.)

I

As with most other fundamental matters in this book, the best statement of our position that the problems of rationality in many-person games cannot be "obviated . . . by a mere recourse to the devices of the theory of probability" is due to von Neumann and Morgenstern:

> Every participant can determine the variables which describe his own actions but not those of the others. Nevertheless those "alien" variables cannot, from his point of view, be described by statistical assumptions. This is because the others are guided, just as he himself, by rational principles—whatever that may mean—and no *modus procedendi* can be correct which does not attempt to understand those principles and the interactions of the conflicting interests of all participants. (1944, p. 11)

This unwillingness to use statistical techniques for games was not original with von Neumann and Morgenstern, however. As early as 1908 Poincaré denied that the laws of chance applied to the "moral sciences," though he was by no means as clear as von Neumann and Morgenstern:

> We are tempted to attribute facts of this nature to chance because their causes are obscure, but this is not true chance. The causes are unknown to us, it is true, and they are even complex; but they are not sufficiently complex, and we have seen that this is the distinguishing mark of "too simple" causes. When men are brought together, they no longer decide by chance and independently of each other, but react upon one another. Many causes come into action, they trouble the men and draw them this way and that, but there is one thing they cannot destroy, the habits they have of Panurge's sheep.[1] (1908, p. 88)

1. In Rabelais' *Gargantua et Pantagruel*, Panurge destroys the flock of a shepherd who has angered him. He does this by purchasing the lead sheep and throwing it into the ocean. The other sheep follow their leader.

Borel made a similar point, somewhat more analytically, in his review of Keynes's *Treatise on Probability*:

> However, there is an important enough case in which the numerical evaluation of probabilities presents some special difficulties, but it does not seem that Mr. Keynes has given to this case the special importance that it appears to me to have, although one could try to relate to it certain examples that he gives. This case is the one in which the event of which the realization is in question is not actually determined and can depend on judgments for which one searches to define the probabilities . . .
>
> Take a simple example. Consider the question of betting on the result of an election, a practice engaged in currently in certain countries. It is clear that it can produce multiple reaction; on the one hand, the partisans of each candidate look to augment his chances by openly betting great sums on him; on the other hand certain voters can be influenced by the desire to vote for the candidate who, according to their judgment, will be elected. Certain bettors who are at the same time voters can have their vote influenced by the desire for gain. A new candidate can surge forward if the bets are large in favor of this combination, etc. Under these conditions, can one admit that the probability of judgment carried by a bet has a determinate numerical value? (1924, p. 58)

The division between games against nature and "games of strategy" (games with other players) in standard works like Luce and Raiffa's *Games and Decisions* (1957) and Blackwell and Girshick's *Theory of Games and Statistical Decisions* (1954) also supports the von Neumann-Morgenstern distinction, *albeit* implicitly.

Drèze is alone among modern writers, to my knowledge, in explicitly denying this division, but his denial does not go so far as to support the use of objective events to determine subjective probabilities. Drèze (1971; cf. 1972, 1960, 1961) holds that the theory he has developed for games against nature generalizes easily to include games of strategy, and hence games of strategy are merely a special type of games against nature, or, more specifically—and the distinction is key—that the normative theory of individual decision-making in games of strategy is merely a special case of the normative theory of decision-making in games against nature: "By successive redefinition of the strategies of a player's opponents, it is always possible to formalize the decision-problem facing a player in a game of strategy as a game against nature, where the states of nature are described with reference to the opponent's strategies" (1972, p. 16). His method is essentially to define probability measures on situations conditionally upon the choice of a strategy by the decision-maker and to use the principle of maximizing expected utility ("moral expectation") to govern choices among strategies.

Drèze's analysis is compatible with ours because all he is talking about is individual rationality. His "redefinition of opponent's strategies" is the same thing as our interesting sets, and his maximizing of expected utility is the same principle we follow in deriving worthy sets from interesting sets, and thus his view of rationality is the same as ours. It is our position, too, that the principles of individual rationality are the same in both games against nature and games of strategy.

Drèze also shares our view that rationality, as we agree on it, is fundamental, and the question of what sets are interesting is secondary, or entirely extra-rational:

> In this vein, we might also speak about two levels of "rationality": the most fundamental level, at which rules of consistency are specified; these rules result in the principle of moral expectation; at a less fundamental level, the "prudential" principle of minimaxing, or the principle of insufficient reason, prove helpful in applying the rule of moral expectation to specific contexts; their claims to "rationality" are however less convincing than those of the consistency rules of games against nature. (Ibid.)

Thus Drèze does not see the linking of external events to probabilities as the role of rationality. The only difference, then, between this book and Drèze's argument is the additional emphasis we place on equilibrium. But this difference is entirely explained by the divergent goals of our inquiries. Drèze is seeking a normative theory. Equilibrium, we stressed, is an empirical requirement. That it does not concern him is not surprising.

Nor has less mathematical economics been any more eager to derive probabilities from external events. Writers such as Knight (1921) and Shackle (1949) have denied the usefulness of numerical probabilities, though not the importance of expectation, in nontrivial economic decision-making, and this position has come to be recognized as a major tenet of the "Austrian" school. Probably the best statement of this position, though, is that of Keynes:

> By "uncertain knowledge," let me explain, I do not mean merely to distinguish what is known from what is only probable. The game of roulette is not subject, in this sense, to uncertainty; nor is the prospect of a Victory bond being drawn. Or, again, the expectation of life is

> only slightly uncertain. Even the weather is only moderately uncertain. The sense in which I am using the term is that in which the prospect of a European war is uncertain, or the price of copper and the rate of interest twenty years hence, or the obsolescence of a new invention, or the position of private wealth-owners in the social system in 1970. About these matters there is no scientific basis on which to form any calculable probability whatever. We simply do not know. (1937, pp. 213–214)

Note that the events cited as uncertain depend on the actions of conscious mutually interdependent agents—players—while the less uncertain events do not.

Keynes, having written one of the twentieth century's major philosophical discussions of probability, was acutely conscious of its role, and portrayed his views on probability as a major and underlying difference between classical economists and himself: "The orthodox theory assumes that we have a knowledge of the future of a kind quite different from that which we actually possess. This false rationalization follows the lines of the Benthamite calculus. The hypothesis of a calculable future leads to a wrong interpretation of the principles of behavior which the need for action compels us to adopt, and to an underestimation of the concealed factors of utter doubt, precariousness, hope, and fear" (ibid., p. 222).

Thus we see that numerical modelling of expectations in games of strategy has been opposed by quite a long and eminent list of writers; there is nothing novel about our position.

II

Can external events *ever* be used to generate probabilities to guide people's actions? The consensus on this question is yes, and an examination of the circumstances that give rise to this answer—games against nature—can show why external events do not always generate probabilities.

Consider a game in which the only two players are Robinson Crusoe and Mother Nature. To be even more specific, suppose Crusoe is deciding whether to climb a tall palm tree, the top of which he cannot see. If Mother Nature has put a coconut at the top of the tree, Crusoe's climb will be worthwhile; if she has not, it will not be. We may even suppose that Crusoe has a payoff function that assigns utilities to the four situations that can occur:

		Mother Nature's Strategy	
		Coconut	No Coconut
Crusoe's Strategy	Climb	10	0
	Don't Climb	5	5

To find out what the equilibria are in this game, and thus what predictions we can make about how it will be played, we need to know Mother Nature's payoff function. There are various views of what Mother Nature's payoff function is—Murphy's Law and the Sermon on the Mount, for instance, provide contrasting positions—but the view that is predominant in probability-using cultures is that Mother Nature is, at the very least, indifferent about what strategy Crusoe chooses. "Now if that is how God clothes the grass in the field which is there today and thrown into the furnace tomorrow, will He not much more look after you, you men of little faith?" is the epigraph for no treatise on decision theory, and it is difficult to imagine how Western science could have developed in a society that took this Gospel seriously.

We will be secular, then, and insist that Mother Nature's payoff be the same in all situations where her strategy is the same. We also restrict our attention to commitments that have this same "indifference-to-Crusoe" property. These two secularity assumptions are the core of modern decision theory, and the reason why games against nature are distinctive. Newcomb's problem, which we discuss in Appendix C, troubles philosophers because it presents as something that looks like a game against nature a circumstance where secularity is uncertain.

To simplify discourse further we will set Mother Nature's payoff equal to one at all situations. This will greatly simplify the analysis, but it will not change the results: the secularity assumptions do the real work. A strategy for Mother Nature will be a probability p for putting coconuts in the tree, and a strategy for Crusoe will be a probability q for climbing the tree. Mother Nature's and Crusoe's payoff functions are thus:

$$f^M(p, q) \equiv 1$$
$$f^c(p, q) = 10\,pq + 5(1 - q),$$

respectively.

First, let us observe that in a certain sense commitments by Crusoe do not really matter. Suppose commitment pattern $g = (g^M, g^c)$ prevails. Whatever g is, Mother Nature's good set will be identical to her possible set, since all situations have the same payoff to her, and her possible set will be identical to Crusoe's acceptable set, since Crusoe is the only other player. Thus Mother Nature's good set will be identical to Crusoe's acceptable set, which will depend on his commitment, but not Mother Nature's. On the other hand, Crusoe's good set is the situations that maximize his payoff in his possible set, which is identical to Mother Nature's acceptable set. Mother Nature's acceptable set depends on her commitment, but not on Crusoe's. Thus for $(g, (p, q))$ to be an equilibrium, (p, q) must maximize Crusoe's payoff in Mother Nature's acceptable set, and be in Crusoe's acceptable set:

$$f^c(p, q) \geq f^c(\tilde{p}, \tilde{q}) \qquad \text{for all } (\tilde{p}, \tilde{q}) \text{ in } A(M, g) \tag{1}$$

and

$$f^c(p, q) \geq (f^c - g^c)(p, \bar{q}) \quad \text{for all } \bar{q} \in (0, 1). \tag{2}$$

Now suppose that $((g^M, g^c), (p, q))$ is an equilibrium but that $((g^M, 0), (p, q))$ is not. Since Mother Nature's acceptable set depends on her commitment alone, $A(M, (g^M, 0)) = A(M, (g^M, g^c))$ and

$$f^c(p, \bar{q}) \geq f^c(\tilde{p}, \tilde{q}) \qquad \text{for all } (\tilde{p}, \tilde{q}) \text{ in } A(M, (g^M, 0)) \tag{3}$$

since $((g^M, g^c), (p, q))$ was by hypothesis an equilibrium. Then it must be the case that (2) does not hold; i.e., that there is some $\bar{q}$ with

$$f^c(p, \bar{q}) > f^c(p, q). \tag{4}$$

Comparing (3) and (4), we see that it must be the case that $(p, \bar{q}) \notin A(M, (g^M, 0))$, so that there must be some $\bar{p}$ such that

$$(f^M - g^M)(\bar{p}, \bar{q}) > (f^M - g^M)(p, \bar{q}). \tag{5}$$

From secularity, though

$$(f^M - g^M)(\bar{p}, \bar{q}) = (f^M - g^M)(\bar{p}, q)$$

and

$$(f^M - g^M)(p, \bar{q}) = (f^M - g^M)(p, q).$$

Combining these with (5), we obtain

$$(f^M - g^M)(\bar{p}, q) > (f^M - g^M)(p, q)$$

whence it follows that (p, q) is not in $A(M, (g^M, g^c))$ and therefore not an equilibrium. Since this is a contradiction, we must conclude that our original supposition was false and its negation true:

$$\text{If } ((g^M, g^c), (p, q)) \text{ is an equilibrium, then so is } ((g^m, 0), (p, q)). \tag{6}$$

Proposition (6) means that in a secular world, shaking one's fist at, negotiating with, and praying to Mother Nature are all equally ineffective. Crusoe's threats and promises cannot in the least bit budge Mother Nature, because she does not care what he does.

Proposition (6) also means that in a secular world we can confine our attention to commitment patterns with $g^c \equiv 0$. Since it is easy to show that if $((g^M, 0), (p, q))$ is an equilibrium and $(p, q) \in A(C, (g^M, g^c))$ then $((g^M, g^c), (p, q))$ is also an equilibrium, all equilibria are simple variants of equilibria with $g^c \equiv 0$. Finding equilibria when $g^c \equiv 0$ is particularly undemanding because of the following result:

$$((g^M, 0), (p, q)) \quad \text{is an equilibrium iff (1).} \tag{7}$$

Necessity, of course, is merely a restatement of (1). To see why (7) should hold in the other direction, note that secularity implies that if $(p, q) \in A(M, g^M)$, then $(p, \tilde{q}) \in A(M, g^M)$ for all $\tilde{q} \in (0, 1)$. Thus (1) implies

$$f^c(p, q) \geq f^c(p, \tilde{q}) \quad \text{for all } \tilde{q} \in (0, 1)$$

which is precisely (2) for $g^c \equiv 0$, and (1) and (2) are sufficient for $((g^M, 0), (p, q))$ to be an equilibrium.

Thus (6) and (7) tell us that equilibria can be found by solving (1). This is trivial, although a little notation is needed. Assume $A(M, g)$ is always closed and let $p^*(g^M)$ denote the greatest p such that there is some q with $(p, q) \in A(M, g)$. (Secularity means that $(p^*, \bar{q}) \in A(M, g)$ for all $\bar{q}$.) Then the equilibrium situations are:

$$\begin{array}{llll} \text{for } g^M & \text{with } p^*(g^M) > .5, & (p^*(g^M), 1) & \\ \text{for } g^M & \text{with } p^*(g^M) = .5, & (.5, q) & \text{where } q \in (0, 1) \\ \text{for } g^M & \text{with } p^*(g^M) < .5, & (p, 0) & \text{where } (p, 0) \in A(M, g). \end{array}$$

Now consider commitments by Mother Nature of the form

$$\begin{aligned} g^M(p, q) &= f^M(p, q) && \text{if } p \neq \hat{p} \\ &= 0 && \text{if } p = \hat{p}. \end{aligned}$$

We call such commitments canonical. Canonical commitments satisfy secularity. If $p^*(g^M) \geq .5$, then the canonical commitment with $\hat{p} = p^*(g^M)$ has the same equilibrium situations as g^M does. If $p^*(g^M) < .5$, then the equilibrium situation with the canonical commitment pattern with $\hat{p} = p^*(g^M)$

is an equilibrium situation with g^M, Crusoe's strategy is the same at the canonical commitment pattern equilibrium situation as at all the g^M-equilibrium situations, and both players' payoffs are the same at the canonical commitment pattern equilibrium situation as they are at the g^M-equilibrium situations. Thus to predict Crusoe's actions and players' payoffs (and to advise Crusoe) all we need to consider are canonical commitments by Mother Nature. Economists in a secular world may safely presume that Mother Nature is making a canonical commitment, and Crusoe a null one.

This information, however, does neither us nor Crusoe much good. There is an equilibrium for any canonical commitment whatsoever by Mother Nature. Because of Mother Nature's vast indifference, the hypothesis that the players are rational does not very severely restrict the situations that might be observed; in particular, it does not restrict at all the behavior that might be observed of Mother Nature. On the other hand, if we know Mother Nature's commitment, rationality permits us to say quite a bit—everything, in fact, that is of interest. This is why game theorists generally analyze games as if they knew Mother Nature's commitment (and why the fifth constituent of an extensive game in chapter four was Mother Nature's mixed strategy). The problem is that rationality tells us nothing about Mother Nature's commitment.

Economists qua students of rationality therefore have nothing to say about this game or other, more complicated games against nature. Studying rationality, though, is not the only source of knowledge, and so, rather than say nothing at all about these games, economists have posited various extra-rational processes in Crusoe's mind to allow them to use events external to the game to predict his behavior in it.

The external events that these processes rely on are previous plays of games "similar" to the game under study, and the basic postulate under which these processes work is that Crusoe acts as if Mother Nature's commitment in "similar" games will be "similar" to her commitment in the game under study. If most other palm trees have coconuts at the top, Crusoe will believe that this one will too, and climb it. This type of postulate is intuitively appealing because there is no reason for us as observers or Crusoe as a player to believe that Mother Nature is making a commitment other than the one she made in similar games, since no commitment is better than any other for her, and Crusoe's commitments make no difference to her whatsoever.

The computational task of these processes, then, is to tease out of the historical record of past "similar" plays what Mother Nature's commitment was then and what it will be in the game under study. How to do it is difficult and controversial. The word "similar" is the crux of the problem.

One can never step in the same river twice, and no game is ever the same as one that was played before. Just how simple-minded does Crusoe believe Mother Nature is? Does Mother Nature use the same commitment only for palm trees at this time of year on this side of the island, or does she use the same commitment for all tall objects? Even if Crusoe does not believe that Mother Nature uses exactly the same commitment for palm trees on both sides of the island, is there some way for him to use his information on what she did on the other side of the island? Is there some way that Crusoe can use his information that King Kong did not find a coconut at the top of the Empire State Building? Different schools of statistical theory and epistemology give different answers about what Crusoe *should* believe, while different schools of expectationist economics give different answers about what Crusoe *does* believe (or, more precisely, what it is that Crusoe acts as if he believed). Such controversies are beyond rationality and unlikely ever to be resolved.

III

Thus we see that external events can be used to generate probabilities only when secularity holds. But secularity holds only in a particularly barren class of games, about which rationality says very little. These methods, then, are in a sense techniques of desperation, and using them in more fertile games is like irrigating tropical rain forests in imitation of Arizona's farming methods, or clothing rich children in hand-me-down's from poor relations.

The reasons why generating probabilities from external events had intuitive appeal for games against nature do not carry over into nonsecular games of strategy. Suppose that it is Friday, not Mother Nature, who puts coconuts in trees, and that Friday cares about whether or not Crusoe climbs the tree. We cannot postulate secularity of Friday. Then canonical commitments have no generality; nor can we act as if Crusoe was making a null commitment.

Even if we should go so far as to allow that Friday is making a canonical commitment, the two reasons for the intuitive appeal of using external events still vanish. For what commitments Friday made in similar games depended on what commitments Crusoe made, and it is because Crusoe is thinking about what his commitment will be that he is pondering what Friday's is; thus he can seriously suspect that Friday's commitment might also change from what it was in those games.

The problem of defining what games are similar, moreover, difficult as it was with games against nature, becomes almost insuperable in games of strategy. Solving it, too, becomes more important: because of secularity no answer to this problem could force Mother Nature to act irrationally (basically because Mother Nature cannot act irrationally) but wrong answers can force Friday into irrationality. In deciding what games of strategy (if any) are similar, Crusoe must take into account Friday's learning more about Crusoe's behavior (something that matters to him but not to Mother Nature) every time the game is played and thus having different information every time. He must also consider Friday's thinking about Crusoe's thought on Friday's learning in the previous games, and so on in infinite regress. Perhaps the only way to resolve this matter is to define similar games as those with isomorphic commitment equilibria. But if we do so we are analyzing games in terms of their internal structure, not external events.

Nor is the problem any easier if Crusoe is not a frequentist. No matter what his philosophy about probability is, he still cannot attribute secularity to Friday and so he cannot appeal to external events of whatever kind to induce probabilities. An exception would be if Crusoe's philosophy of probability were a necessarism that derived probabilities from the commitment equilibria, but such necessarism would not use external events; it would represent the harmless rhetorical use of the work "expectations" that we described in chapter 1.

IV

Indeed, there is no way of analyzing games with rational players except in terms of commitment equilibria. We first made this point at the end of chapter 3 and are repeating it now only for emphasis. Whatever method we wish to use to arrive at probabilities, it will lead us astray unless it leads us to commitment equilibria.

For suppose that Crusoe believed that Friday was making a canonical commitment to put a coconut on top of the tree with probability $\hat{p}$. Perhaps he considered only a few nearby trees similar, in which case he would be said to have "adaptive expectations," or perhaps he used the best system of regression equations economists could come up with to explain his past failures and successes in finding coconuts (or fruits) on top of trees (or tall things), in which case he might be said to have "rational expectations."[2]

2. These are perhaps not what proponents would see as rational expectations in the strict sense, but only an empirically implementable approximation to it. In some strict senses, rational expectations becomes the necessarist position in which the use of the word "expectations" is only a harmless rhetorical device. If rational expectations is understood in this sense, the question we are discussing is whether the theory is well served by its empirical implementation.

Or maybe he might have used some other events in some nonfrequentist fashion. The particular mechanism is immaterial.

His good set, then, is all the situations $(\hat{p}, q)$ that maximize his utility given that there is a probability $\hat{p}$ that a coconut is in the tree. It is exactly the same as his worthy set if his interesting set is all situations with $p = \hat{p}$: whether or not there will be an equilibrium depends on whether Friday will in fact set $p = \hat{p}$: whether Friday's payoff function and Crusoe's commitment are such there is some situation $(\hat{p}, q)$ in both good sets. (If Crusoe's commitment is also canonical, then a situation will be associated with a commitment equilibrium if and only if it is a Nash equilibrium.) If there is no equilibrium with $p = \hat{p}$ and Crusoe's commitment, then rationality will prevent Friday from choosing $p = \hat{p}$.

Friday's actions depend on the structure of the game, not on his past action.

V

What, then, can account for the popularity of expectations derived from past external events in economic modelling? Let us consider the type of games and the manner in which expectations are most commonly used.

These are extensive games in which something called a "temporary equilibrium" is sought. It works like this: the information sets of the game are partitioned into two sets, the "present" and the "future." The present includes the origin, and no vertex in any information set in the present comes after any vertex in any information set in the future. Players' interesting sets of behavioral strategy situations are determined by their expectations, and their worthy sets by the usual maximizations. Ordinary equilibria, if they exist, would be behavioral strategy situations that are worthy for all players, but temporary equilibria are sets of behavioral strategy situations that must meet two less stringent criteria: these sets must include at least one behavioral strategy situation that is worthy for each player and all behavioral strategy situations in the set must have the same local strategies at all information sets in the present.

All equilibria are temporary equilibria, then, but the converse is not true. Expectations can create interesting sets that yield temporary equilibria that are divergent behavioral strategy situations. Consider the two-person game with the payoff bi-matrix:

		Player 2	
		L	R
Player 1	L	0, 5	5, 0
	R	5, 5	4, 0

Let player 1 move first, but let player 2 be ignorant of player 1's move. One temporary equilibrium of this game can be arrived at by considering player 1's information set the present and player 2's information set the future. Let player 1's expectation be that player 2 will choose R and player 2's, that player 1 will choose L. Given this partition and these expectations, the temporary equilibrium will be the set {LL, LR}. But neither of the situations could ever be in an equilibrium. The situation LL could never be an equilibrium because it is not individually improving for player 1 (he can assure himself of 4 by choosing R). The situation LR could never be in an equilibrium because it is not individually improving for player 2 (he can assure himself of 5 by choosing L).

The search for temporary equilibria is thus not fully within the tradition of rationality. This is not to say that temporary equilibria and the extra-rational expectations processes associated with them are not worth studying or that no phenomena will ever be found that rationality cannot explain and temporary equilibria can. All that it means is that there is a presumption for exhausting the possibilities of rationality first. If there is no way—or even no reasonably simple way—of describing the phenomena we are interested in as equilibria, then by all means we should consider them as temporary equilibria. But if the phenomena can be described as equilibria, there is no reason to settle for a temporary equilibrium description.

So we turn now to seeing how well economic phenomena can be described as commitment equilibria.

PART TWO ▪ SPECIFIC

6 ▪ Small Simple Economies

Our little systems have their day;
They have their day and cease to be . . .
ALFRED LORD TENNYSON, *In Memoriam*

Can we maintain that people act rationally? We saw in chapter 3 that it did not involve any contradiction to assert that people acted rationally; this was because commitment equilibria existed in most games. But the fact that we can assert something without contradicting ourselves does not mean it is true. The question we must now consider is whether there are commitment equilibria that resemble the occurrences we observe in the world.

To do this, we must consider the specific games we are interested in—those that resemble actual economies. Our method for these games will be to see whether they have commitment equilibria associated with any members of various families of commitment patterns. If they do, and if these equilibria resemble things that happen in actuality, then we will be happy—both with rationality in general, and with the family of commitment patterns in particular. If either count fails, we will continue our search for other families of commitment patterns. One might wish to identify "families of commitment patterns" with "institutions"; then the search for usable families of commitment patterns becomes a search for institutions that are both logically coherent (because they are associated with commitment equilibria) and empirically satisfying (because their equilibria are what happens).

That we need axioms beyond simple rationality before we can make testable statements should not be surprising; nor does it indicate any weakness in the concept of commitment equilibrium. Most scientific theories require many, many axioms before they can generate testable statements. But how does postulating a family of commitment patterns differ from postulating a type of expectations? Both steps, to be sure, go beyond rationality, but working with commitment patterns does so in a way that is sure not to contradict rationality; we have seen that with expectations—unless we treat them as a rhetorical device only—there is no such guarantee. All commitment pattern statements can be paraphrased in expectation-language, but only noncontradictory expectation statements can be paraphrased in commitment-language. There is simply no need for expectation-language. (Expectation-language also carries with it two misleading connotations about the link between rationality and predictions: the first is that the problem would not exist in atemporal economies, and the second is that the necessary link is private and psychological, not social and institutional.)

A system where we did not have to postulate families of commitment patterns would of course be more elegant, simpler, and more desirable. Perhaps there is some way of assigning commitment pattern families to games flawlessly, or with a high degree of reliability. Surely such a system is worth searching for, but if it exists I do not know what it is.

With this chapter, then, we have finally reached the stage where we can talk about subjects vaguely resembling economics. We start with the simplest of subjects—atemporal economies with only a few goods and a few agents. These economies are too simple, in fact, to have any empirical content, but they are building blocks and mental training grounds. For all their simplicity, though, they allow us to see a surprisingly large number of things: how Walrasian competitive equilibrium is a special type of commitment equilibrium, how money acts as a medium of exchange, why trust alone is inadequate in a monetary economy, and even a little bit about how the Brehon code, the legal system of preconquest Ireland, worked. Complications and more serious attempts to approximate reality follow in subsequent chapters.

One terminological note: from now on, when we say "equilibrium" without a modifier, we will mean "commitment equilibrium." This convention will shorten the text.

I

Let us begin with an economy with two players (1 and 2, as usual), each of whom is endowed with a single unit of different indivisible good. Player 1 prefers player 2's good to the one he is endowed with, and similarly player 2 prefers player 1's good to his own. Each, however, prefers his own good to nothing at all. For the sake of definiteness, let us say that each values his own good at 1 and the other's good at 5. Assume also that utility is simply additive: each player values having both goods at 6.

Each player controls his own endowment, and that only. Thus each has only two strategies available to him: he can keep his good (and consume it), or he can give it to the other player. From this discussion we can construct a payoff matrix:

		Player 2	
		Give	Keep
Player 1	Give	5, 5	0, 6
	Keep	6, 0	1, 1

Notice that this bi-matrix is identical to the prisoners' dilemma bi-matrix in chapter 2 (except for the names of strategies): trade is the same game as prisoners' dilemma. Thus there are two kinds of equilibria: autarky (both keeping) with the null commitment pattern, and trade (both giving) with a commitment pattern in which each player subtracts an amount greater than one from his payoff in the situation where he alone keeps.

There should be nothing counterintuitive about this analysis. What can make greedy rational people give away things they like? They will do so only if they can contrive making certain situations where they keep the good more unpleasant than those situations actually are. Trade can take place only if players selectively reduce their payoff functions through promises and other strategic moves.

(It may be objected that the possibility of "enforceable contracts" distinguishes exchange economies from prisoners' dilemma games. "Enforceable contracts," though, are the same as commitments: entering into an enforceable contract means arranging for a bad thing to happen to oneself under certain circumstances—arranging, that is for certain subtractions from one's payoff matrix. The objection might be restated then, that certain types of commitments that are available to traders are not available to prisoners—it is an objection, in short, to the free disposal of utility axiom for the game with prisoners. Hence the objection could be met by saying that exchange economies are the same as the free-disposal version of prisoners' dilemma.)

Thus, Pareto improvements never come without the proper commitments, and sometimes they do not come at all. That is why our methods will be able to explain persistent inefficiencies like unemployment and discrimination.

II

Now let us consider bilateral exchange with divisible, rather than indivisible goods.

Let player 1 be endowed with one unit of good x, and let player 2 be endowed with one unit of good y. Thus a strategy for player 1 is an amount of good x to give to player 2, and a strategy for player 2 is an amount of good y to give to player 1. We assume that each player's utility is given by the same Cobb-Douglas function. We have:

$$S_1 = \{x_2 \mid 0 \leq x_2 \leq 1\}$$
$$S_2 = \{y_1 \mid 0 \leq y_1 \leq 1\}$$
$$f_1(x_2, y_1) = (1 - x_2)^{\alpha} y_1^{\beta}, \quad \alpha + \beta = 1$$
$$f_2(x_2, y_1) = x_2^{\alpha}(1 - y_1)^{\beta}, \quad \alpha + \beta = 1.$$

The null commitment pattern and autarky, of course, form one equilibrium of this game. We will look for other equilibria involving two families of commitment patterns.

The first family of commitment patterns that we wish to study is the family G^N of "naked trade" commitment patterns.

A commitment pattern g^N is in the family G^N of *naked trade commitment patterns* if there is a vector $(\bar{x}_2^1, \bar{x}_2^2, \bar{y}_1^1, \bar{y}_1^2)$, with each element on the unit interval, such that g^N can be expressed:

$$\begin{aligned} g_1^N(x_2, y_1) &= f_1(x_2, y_1) && \text{if } x_2 < \bar{x}_2^1 \text{ and } y_1 \geq \bar{y}_1^1 \\ &= 0 && \text{otherwise} \end{aligned}$$

$$\begin{aligned} g_2^N(x_2, y_1) &= f_2(x_2, y_1) && \text{if } y_1 < \bar{y}_1^2 \text{ and } x_2 \geq \bar{x}_2^2 \\ &= 0 && \text{otherwise.} \end{aligned}$$

Player 1's commitment can be stated in words (addressed to player 2) as: "I promise to give you at least $\bar{x}_2^1$ if you give me at least $\bar{y}_1^1$. May lightning strike me dead if you give me at least $\bar{y}_1^1$ and I give you less than $\bar{x}_2^1$." Similarly player 2's commitment is, "I promise to give you at least $\bar{y}_1^2$ if you give me at least $\bar{x}_2^2$. May lightning strike me dead if you give me at least $\bar{x}_2^2$ and I give you less than $\bar{y}_1^2$."

This naked trade commitment pattern is illustrated in the Edgeworth box of figure 2. Player 1's promise has made the shaded rectangular region marked (A) a region of zero utility for him; player 2's promise has made the rectangular region marked (B) a region of zero utility for him. Player 1's promise affects the northeast corner of the Edgeworth box, where his utility is greatest; the same relationship holds for player 2 and the southwest corner.

Now consider the acceptable situations for player 2 in this game, $\langle\{1,2\}, S, f - g^N\rangle$. If $x_2 \geq \bar{x}_2^2$, player 2 is best off if $y_1 = \bar{y}_1^2$. If $x_2 < \bar{x}_2^2$, player 2 is best off if $y_1 = 0$. Hence

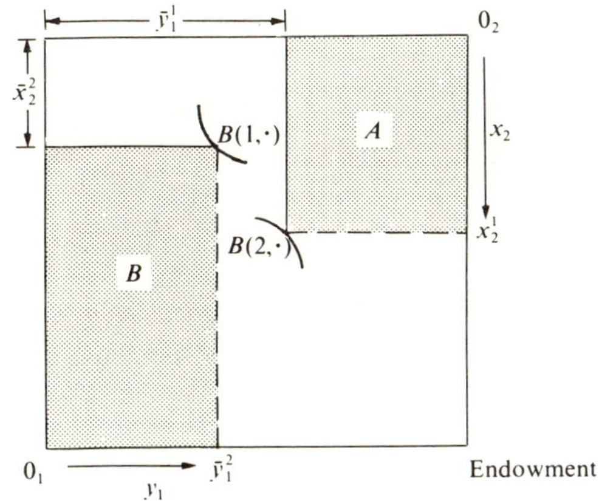

Figure 2

$$A(2, g^N) = \{(x_2, y_1) \mid x_2 \geq \bar{x}_2^2 \quad \text{and} \quad y_1 = \bar{y}_1^2\}$$
$$\cup \{(x_2, y_1) \mid x_2 < \bar{x}_2^2 \quad \text{and} \quad y_1 = 0\}.$$

Since player 2 is player 1's only opponent,

$$A(2, g^N) = P(1, g^N)$$

and a good situation for player 1 is one that maximizes

$$f_1(x_2, y_1) = (1-x_2)^\alpha \, y_1^\beta$$

in $A(2, g^N)$. Clearly such a maximum will never be achieved in the second subset of $A(2, g^N)$, since $y_1 = 0$ there means that player 1's utility vanishes. The elements of the first subset of $A(2, g^N)$ differ only in their values of x_2, and player 1 is better off the smaller the value of x_2. Thus $(\bar{x}_2^2, \bar{y}_1^2)$ maximizes $f_1(\cdot)$ in $A(2, g^N)$:

$$B(1, g^N) = \{(\bar{x}_2^2, \bar{y}_1^2)\}.$$

In the Edgeworth box, player 1's good set consists only of the corner point of player 2's forbidden rectangle. By a similar argument $B(2, g^N) = \{(\bar{x}_2^1, \bar{y}_1^1)\}$. The intersection of good sets will be nonempty, of course, only when

$$\begin{aligned} \bar{x}_2^2 &= \bar{x}_2^1 \triangleq \bar{x}_2 \\ \bar{y}_1^2 &= \bar{y}_1^1 \triangleq \bar{y}_1 \end{aligned} \tag{1}$$

and then will consist of the point $(\bar{x}_2, \bar{y}_1)$. Thus there will be no equilibria associated with commitment patterns in the naked trade family that do not satisfy (1); however, there will be an equilibrium with $(\bar{x}_2, \bar{y}_1)$ with any

Figure 3

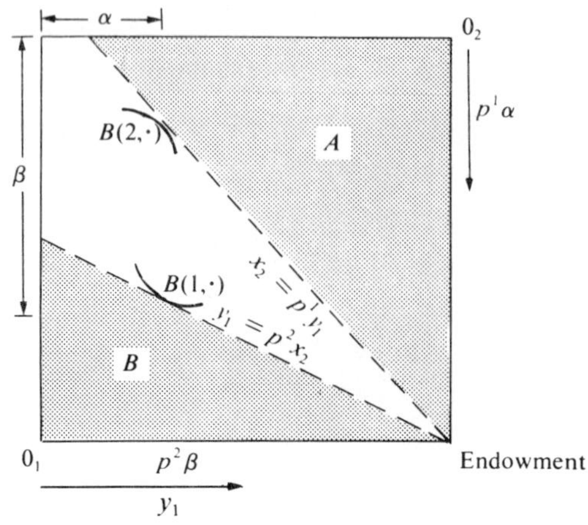

naked trade commitment pattern that satisfies (1). Thus there will be a naked trade equilibrium for every point in the Edgeworth box. With more general endowments, this result becomes that there will be a naked trade equilibrium associated with every point weakly Pareto-superior to the endowment point.

A price system is another type of commitment pattern that can be used, and it is obviously one that we should study at some length. A price system (at least as we take the term to be understood in our simple example) depends on two parameters (as opposed to four for naked trades) which we call p^1 and p^2. These parameters may be any positive numbers. Under a price system, player 1 promises: "Whatever amount y_1 you give me, I will give you at least the amount $p^1 y_1$ of x." Player 2 promises: "Whatever amount x_2 you give me, I will give you at least the amount $p^2 x_2$ of y."

Let G^P denote the family of commitment patterns g^P that are price systems. A commitment pattern g^P is in G^P if there is a vector $(p^1, p^2) \in \mathbf{R}^2_+$ such that g^P can be expressed:

$$\begin{aligned} g_1^P(x_2, y_1) &= f_1(x_2, y_1) && \text{if} \quad x_2 < p^1 y_1 \\ &= 0 && \text{otherwise} \end{aligned}$$

$$\begin{aligned} g_2^P(x_2, y_1) &= f_2(x_2, y_1) && \text{if} \quad y_1 < p^2 x_2 \\ &= 0 && \text{otherwise.} \end{aligned}$$

Figure 3 illustrates a price commitment pattern. Like a naked trade commitment pattern, a price commitment pattern makes the northeast corner of the Edgeworth box a region (marked (A) in figure 3) of zero utility for player 1, and the southwest corner (marked (B) in figure 3) a region of zero utility for player 2. Naked trade zero utility regions are always rectangular while price zero utility regions are triangular or quadrangular; the naked trade regions may or may not touch or overlay, while the price system regions always come together at the endowment point. Player 2's acceptable situations are

$$A(2, g^p) = \{(x_2, y_1) \mid y_1 = p^2 x_2\},$$

and

$$A(2, g^p) = P(1, g^p).$$

Thus good situations for player 1 maximize his utility subject to $y_1 = p^2 x_2$. By the usual calculation we have

$$B(1, g^p) = \{(\beta, p^2 \beta)\}.$$

Similarly

$$B(2, g^p) = \{(p^1 \alpha, \alpha)\}.$$

The two good sets will coincide if and only if

$$p^1 = 1/p^2 = \beta/\alpha \tag{2}$$

in which case their common element will be (β, α). Note that this is the Walrasian equilibrium.

Thus only those commitment patterns in G^p that satisfy (2) are associated with commitment equilibria, and all such commitment equilibria involve the Walrasian equilibrium situation.

That the Walrasian equilibrium is the only commitment equilibrium with a price system commitment pattern does not, of course, mean that it is the only commitment equilibrium. We have already seen that a multitude of commitment equilibria with naked trades exist. There are even some very interesting equilibria with commitment patterns very similar to a price system.

Suppose, for instance, that both players agree on a price different from the equilibrium price. Then player 2's good point on the price line will differ from player 1's; and lack of agreement rules out an equilibrium with this price line. To eliminate this conflict within the set of pure price systems we would have to switch to another price line. An alternative would be to change a player's commitment pattern to prevent him from deviating from the other player's good point. The way to do this is for the player to "ration" his sale of his good to the other player to the amount he would sell at his most favored point on the price line. This commitment pattern eliminates the zone of conflict and is associated with a commitment equilibrium more favorable to the rationing player than any other point on the prevailing

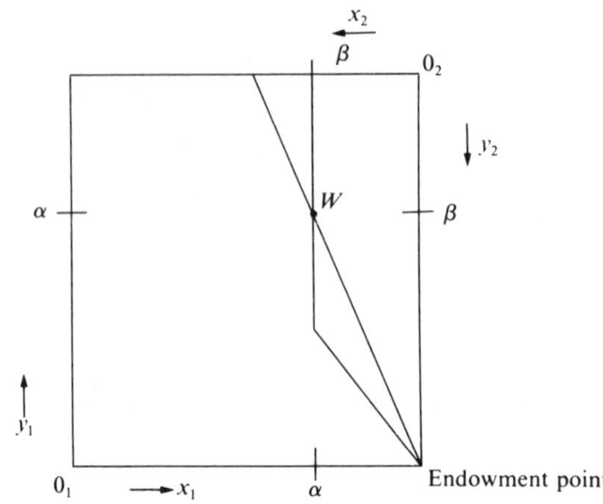

Figure 4

price line. It gives the rationed player, moreover, a result better than the Walrasian equilibrium.

We can provide a concrete example of this phenomenon; it is illustrated in the Edgeworth box of figure 4. Let g^R be given by:

$$\begin{aligned} g_1^R(x_2, y_1) &= f_1(x_2, y_1) \quad \text{if} \quad x_2 < py_1 \\ & \qquad\qquad\qquad\quad \text{or} \quad x_2 > \beta \\ &= 0 \qquad\qquad\quad \text{otherwise} \end{aligned}$$

$$\begin{aligned} g_2^R(x_2, y_1) &= f_2(x_2, y_1) \quad \text{if} \quad y_1 < (1/p)x_2 \\ &= 0 \qquad\qquad\quad \text{otherwise} \end{aligned}$$

where we assume $p > \beta/\alpha$, the Walrasian price ratio. For player 1, the acceptable situations have

$$\begin{aligned} x_2 &= py_1 \quad \text{if} \quad y_1 \leq \beta/p \\ &= \beta \quad\ \ \text{if} \quad y_1 \geq \beta/p. \end{aligned}$$

For player 2 the acceptable situations have, as before $y_1 = (1/p)x_2$.

As before, $B(1, g^R) = \{(\beta, p\beta)\}$, but finding $B(2, g^R)$ is more complicated. The goodness problem

$$\max_{x_2, y_1} \ x_2^\alpha(1 - y_1)^\beta$$

s.t.

$$\begin{aligned} x_2 &= py_1 \quad \text{if} \quad y_1 \leq \beta/p \\ &= \beta \quad\ \ \text{if} \quad y_1 \geq \beta/p \end{aligned}$$

cannot be solved with only the first constraint binding since $\beta/p < \alpha$; rather the solution is at the kink in figure 4:

$$B(2, g^R) = \{(\beta, p\beta)\}.$$

Thus (g^R, (β, $p\beta$)) is an equilibrium.

It is easy to show that player 1 is worse off in this equilibrium and player 2 is better off than in the Walrasian equilibrium. We saw above that in the Walrasian equilibrium

$$\begin{aligned} y_1 &= \alpha \\ x_2 &= \beta. \end{aligned}$$

x_2 has the same value at both of the equilibria. In the rationing equilibrium, however, y_1 is smaller. Since greater y_1 helps player 1 and hurts player 2, the conclusion is obvious.

III

Use of money can add a new wrinkle to our discussion of the two-person two-good economy. Since most economic transactions are by money, not by barter, it seems worthwhile to see how money works.

The type of money that we will use is absolutely worthless—it enters into no utility function—and not even inherently scarce. It acquires its "value" solely by social convention. It is thus quite similar to a checking account or a credit card. Such money is thus a bit more ethereal than the fiat or commodity money that economists more commonly use, but it seems no more ethereal than the real thing: people accept checks because they will make accounting entries and write checks themselves. Nothing with substance moves; there is only a series of debit and credit entries on agents' accounting books.

The players' strategy sets must be expanded when we consider an economy with money. Each player must determine not only the amount of his good that he will give to the other player, but also the amount of money he will give the other player. Thus a strategy for player 1 is a pair (x_2, m_2^1) where m_2^1 denotes the amount of money player 1 gives to player 2, and a strategy for player 2 is a pair (y_1, m_1^2) where m_1^2 denotes the amount of money player 2 gives to player 1. We call this new strategy space S^m. We need a new payoff function:

$$f^m((x_2, m_2^1), (y_1, m_1^2)) \triangleq f(x_2, y_1).$$

The players $\{1, 2\}$ remain the same, but the game $\langle\{1, 2\}, S^m, f^m\rangle^*$ which we will be studying here is, of course, a different game from $\langle\{1, 2\}, S, f\rangle^*$ which we studied in the previous section.

Let us experiment with the following price system commitment pattern:

$$g_1((x_2, m_2^1), (y_1, m_1^2)) = f_1(x_2, y_1) \qquad \text{if} \quad x_2 < p^1 m_1^2 \qquad (3a)$$

$$\qquad \text{or if} \quad m_2^1 > m_1^2 \qquad (3b)$$

$$= 0 \qquad \text{otherwise} \qquad (3c)$$

$$g_2((x_2, m_2^1), (y_1, m_1^2)) = f_2(x_2, y_1) \qquad \text{if} \quad y_1 < p^2 m_2^1 \qquad (3d)$$

$$\qquad \text{or if} \quad m_1^2 > m_2^1 \qquad (3e)$$

$$= 0 \qquad \text{otherwise.} \qquad (3f)$$

In (3a), player 1 promises to give player 2 at least the amount $p^1 m_1^2$ of x if player 2 writes a check for m_1^2. In (3d), player 2 promises to give player 1 the amount $p^2 m_2^1$ of y if player 1 writes a check for m_2^1. In (3b) and (3e) players 1 and 2 respectively promise that they will not overdraw their checking accounts.

If player 2 chooses the strategy (y_1, m_1^2), player 1's acceptable situations are those which satisfy:

$$x_2 = p^1 m_1^2 \qquad (4a)$$

$$m_2^1 \leq m_1^2. \qquad (4b)$$

Similarly if player 1 chooses the strategy (x_2, m_2^1), player 2's acceptable situations are those which satisfy

$$y_1 = p^2 m_2^1 \qquad (5a)$$

$$m_1^2 \leq m_2^1. \qquad (5b)$$

Note that both players' acceptable situations are quite numerous; since money does not enter into the payoff function a player's only concern at this level is avoiding an overdraft. Note also that while the amount of good a player receives from the other player matters to the recipient, the recipient treats it as a fait accompli that does not affect his choice of strategies.

For a situation $((x_2, m_2^1), (y_1, m_1^2))$ to be an NE, both (4) and (5) must be satisfied. Combining (4b) and (5b): $m_1^2 \geq m_2^1 \geq m_1^2$ hence

$$m_1^2 = m_2^1 \triangleq m. \qquad (6)$$

For any $m > 0$, then, $((p^1\ m, m), (p^2\ m, m))$ is an NE of $\langle\{1, 2\}, S^m, f - g\rangle$; there are no other NEs.

For an equilibrium to be possible with g, there must be Unquestioned Superiority among these NEs. For there to be Unquestioned Superiority, the best NE for player 1 must also be the best NE for player 2. For each value of m there is a unique NE; thus we may consider each player's utility at that NE as a function of m. Let M_i denote the m that maximizes player i's utility, $i = 1, 2$. Then Unquestioned Superiority means $M_1 = M_2$.

To find M_1 we must maximize

$$\ln v_1(m) = \alpha \ln(1 - p^1 m) + \beta \ln p^2 m.$$

Differentiating with respect to m

$$\frac{\partial \ln v_1(m)}{\partial m} = \frac{-\alpha p^1}{1 - p^1 m} + \frac{\beta}{m} = 0,$$

whence

$$M_1 = \beta / p^1. \tag{7}$$

Similarly for player 2 we must maximize

$$\ln v_2(m) = \alpha \ln p^1 m + \beta \ln(1 - p^2 m),$$

whence

$$M_2 = \alpha / p^2. \tag{8}$$

Comparing (7) and (8), a necessary condition for an equilibrium is

$$\beta / p^1 = \alpha / p^2, \quad \text{or}$$

$$p^1 / p^2 = \beta / \alpha \tag{9}$$

(which is the Walrasian equilibrium price ratio). From (7), (8), (4a), (5a),

$$x_2 = (\beta / \alpha) \alpha = \beta \tag{10}$$

$$y_1 = \alpha$$

(which again is the Walrasian equilibrium).

Equations (9) and (10) are necessary for an equilibrium, but are they sufficient? Consider player 1 and set $p^2 = 1$ as numéraire. The set of possible points $P(1, g)$ for player 1 are given by (5):

$$P(1, g) = \{((x_2, m_2^1), (y_1, m_1^2)) \mid y_1 = m_2^1, m_1^2 \leq m_2^1\}. \tag{11}$$

Player 1's utility at (10) is

$$(1 - \beta)^\alpha \alpha^\beta = \alpha.$$

By the possible point theorem the question becomes whether there is a situation $s \in P(i, g)$ such that $f_1(s) > \alpha$. Of course there is: x_2 can be made as small as desired and m_2^1 and hence y_1, as large as desired in $P(1,$

g); a utility of 1 (the physical maximum) is attainable. Thus there is no equilibrium with a commitment pattern like g.

Why does this commitment pattern fail? Essentially because it lacks "enforcement." Compare the commitment pattern in (3) with, for instance, the commitment pattern in the prisoners' dilemma game where neither player confessed. In prisoners' dilemma, player 2 "enforces" good conduct on player 1 because player 1 knows that if he confesses, player 2 will also. Similarly in barter, player 2 "enforces" good conduct on player 1 because player 1 knows that if he reduces the amount of good x he gives to player 2, player 2 will reduce the amount of good y he gives to player 1. In (3) and (11), per contra, there is no enforcement: player 2 will act the same way no matter whether player 1 gives him the good x to which he is "entitled" or not; no matter whether player 1 overdraws his checking account or not. (Symmetrical statements, of course, hold for player 2.) The enforcement problem is a major difference between barter and monetary economies, and is the reason why the commitment pattern in (3) does not have an equilibrium.

Several ways of providing the required enforcement come to mind. The first way would be to add a third player, an Enforcer, who is indifferent among all situations in the game involving players 1 and 2, but who threatens to employ a strategy that will reduce that player's payoff to zero against any player who deviates from "good conduct." There are two problems with this approach: the first is that "good conduct" is not well-defined and tyrannical outcomes are not what we are interested in at this point; the second is that an additional player can be a large complication. We will forgo the Enforcer at this point, therefore, although we will need a player something like this when we talk later about less simple and more realistic matters.

The approach we take, then, will be more in the spirit of the prisoners' dilemma and barter games, where each player enforced good conduct on the other. Each player will honor the other's checks only if the other is not a "deadbeat." This is not a bad approximation to reality—one very important reason why people pay their bills is that they anticipate serious problems if their credit ratings are bad.[1] Thus we consider the revised commitment pattern g':

$$g_1'((x_2, m_2^1), (y_1, m_1^2)) = f_1(x_2, y_1) \qquad \text{if } x_2 < \rho^1 m_1^2 \text{ and } y_1 \geq \rho^2 m_2^1 \text{ and } m_1^2 \leq m_2^1 \tag{12a}$$

1. It is a good approximation to the Brehon code: "he who evades his legal responsibilities shall not be paid by God or man" (Brehon Laws I.113).

$$\text{or if} \quad m_1^2 < m_2^1 \tag{12b}$$

$$= 0 \qquad \text{otherwise} \tag{12c}$$

$$g_2'((x_2, m_2^1), (y_1, m_1^2)) = f_2(x_2, y_1) \qquad \text{if} \quad y_1 < \rho^2 m_2^1 \tag{12d}$$

$$\text{and} \quad x_2 \geq m_1^2$$
$$\text{and} \quad m_1^2 \geq m_2^1$$

$$\text{or if} \quad m_2^1 < m_1^2 \tag{12e}$$

$$= 0 \qquad \text{otherwise.}$$

We can, in fact, further simplify the commitment pattern by removing (12b) and (12e), since they are used only for (4b) and (5b) which now follow from (12a) and (12d) if trade takes place: One does not have to promise not to overdraw, one need only to be threatened with the consequences. With g' as in (12), the argument of (4)–(10) goes through exactly as before. In particular, the necessary conditions in (9) and (10) for an equilibrium are still necessary.

The test is the possible point theorem. Substituting (12) for (3) we have for player 1's possible point set $P(1, g')$:

$$P(1, g') = \{(x_2, m_2^1), (y_1, m_1^2) \mid y_1 = m_2^1,\ x_2 \geq (\beta/\alpha) m_1^2 \text{ and } m_1^2 \geq m_2^1\} \tag{13}$$
$$\cup \{(x_2, m_2^1), (y_1, m_1^2) \mid y_1 = 0 \text{ and } x_2 < (\beta/\alpha) m_1^2 \text{ or } m_1^2 < m_2^1\}.$$

For all points in the second subset, $f_1(\cdot)$ since $y_1 = 0$; hence these present no problem. To apply the possible point theorem, then, we must find the situation in the first subset of $P(1, g')$ that maximizes player 1's utility. It is obvious that at such a maximizing point equality will hold in each of the three expressions that define the subset. Then we can write player 1's utility as a function $v_1(\cdot)$ of $m = m_1^2 = m_2^1$:

$$\ln v_1(m) = \alpha \ln(1 - (\beta/\alpha)\, m) + \beta \ln m.$$

This is precisely the same expression we maximized before in trying to find Unquestioned Superiority, with the constraints $\rho^1 = \beta/\alpha$. Thus

$$m = M_1 = \beta/\rho^1 = \alpha.$$

In (13):

$$y_1 = \alpha, \quad x_2 = \beta.$$

Hence no point in $P(1, g')$ is more favorable to player 1 than the proposed equilibrium NE. Similar reasoning prevails for player 2. Thus the "Walrasian" equilibrium

$$(g', ((\beta, \alpha), (\alpha, \alpha))$$

is a commitment equilibrium of $\langle \{1, 2\}, S^m, f^m \rangle$. All other equilibria in this family are "inflationary" replicas of this: pairs with all prices and money multiplied by the same constant.

IV

We have exhausted for now the interesting things we can do with two players. Let us expand by adding a third player and a third good. With three players and three goods, we can pose some new questions about a barter economy.

Specifically, let the three goods be called x, y and z, and let player 1's endowment be a unit of x, and nothing else, player 2's endowment be a unit of y, and nothing else, and player 3's endowment be a unit of z, and nothing else. Let each player gain positive utility from consumption of his own good and one other. To make the problem interesting, let the other good for player 1 be y, for player 2 be z, and for player 3 be x.

Specifically let:

$$u_1(\cdot) = x_1^\alpha y_1^\beta$$
$$u_2(\cdot) = y_2^\alpha z_2^\beta$$
$$u_3(\cdot) = z_3^\alpha x_3^\beta.$$

The Walrasian equilibrium for this economy is given by the price relation $p_x = p_y = p_z$ and the following allocation:

	Player 1	Player 2	Player 3
Good x	α	0	β
Good y	β	α	0
Good z	0	β	α

First let us consider price system games without money. The players' strategy sets are given by

$$S = S_1 \times S_2 \times S_3$$

$$S_1 = \{(x_1, x_2, x_3) \in \mathbf{R}_+^3 | \sum_i x_i = 1\}$$

$$S_2 = \{(y_1, y_2, y_3) \in \mathbf{R}_+^3 | \sum_i y_i = 1\}$$

$$S_3 = \{(z_1, z_2, z_3) \in \mathbf{R}^3_+ | \sum_i z_i = 1\}$$

and payoff functions are given by $f_i(\cdot) = u_i(\cdot)$. As usual, no trade is the sole NE of $\langle \{1, 2, 3\}, S, f \rangle$. The game we are interested in is $\langle \{1, 2, 3\}, S, f \rangle^*$.

The first commitment pattern we wish to look at we can call "nonmeddlesome" barter. By "nonmeddlesome" we mean that for any two players, the amount the first gives the second depends only on the amount the second gives the first; what either player does with the third player is entirely irrelevant to the transaction between the first two players. In general, $g^{PN} \in G^{PN}$, the set of nonmeddlesome price system commitment patterns, if there is a vector $\rho = (\rho_2^1, \rho_3^1, \rho_1^2, \rho_3^2, \rho_1^3, \rho_2^3) \in \mathbf{R}^6_+$ such that g^{PN} can be expressed:

$$\begin{aligned} g_1^{PN}(\cdot) &= f_1(\cdot) \quad \text{if} \quad x_2 < \rho_2^1 y_1 \quad \text{or if} \quad x_3 < \rho_3^1 z_1 \\ &= 0 \quad \text{otherwise} \end{aligned} \tag{14}$$

$$\begin{aligned} g_2^{PN}(\cdot) &= f_2(\cdot) \quad \text{if} \quad y_1 < \rho_1^2 x_2 \quad \text{or if} \quad y_3 < \rho_3^2 z_2 \\ &= 0 \quad \text{otherwise} \end{aligned}$$

$$\begin{aligned} g_3^{PN}(\cdot) &= f_3(\cdot) \quad \text{if} \quad z_1 < \rho_1^3 x_3 \quad \text{or if} \quad z_2 < \rho_2^3 y_3 \\ &= 0 \quad \text{otherwise.} \end{aligned}$$

Thus what each player promises to give depends only on what he has received from the player to whom the gift is contemplated.

(14) allows us to characterize acceptable situations. These have, for player 1

$$\begin{aligned} x_2 &= \rho_2^1 y_1 \\ x_3 &= \rho_3^1 z_1 \end{aligned}$$

for player 2

$$\begin{aligned} y_1 &= \rho_1^2 x_2 \\ y_3 &= \rho_3^2 z_2, \end{aligned}$$

and for player 3

$$\begin{aligned} z_1 &= \rho_1^3 x_3 \\ z_2 &= \rho_2^3 y_3. \end{aligned}$$

Thus, we have

$$P(1, g^{PN}) = \{s | y_1 = \rho_1^2 x_2,\ y_3 = \rho_3^2 z_2,\ z_1 = \rho_1^3 x_3,\ z_2 = \rho_2^3 y_3\}$$

and hence, by maximization

$$B(1, g^{PN}) = \{s | x_2 = \beta,\ y_1 = \rho_1^2 \beta,\ z_1 = x_3 = 0\}$$

if $\rho_3^2 \rho_2^3 = 1$, and

$$B(1, g^{PN}) = \{s \mid x_2 = \beta,\ y_1 = \rho^2_1\beta,\ z_1 = x_3 = y_3 = z_2 = 0\},$$

if not.

Similarly

$$B(2, g^{PN}) = \{s \mid y_3 = \beta,\ z_2 = \rho^3_2\beta,\ x_2 = y_1 = 0\}$$

if $\rho^1_3\,\rho^3_1 = 1$, and

$$B(2, g^{PN}) = \{s \mid y_3 = \beta,\ z_2 = \rho^3_2\beta,\ x_2 = y_1 = x_3 = z_1 = 0\}$$

if not.

Without even considering $B(3, g^{PN})$, then, we can see that there will never be an equilibrium with a nonmeddlesome commitment pattern because players 1 and 2 will never agree on x_2 and y_1, no matter what the value of ρ. Thus a commitment pattern like g^{PN} is useless.

The reason why it is useless is easy to see. Player 1 wants what player 2 has, but player 2 does not want what player 1 has. Instead player 2 wants what player 3 has, and player 3 wants, not what player 2 has, but what player 1 has. Trade, to be effective, must be more roundabout than the nonmeddlesome price system will allow.

Three ways to correct this difficulty come to mind immediately. The first way is to allow players to buy goods which have no utility for them in order to resell them to players who value them. Such activity, however, is impossible to model in an atemporal context, since each player's feasible donations to the others depend on what the others give him, and thus will not be determined until after the game has begun.

The second way to correct the difficulty is by using a "meddlesome" commitment pattern. A meddlesome price system is one like g^{md}:

$$\begin{aligned} g^{md}_1(\cdot) &= f_1(\cdot) && \text{if} \quad x_3 < \rho^1 y_1 \\ &= 0 && \text{otherwise} \\[1ex] g^{md}_2(\cdot) &= f_2(\cdot) && \text{if} \quad y_1 < \rho^2 z_2 \\ &= 0 && \text{otherwise} \\[1ex] g^{md}_3(\cdot) &= f_3(\cdot) && \text{if} \quad z_2 < \rho^3 x_3 \\ &= 0 && \text{otherwise.} \end{aligned}$$

A necessary condition for $\langle \{1, 2, 3\}, S, f - g^{md} \rangle$ to have an NE with trade is $\rho^1 \rho^2 \rho^3 = 1$, and it can be shown that the only commitment equilibria with g^{md} is that corresponding to the Walrasian equilibrium with all prices equal.

The promises in g^{md} are rather unusual, though. Player 1 promises player 2: "If you give me y_1 of y, I won't give you anything, but I'll give player 3 the amount $\rho^1 y_1$ of x." Player 2 promises player 3: "If you give me z_2 of z, I will give player 1 the amount $\rho^2 z_2$ of y." And player 3 promises player 1,

"If you give me x_3 of x, I will give player 2 the amount $\rho^3 x_3$ of z." In one sense, these promises accomplish in an atemporal context the type of sale-and-resale that we suggested as the first way out of the difficulty of roundabout trade: player 2, for instance, instead of ever holding any of good x himself, can arrange for player 1 to deliver the appropriate amount of it directly to player 3; in return, he receives good z from player 3. This interpretation is, however, somewhat metaphorical: the plain fact is that the subject of discussions between two players is not solely what goods are exchanged between the two, but also how a third player is treated. This is the reason we have called the commitment pattern "meddlesome," and why there are doubts about its general usefulness.

The third way out of the roundaboutness problem is, of course, money. A player can sell his good to the player who desires it, receive money in return, and use this money to buy the good he desires from the third player. This approach seems to be fairly realistic; indeed, roundabout trade seems to be the basic reason why a "medium of exchange" is useful. However, because of the "enforcement" provisions there may be some questions about whether this sort of monetary economy is truly less meddlesome than a barter economy.

To study a monetary economy, as we saw in the previous section, we must define a new game $\langle \{1, 2, 3\}, S^m, f^m \rangle$. To reduce the dimensionality of strategy space, we will assume that no player gives any of his good to the player who does not derive any utility from it, or any of his money to the player whose good he derives no utility from. Thus a strategy for player 1 is a pair (x_3, m_2^1), a strategy for player 2 is (y_1, m_3^2), and a strategy for player 3 is (z_2, m_1^3). As before, f^m maps from S^m by ignoring monetary phenomena, and assigning utilities to real phenomena only.

Let us then look at the commitment pattern g^m:

$$
\begin{array}{lll}
g_1^m((x_3, m_2^1), (y_1, m_3^2), (z_2, m_1^3)) = f_1(\cdot) & \text{if } x_3 < \rho^1 m_1^3 & (15a) \\
 & \text{and } m_1^3 \leq m_3^2 & \\
 & \text{or if } y_1 \neq \bar{\rho}^2 m_2^1 & (15b) \\
\qquad = 0 & \text{otherwise} & \\
g_2^m(\cdot) = f_2(\cdot) & \text{if } y_1 < \rho^2 m_2^1 & (15c) \\
 & \text{and } m_1^3 \geq m_2^1 & \\
 & \text{or if } z_2 \neq \bar{\rho}^3 m_3^2 & (15d) \\
\qquad = 0 & \text{otherwise} & \\
g_3^m(\cdot) = f_3(\cdot) & \text{if } z_2 < \rho^3 m_3^2 & (15e) \\
 & \text{and } m_2^1 \geq m_3^2 & \\
 & \text{or if } x_3 \neq \bar{\rho}^1 m_1^3 & (15f) \\
\qquad = 0 & \text{otherwise.} &
\end{array}
$$

Each player's commitment in (15) has two parts. Each player as a seller promises to deliver to his buyer at least the amount determined by the buyer's payment of money to him and his own asking price ρ^i. This is done in (15a), (15c), and (15e). This promise is contingent on the buyer's check not bouncing. Each player as a buyer promises to pay his seller j neither more nor less than his (the buyer's) bid price $\bar{\rho}^j$ for each unit of good delivered. This is done in (15b), (15d) and (15f).

Acceptable sets also have two parts, depending on whether buyers overdraw. Thus we have

$$A(1, g^m) = A^1(1, g^m) \cup A^2(1, g^m)$$

$$A(2, g^m) = A^1(2, g^m) \cup A^2(2, g^m)$$

$$A(3, g^m) = A^1(3, g^m) \cup A^2(3, g^m),$$

where

$$A^1(1, \mathrm{g}^m) = \{s \mid x_3 = \rho^1 m_1^3,\ y_1 = \bar{\rho}^2 m_2^1,\ m_1^3 \leq m_3^2\}$$

$$A^2(1, g^m) = \{s \mid x_3 = 0,\ y_1 = \bar{\rho}^2 m_2^1,\ m_1^3 > m_3^2\}$$

$$A^1(2, g^m) = \{s \mid y_1 = \rho^2 m_2^1,\ z_2 = \bar{\rho}^3 m_3^2,\ m_2^1 \leq m_1^3\}$$

$$A^2(2, g^m) = \{s \mid y_1 = 0,\ z_2 = \bar{\rho}^3 m_3^2,\ m_2^1 > m_1^3\}$$

$$A^1(3, g^m) = \{s \mid z_2 = \rho^3 m_3^2,\ x_3 = \bar{\rho}^1 m_1^3,\ m_3^2 \leq m_2^1\}$$

$$A^2(3, g^m) = \{\mathrm{s} \mid z_2 = 0,\ x_3 = \bar{\rho}^1 m_1^3,\ m_3^2 > m_2^1\}.$$

The possible set for player 1 is

$$\begin{aligned} P(1, g^m) &= A(2, g^m) \cap A(3, g^m) \\ &= [A^1(2, g^m) \cap A^1(3, g^m)] \cup [A^1(2, g^m) \cap A^2(3, g^m)] \\ &\quad \cup [A^2(2, g^m) \cap A(3, g^m)]. \end{aligned}$$

Consider $A^1(2, g^m) \cap A^2(3, g^m)$. In $A^2(3, g^m)$, $z_2 = 0$. In $A^1(2, g^m)$, $z_2 = \bar{\rho}^3 m_3^2$, where $\bar{\rho}_3^2$ is positive. Hence in the intersection, if it is nonempty, $m_3^2 = 0$. In $A^2(3, g^m)$, however, $m_3^2 > m_2^1$. Hence in the intersection, $0 > m_2^1$. But this is impossible. Thus

$$A^1(2, g^m) \cap A^2(3, g^m) = \emptyset.$$

In $A^2(2, g^m)$, $y_1 = 0$. Thus in the intersection of $A^2(2, g^m)$ with anything, $f_1(\cdot) = 0$. The good set for player 1 will not be in $A^2(2, g^m)$ if a positive payoff can be achieved anywhere in $P(1, g^m)$.

So we are left to consider only

$$A^1(2, g^m) \cap A^1(3, g^m).$$

In $A^1(2, g^m)$, $z_2 = \bar{\rho}^3 m_3^2$. In $A^1(3, g^m)$, $z_2 = \rho^3 m_3^2$. Thus the intersection will be empty unless

$$\bar{\rho}^3 = \rho^3. \tag{16}$$

If (16) does not hold, player 1's good set is in $A^2(2, g^m)$ and at any equilibrium $f_1(\cdot) = 0$. If (16) holds, then player 1's goodness problem is

$$\max_s \quad f_1(s) = (1 - x_3)^\alpha y_1^\beta, \text{ s.t.}$$

$$s \in [A^1(2, g^m) \cap A^1(3, g^m)]$$
$$= \{s \mid y_1 = \rho^2 m_2^1,\ z_2 = \rho^3 m_3^2,\ m_2^1 \leq m_1^3,\ x_3 = \bar{\rho}^1 m_1^3,\ m_3^2 \leq m_2^1\}.$$

Solving this, we find that player 1's good set is

$$B(1, g^m) = \{s \mid m_3^2 \leq m_2^1 = m_1^3 = \beta/\bar{\rho}^1,\ y_1 = (\rho^2/\bar{\rho}^1)\beta,$$
$$z_2 = \rho^3 m_3^2,\ x_3 = \beta\}$$

if (16) holds, and

$$B(1, g^m) = A^2(2, g^m) \cap A(3, g^m),$$

if (16) fails.

By similar reasoning for players 2 and 3

$$B(2, g^m) = \{s \mid m_1^3 \leq m_2^1 = m_3^2 = \beta/\bar{\rho}^2,\ y_1 = \beta,\ z_2 = (\rho^3/\bar{\rho}^1)\beta,$$
$$x_3 = \rho^1 m_1^3\}$$

if

$$\rho^1 = \bar{\rho}^1, \tag{17}$$

and

$$B(2, g^m) = A^2(3, g^m) \cap A(1, g^m),$$

if not;

$$B(3, g^m) = \{s \mid m_2^1 \leq m_1^3 = m_3^2 = \beta/\bar{\rho}^3,\ y_1 = \rho^2 m_2^1,\ z_2 = \beta,$$
$$x_3 = (\rho^1/\bar{\rho}^3)\beta\}$$

if

$$\rho^2 = \bar{\rho}^2, \tag{18}$$

and

$$B(3,g^m) = A^2(1,g^m) \cap A(2,g^m)$$

if not.

If (16), (17), and (18) hold—if buyers and sellers agree on price—then we have a Walrasian equilibrium, if any; for the good sets will have a nonempty intersection only if

$$\rho^1 = \rho^2 = \rho^3 \triangleq \rho$$

and the only situation in that intersection will have

$$m_2^1 = m_3^2 = m_1^3 = \beta/\rho, \; y_1 = z_2 = x_3 = \beta.$$

Should any of (16), (17), and (18) fail there will be no equilibrium. If one fails while the other two hold, then the intersection of the good sets with positive payoffs will have positive values for y_1, z_2, and x_3. The good set for the player with zero payoff will have a zero value for one of these three variables. If two or more fail, the intersection of the good sets will be empty unless at least one of

$$A^2(2,g^m) \cap A^2(1,g^m)$$

$$A^2(2,g^m) \cap A^2(3,g^m)$$

$$A^2(1,g^m) \cap A^2(3,g^m)$$

is nonempty. But all are empty. Consider, for instance, $A^2(1,g^m) \cap A^2(3,g^m)$. In $A^2(1,g^m)$, $m_1^3 > m_3^2$. In $A^2(3,g^m)$, $m_3^2 > m_2^1$. Hence in the intersection

$$m_1^3 > m_2^1. \tag{19}$$

In $A^2(1,g^m)$, $x_3 = 0$. In $A^2(3,g^m)$, $x^3 = \bar{\rho}^1 m_1^3$, $\bar{\rho}^1 > 0$. Hence in the intersection $m_1^3 = 0$. Combining this with (19) we conclude $0 > m_2^1$, which is impossible. Thus this intersection is empty. The demonstration for the other two intersections is similar.

V

These problems, as we have seen, can grow very large, even if we strive determinedly to deal with only the most elementary of systems. The difficulties can only increase as we progress, since our true interests lie in problems that are not at all elementary.

A more powerful method, however, is available. We call it "supergoodness." Let $\hat{P}(i,g)$ denote an arbitrary superset of $P(i,g)$:

$$\hat{P}(i,g) \supset P(i,g).$$

We will call $\hat{P}(\cdot,\cdot)$ *player i's super-possible set*. Next we define i's *supergood set* $\hat{B}(i,g)$ as the elements in $\hat{P}(i,g)$ that maximize i's payoff:

$$\hat{B}(i,g) \triangleq \{s \in \hat{P}(i,g) \mid (\forall \tilde{s} \in \hat{P}(i,g))\, f_i(s) \geq f_i(\tilde{s})\}.$$

Then we have the following theorem:

Theorem 9. (Supergoodness) *If* $s \in [\bigcap_i \hat{B}(i,g) \cap N(g)]$, *then* (g,s) *is an equilibrium.*

Proof. Since $s \in N(g)$ by hypothesis, we must show that s is not beaten. Suppose (g', s') beats (g,s) through i. Then by the possible point theorem $s' \in P(i,g)$ and

$$f_i(s') > f_i(s). \tag{20}$$

Since $s' \in P(i,g)$ and $P(i,g) \subset \hat{P}(i,g)$, we know $s' \in \hat{P}(i,g)$. Since, then, (20) and $s' \in \hat{P}(i,g)$, we conclude $s \notin \hat{B}(i,g)$. Hence $s \notin [\bigcap_i \hat{B}(i,g) \cap N(g)]$, a contradiction. ■

The Supergoodness Theorem is useful because NEs are easy to come by: in most of the games we deal with, NEs require only that the commitment pattern exhibit a very slight degree of internal consistency and that players honor the commitments they make. The theorem allows us to add anything we wish—even impossible situations, old shoes, Genghis Khan, or your neighbor's dog—to any player's acceptable set before we perform the difficult maximizations, and lets us change what we add when we do the next maximization. Of course, adding old shoes does not make maximization problems easier. What does make them easier is dropping constraints—and since dropping constraints is the same thing as adding to acceptable sets, the Supergoodness Theorem allows us to drop almost at will. "Almost" because there is a final accounting—the intersection of the supergood sets must be nonempty. If it is empty we can conclude nothing, since it might have been nonempty if we had chosen different superpossible sets. Thus there is some art involved in choosing which constraints to ignore in finding which player's supergood set.

Supergoodness, moreover, while it is perhaps primarily a crutch for lazy mathematicians, also allows us to understand more fully what is meant by Walrasian equilibrium, and why it so often, as we have seen in this chapter, coincides with a commitment equilibrium. The Walrasian equilibrium problem may be formulated, roughly, like this: There is a price commitment pattern. Each agent is imagined to solve a maximization problem in which the maximand is his utility, the instruments are the amounts of goods and services he gives to others and receives from others, and constraints are of two types. The agent is constrained, first, by his inability to give out and keep more than his initial endowment, and second, by the fact that the amount of goods and services he receives from others is determined by the amounts he gives them, with the precise relationship between what is given and what is received being given by the price system. These two types of constraint are generally consolidated into one expression called a budget constraint. A price system is called a Walrasian equilibrium price system if the solutions to the agents' maximization problems are consistent with one another in the sense that for each commodity the amounts that agents want to give to each other are the same as the amounts they want to receive from each other. It has, of course, been shown that in many cases Walrasian equilibria exist.

Now suppose we were trying to find a commitment equilibrium involving a price commitment pattern. If we used the goodness theorem, we would also maximize each agent's utility. The goodness problem, however, would differ from the agent's Walrasian maximizing problem in two respects: first, the maximization would be over all the transactions in the economy, and, second, the constraints would be all the feasibility constraints and all the acceptability constraints (except the agent's own) in the economy. The Walrasian maximization problem, by contrast, is over only those transactions that affect the agent directly as a donor or recipient. It includes only those feasibility constraints that limit what the agent himself can give away, and only the acceptability constraints that limit what others give the agent himself.

If we proceed by supergoodness, however, we can ignore this difference. Specifically, supergoodness allows us to drop all constraints in an agent's goodness problem that do not appear in the agent's Walrasian maximization problem. In this case, the agent's supergood set consists only of situations where his transactions are identical with the transactions that solve his Walrasian maximization problem. The supergood sets formed in this manner have a nonempty intersection iff the solutions to agents' Walrasian maximization problems are consistent with one another. If they are consistent, the Walrasian and commitment equilibria coincide.

We see, then, that Walrasian equilibrium is a very specialized kind of commitment equilibrium and Walrasian rationality is a specialized kind of commitment rationality. This is just a further instance of our general result in chapter 3.

7 ▪ Simple Economies with Time

And indeed there will be time
To wonder, "Do I dare?" and, "Do I dare?"
T. S. ELIOT, "The Lovesong of J. Alfred Prufrock"

Atemporal worlds are nice, but most things that are interesting occur in time. People learn things as their lives progress. Atemporal games, for instance, cannot deal with production, because employers cannot reasonably be expected to decide how much output to supply to customers until they know how much labor workers have provided and thus what the level of output is. Fortunately, in chapter 4 we have already seen how to treat the extensive games that can formalize these difficulties, and although we dealt there primarily with finite games, we should have no difficulty applying this theory to economic games.

I

Let us start with a simple problem, and consider a world with two players, no money, one good, and two time periods. The good is durable, and we will refer to it as y. Player 1 receives one unit of good in period 1, and none in period 2. Player 2 receives one unit of good in period 2, but nothing in period 1. Each player's utility is the same Cobb-Douglas function of first and second period consumption. If we denote by c_t^i the amount of good consumed by player i at time t, we have

$$\ln u_i = \alpha \ln c_1^i + \beta \ln c_2^i, \quad \alpha + \beta = 1.$$

We will confine our attention to pure strategies, and perfect equilibria. The first vertex in the game belongs to player 1. A local strategy for player 1 at this information set is a pair of nonnegative numbers (y_2^1, c_1^1): y_2^1 is the amount of good he will give player 2 at this time, and c_1^1 is the amount he will consume in this period. This local strategy is subject to the constraint

$$y_2^1 + c_1^1 \leq 1 \tag{1}$$

i.e., player 1 cannot use more than his endowment.

Whatever (y_2^1, c_1^1) player 1 chooses, the next information set belongs to player 2. For each (y_2^1, c_1^1) that player 1 chooses there is in fact a different information set for player 2. His local strategy at any one of these information sets is a triplet (c_1^2, y_1^2, c_2^2) of first period consumption c_1^2, second period donation to player 1 y_1^2, and second period consumption c_2^2. The local strategy at the information set associated with (y_2^1, c_1^1) is subject to the constraints:

$$c_1^2 \leq y_2^1 \tag{2}$$

$$y_1^2 + c_2^2 \leq 1 + y_2^1 - c_1^2. \tag{3}$$

Player 2 cannot consume more in period 1 than he receives from player 1 then, and he cannot use in period 2 more than the unit he is endowed with and whatever he saves from period 1.

The final information set belongs to player 1, and there is one corresponding to every pair of (y_2^1, c_1^1) and (c_1^2, y_1^2, c_2^2) previously picked by players 1 and 2 respectively. (Equivalently we could put all vertices with the same c_2^2 in the same information set.) At each of these information sets player 1 chooses a second-period consumption c_2^1 subject to

$$c_2^1 \leq 1 - y_2^1 - c_1^1 + y_1^2. \tag{4}$$

Second-period consumption cannot exceed savings from period 1 plus period 2 donations from player 2.

Let us examine the following family of commitment patterns:

$$g_1(\cdot) = f_1(\cdot) \quad \text{if } y_1^2 < \bar{\rho} y_2^1 \tag{5a}$$
$$= 0 \quad \text{otherwise}$$

$$g_2(\cdot) = f_2(\cdot) \quad \text{if } y_1^2 < \rho y_2^1 \tag{5b}$$
$$\text{or if } y_1^2 > \rho y_2^1 \tag{5c}$$
$$= 0 \quad \text{otherwise}$$

(5b) gives, as it were, player 2's primary promise: he promises to repay player 1 at least ρ times whatever is received in period 1. (5a) and (5c) are essentially enforcement commitments: in (5a) player 1 lets it be known that he will be mortified if he is not sufficiently repaid, while in (5c) player 2 invokes similar mortification upon himself if his repayment is too great.

Let us consider first situations acceptable to player 2. Since it is perfection we are interested in, we will act as if each of player 2's information sets is reachable. Whatever (y_2^1, c_1^1) is, then, player 2's acceptability problem is

$$\max_{c_1^2, y_1^2, c_2^2} \alpha \ln c_1^2 + \beta \ln c_2^2$$

subject to (2), (3), and

$$y_1^2 \geq \rho y_2^1$$
$$y_1^2 \leq \rho y_2^1.$$

These last two inequalities obviously imply

$$y_1^2 = \rho y_2^1 \tag{6}$$

which, together with

$$c_1^2 = \min[y_2^1, \alpha(1 + (1 - \rho) y_2^1)] \tag{7}$$

$$y_1^2 + c_2^2 = 1 + y_2^1 - c_1^2 \tag{8}$$

give the necessary and sufficient conditions that all its local strategies for player 2 have to meet for a situation to be acceptable (with perfection) for player 2.

Acceptability for player 1 is a bit more complicated, since player 2's response to a choice at the origin must be anticipated. A strategy for player 2 is a choice of (c_1^2, y_1^2, c_2^2) at every information set (y_2^1, c_1^1). Thus for an arbitrary strategy of player 2 we may write

$$y_1^2 = y_1^2 (y_2^1, c_1^1)$$

(and similar expressions for c_1^2 and c_2^2 but these do not interest us). Then to find acceptable situations for player 1 we must

$$\max_{c_1^1, y_2^1, c_2^1} \alpha \ln c_1^1 + \beta \ln c_2^1,$$

subject to:

$$\bar{\rho}\, y_2^1 \geq y_1^2 (c_1^1, y_2^1) \tag{9}$$

$$y_2^1 + c_1^1 \leq 1 \tag{1}$$

$$c_2^1 \leq 1 - y_2^1 - c_1^1 + y_1^2(c_1^1, y_2^1). \tag{4}$$

Clearly (9) will be binding if either (1) or (4) are, and both of them will be. Thus we know that (9) will be binding at any situation acceptable to player 1. There are obviously other conditions for acceptability, but supergoodness will let us ignore them.

To find the values of the variables at good situations for player 1, we maximize his utility subject to feasibility and acceptability to player 2:

$$\max_{\text{(all variables)}} \quad \alpha \ln c_1^1 + \beta \ln c_2^1, \quad \text{s.t.}$$

$$y_2^1 + c_1^1 \leq 1 \tag{1}$$

$$c_1^2 \leq y_2^1 \tag{2}$$

$$y_1^2 + c_2^2 \leq 1 + y_2^1 - c_1^2 \tag{3}$$

$$c_2^1 \leq 1 - y_2^1 - c_1^1 + y_1^2 \tag{4}$$

$$y_1^2 = \rho y_2^1 \tag{6}$$

$$c_1^2 = \min[y_2^1, \alpha(1 + (1 - \rho) y_2^1)] \tag{7}$$

$$y_1^2 + c_2^2 = 1 + y_2^1 - c_1^2. \tag{8}$$

Since (8) implies it, (4) may be ignored; by supergoodness we will choose to ignore (8) as well. Similarly we will drop (2) and (7). Clearly (4) will be binding; we will substitute from (6) and use its RHS in the maximand. Thus the supergoodness problem is:

$$\max_{c_1^1, y_2^1,} \alpha \ln c_1^1 + \beta \ln(1 - c_1^1 + (\rho - 1) y_2^1), \text{ s.t.}$$

$$y_2^1 + c_1^1 \leq 1. \tag{1}$$

There are three cases to consider:

(1-A) If $\rho - 1 < 0$ then

$$y_2^1 = y_1^2 = 0$$
$$c_1^1 = \alpha, \quad c_2^1 = \beta.$$

(1-B) If $\rho - 1 = 0$, y_2^1 can take on any value less than or equal to β and

$$y_1^2 = \rho y_2^1 = y_2^1$$
$$c_1^1 = \alpha, \quad c_2^1 = \beta.$$

(1-C) If $\rho - 1 > 0$

$$y_2^1 = \beta, \quad y_1^2 = \rho\beta$$
$$c_1^1 = \alpha, \quad c_2^1 = \rho\beta.$$

For player 2, we take the supergoodness problem as

$$\max_{c_1^1, c_1^2, c_2^2, y_1^2(\cdot), y_2^1} \alpha \ln c_1^2 + \beta \ln c_2^2, \text{ s.t.}$$

$$c_1^2 \leq y_2^1 \tag{2}$$

$$y_1^2(c_1^1, y_2^1) + c_2^2 \leq 1 + y_2^1 - c_1^2 \tag{3}$$

$$\bar{\rho} y_2^1 = y_1^2(c_1^1, y_2^1). \tag{9'}$$

Since all that matters to this optimization problem is the value of $y_1^2(\cdot)$ at (c_1^1, y_2^1) and there are no continuity constraints, we need not maximize over the function, but only over the value, which we will write simply as y_1^2. Thus we have

$$\bar{\rho}y_2^1 = y_1^2. \tag{9^{11}}$$

Notice however that

$$y_1^2 = \rho y_2^1 \tag{6}$$

is a necessary condition for a situation to be good for player 1. There is no equilibrium except when equations (6) and (9^{11}) both hold; thus there is no equilibrium with trade unless $\rho = \bar{\rho}$ which we henceforth assume to be the case.

Returning to player 2's supergoodness problem, we see that clearly (3) will be binding. Using (9^{11}) and substituting from (3) into the maximand, we have

$$\max_{c_1^2} \alpha \ln c_1^2 + \beta \ln(1 - c_1^2 + (1 - \rho)y_2^1), \text{ s.t.}$$

$$c_1^2 \leq y_2^1 \tag{2}$$

Again there are three cases:

(2-A) If $\rho - 1 < 0$ then $(1 - \rho) > 0$ and the supergoodness problem has no solution, as y_2^1 increases beyond all bounds.

(2-B) If $\rho - 1 = 0$ then $c_1^2 = \alpha$ and $c_2^2 = \beta$ and y_2^1 can take any value greater than or equal to α, and $y_1^2 = y_2^1$.

(2-C) If $\rho - 1 > 0$, then $(1 - \rho) < 0$

$$c_1^2 = \alpha/\rho \quad c_2^2 = \beta$$
$$y_2^1 = \alpha/\rho \quad y_1^2 = \alpha.$$

Now we must find out if there are any circumstances under which the two sets of supergoodness solutions agree.

Clearly they will never agree if cases (1-A) and (2-A) prevail, for in the former y_2^1 vanishes while in the latter it increases beyond all bounds. Even if we modified our supergoodness approach and included a few more constraints, it is unlikely that we could produce agreement in this case, for when $\rho < 1$, the players' interests are fundamentally opposed.

Agreement is not impossible in the B cases. When $\rho = 1$, a situation with any value $y_2^1 \leq \beta$ is supergood for player 1, while a situation with any value $y_2^1 \geq \alpha$ is supergood for 2. Thus there can be agreement iff

$$\alpha \leq \beta \tag{10}$$

in which case any y_2^1 satisfying $\alpha \leq y_2^1 \leq \beta$ will be supergood for both players. Then it is easy to verify that the doubly supergood situations with

$$y_2^1 = y_1^2$$
$$c_1^1 = c_1^2 = \alpha$$
$$c_2^1 = c_2^2 = \beta$$

are NEs and hence (by the Supergoodness Theorem) equilibria with the $\bar{\rho} = \rho = 1$ commitment pattern, provided (10) holds. (10), however, is a rather unusual condition—it requires that players value future consumption at least as highly as present. Economists, however, generally believe that the contrary is true; hence the equilibrium we have found cannot leave us satisfied.

Fortunately, agreement is possible in the C cases iff (10) does not hold. When $\rho > 1$, player 1's supergood situations have $y_2^1 = \beta$ while player 2's supergood situations have $y_2^1 = \alpha / \rho$. For agreement we need $\beta = \alpha / \rho$, i.e., $\rho = \alpha / \beta$. Now $\rho = \alpha / \beta > 1$ as required for case C iff

$$\alpha > \beta \tag{11}$$

i.e., iff (10) fails. It is easy to verify that given $\rho = \alpha / \beta$, players 1 and 2 agree on the remaining variables:

$$c_2^1 = y_1^2 = c_1^1 = \alpha$$
$$c_1^2 = y_2^1 = c_2^2 = \beta$$

and that the situations with these values are NEs. Hence those situations, along with the $\bar{\rho} = \rho = \alpha / \beta$ commitment pattern, are equilibria whenever (11) holds. Thus we have found equilibria for every possible value of α and β.

There is nothing unusual about these results. When future consumption is at least as valuable as present, players will trade future against present equally, many situations are compatible with equilibrium and each player will follow the same pattern of increasing consumption. In the normal case where present is preferred to future, there will be a premium on present consumption, each player will follow a pattern of even consumption over time, and the player whose endowment is of the more valuable good—the present time good—will be better off than the one who receives his endowment later.

The results also coincide with a Walrasian equilibrium. Although we talked about "supergood sets" and "agreement" while the Walrasian approach talks about "demand correspondences" and "market clearing," because of the way we chose super-acceptable sets the mathematical operations we performed were the same as those that would be performed to find a Walrasian equilibrium.

Note, however, that we never considered "expectations," even though in any actual play of the game player 1 would no doubt think about how much, if anything, player 2 would repay him in period 2, and these thoughts would influence his actions in period I. Our interest, though, is not psychology. Only the patterns of actions and commitments that are equilibria will leave all players without regret at how they played the game—that is one way we defined equilibrium. If an actual play is not an equilibrium somebody is making a mistake. (In this sense every commitment equilibrium is a rational expectations equilibrium.) I do not wish to deny that people make mistakes; original sin has been said to be the only empirically verifiable proposition of theology. Psychology may in fact be able to say some interesting things about how people make mistakes. But economics has been well served heretofore by its assumption of rationality, and a disquisition on mistakes and irrationality could hardly be called economics.

II

The problem we have just discussed did not involve money, although it could have. If it did, it would have had to use the "credit-card money" we used in chapter 6. This was sort of slippery stuff that had the property of coming from nothing and disappearing by the end of the problem. People had to be looking over each others' shoulders constantly to prevent abuses, but everyone wandered around with omnipotent credit cards and unlimited overdraft privileges.

With explicit time, we can consider another, perhaps more realistic, kind of money: paper money (or certified checks). Like credit-card money, paper money is not desired for itself: it enters into no one's utility function. It differs from credit-card money in two important respects. First, someone has a fixed endowment of it at the beginning of the game; it does not spring into being merely by assertions. Second, the constraints against overspending are technological, not part of the commitment pattern: if all you have is five dollars, you cannot give away more than five dollars no matter what the other players think or do.

Paper money, however, makes eschatology a crucial issue. Suppose there is a day on which the world will end. The folk saying is true about paper money: you can't take it with you. Hence we may be assured that there will be no going-out-of-business sales the day before Armageddon, since the merchants will never be able to spend and thereby enjoy the money they would realize from those sales. In general, then, money will be useless the day before Armageddon, and so no one will want to hold any money balance at the end of the day before the day before Armageddon. Thus money will be useless then too. In this manner we can continue backwards as long as we wish, and conclude that no one will ever want to hold paper money if the world will end someday, no matter how far in the future Armageddon is.

To understand paper money, then, we must assume away the end of the world (a bold assumption, indeed). We will consider an overlapping generations game à la Samuelson (1958) with a countable infinity of players and a countable infinity of time periods. Denote by $t = 1, 2, \ldots$, the time periods. In each period a new player is "born," and we will name him after his birthday. Player t "lives" for two periods: in period t he is endowed with one unit of a durable good, and in period $(t + 1)$ he is endowed with nothing. He consumes c_t^t in period t and c_t^{t+1} in period $(t + 1)$, and his utility is given by

$$\ln u_t = \alpha \ln c_t^t + \beta \ln c_t^{t+1}.$$

The biological language in quotation marks is, of course, merely motivational: it is just as easy to imagine all the players existing forever, but with nonnull moves only in the periods we have called their lives.

Trade with the unborn and dead being impossible, we allow player t to choose an amount y_{t-1}^t to give to player $(t - 1)$ at period t and to receive an amount from player $(t + 1)$ at period $(t + 1)$. Each player also chooses a consumption amount at the end of each period, subject to the constraints

$$c_t^t \leq 1 - y_{t-1}^t \tag{12}$$

$$c_t^{t+1} \leq 1 - y_{t-1}^t + y_t^{t+1} - c_t^t. \tag{13}$$

Barter is entirely unpromising in this world, because there is nothing that player $(t - 1)$ can give to player t that player t does not have already. Without money there will be no trade. Let player t, therefore, receive m_t^{t-1} in money from player $(t - 1)$ at period t, and choose m_{t+1}^t to give to player $(t + 1)$ at period $(t + 1)$. We take m_1^0 to be the exogenously fixed amount of paper money that player 1 has on hand when the game begins and require, as a technological constraint, that money outlays do not exceed money income:

$$m_{t+1}^t \leq m_t^{t-1} \quad t = 1, 2, \ldots \tag{14}$$

We will look at both price and naked trade commitment patterns for this game. First, price:

$$g_t(\cdot) = f_t(\cdot) \quad \text{if} \quad p^t y_{t-1}^t < m_t^{t-1} \tag{15a}$$

$$t = 2, 3, \ldots$$

$$\text{or if} \quad \bar{p}^{t+1} y_t^{t+1} < m_{t+1}^t \tag{15b}$$

$$= 0 \quad \text{otherwise}$$

$$g_1(\cdot) = f_1(\cdot) \quad \text{if} \quad \bar{p}^2 y_1^2 < m_2^1. \tag{15c}$$

Let us consider some necessary conditions for a situation to be acceptable to player $\tau > 1$. Since we will be using supergoodness to find equilibria we need not search for sufficiency. From the price commitment pattern, and the uselessness of excess donations, a situation will be acceptable to τ only if

$$p^\tau y^\tau_{\tau-1} = m^{\tau-1}_\tau, \quad \tau > 1 \tag{16}$$

$$\bar{p}^{\tau+1}\, y^{\tau+1}_\tau \geq m^\tau_{\tau+1}, \quad \tau > 1 \tag{17}$$

For $\tau = 1$, we have only the analogue of (17)

$$\bar{p}^2 y^2_1 \geq m^1_2. \tag{18}$$

To be precise, we should have specified $y^{\tau+1}_\tau$ and y^2_1 as functions of previous variables, since they will differ on different information sets for players $(\tau + 1)$ and 2 respectively. As we saw in the previous example, however, these distinctions will disappear when we look for supergoodness; so there is no sense loading up on notation that we will just throw away.

Consider now the supergoodness problem for a player $t > 1$. The goodness problem has an infinity of constraints, but we will ignore all of these except the technological constraints (13) for t and (14) for $\tau \leq t$, and the acceptability constraints (16) for $\tau = t + 1$ and (17) for $\tau = t - 1$. Thus the supergoodness problem is

$$\max_{\substack{c^t_t,\, c^{t+1}_t,\, y^t_{t-1},\, y^{t+1}_t \\ m^{\tau-1}_\tau,\, \tau < t+1}} \alpha \ln c^t_t + \beta \ln c^{t+1}_t, \quad \text{s.t.}$$

$$c^{t+1}_t \leq 1 - y^t_{t-1} + y^{t+1}_t - c^t_t \tag{13}$$

$$m^t_{t+1} \leq m^{t-1}_t \tag{14}$$

$$m^\tau_{\tau+1} \leq m^{\tau-1}_\tau \quad \forall \tau < t \tag{14'}$$

$$p^{t+1}\, y^{t+1}_t = m^t_{t+1} \tag{16}$$

$$\bar{p}^t\, y^t_{t-1} \geq m^{t-1}_t. \tag{17}$$

It is easy to show from Lagrangian expressions that (17) must be binding if trade takes place. We know that for a situation to be acceptable to t: $p^t\, y^t_{t-1} = m^{t-1}_t$ which hence is a necessary condition for an NE. But (17) binding means that in any supergood situation for t and hence in any intersection of supergood sets $\bar{p}^t\, y^t_{t-1} = m^{t-1}_t$. Since equilibrium situations are the intersection of all supergood sets and the set of NEs, this particular supergoodness approach will yield an equilibrium situation with trade only if $\bar{p}^t = p^t$ which we shall henceforth assume to be the case.

It should also be clear that (13) and (14) will be binding. Substituting (13), (14), (16), and (17) in the maximand, the problem becomes

$$\max_{c_t^t,\, m_t^{t-1},\, m_\tau^{\tau+1}} \alpha \ln c_t^t + \beta \ln \left(1 - c_t^t + m_t^{t-1} \left[\frac{1}{p^{t+1}} - \frac{1}{p^t}\right]\right) \quad , \text{ s.t.}$$

$$m_{\tau+1}^{\tau} \leq m_\tau^{\tau-1} \qquad \forall \tau < t. \qquad (14^1)$$

Once again, there are three cases to consider:

(t-A) If $(1/p^{t+1}) - (1/p^t) > 0$, then m_t^{t-1} should be as large as possible. Then (14^1) will be binding for all $\tau < t$ and hence $m_t^{t-1} = m_1^0$. The full solution becomes

$$c_t^t = \alpha\left(1 + m_1^0 \left[\frac{1}{p^{t+1}} - \frac{1}{p^t}\right]\right)$$

$$c_t^{t+1} = \beta\left(1 + m_1^0 \left[\frac{1}{p^{t+1}} - \frac{1}{p^t}\right]\right)$$

$$y_{t-1}^t = \frac{m_1^0}{p^t}$$

$$y_t^{t+1} = \frac{m_1^0}{p^{t+1}} \,.$$

(t-B) If $(1/p^{t+1}) - (1/p^t) = 0$, then any value of m_t^{t-1} is a solution; hence any weakly monotonically decreasing sequence

$$m_1^0, m_2^1, m_3^2, \ldots, m_{t-1}^{t-2}, m_t^{t-1}$$

is a solution and

$$c_t^t = \alpha \qquad c_t^{t+1} = \beta$$

$$y_{t-1}^t = \frac{m_t^{t-1}}{p^t} \qquad y_t^{t+1} = \frac{m_t^{t-1}}{p^{t+1}}$$

is the full solution.

(t-C) If $(1/p^{t+1}) - (1/p^t) < 0$ then $m_t^{t-1} = 0$, and any weakly monotonically decreasing sequence $m_1^0, m_2^1, m_3^2, \ldots, m_{t-1}^{t-2}$ will be a solution. The rest of the solution is:

$$c_t^t = \alpha \qquad c_t^{t+1} = \beta$$

$$y_{t-1}^t = y_t^{t+1} = 0.$$

In addition, the solution implies $m_\tau^{\tau-1} = 0$ for $\tau > t$.

For $t = 1$, the supergoodness problem is

$$\max_{c_1^1,\, c_1^2,\, y_1^2,\, m_2^1} \alpha \ln c_1^1 + \beta \ln c_1^2 \text{ s.t.}$$

$$c_1^2 \leq 1 + y_1^2 - c_1^1 \tag{13-1}$$

$$m_2^1 \leq m_1^0 \tag{14-1}$$

$$p^2 y^2 = m_2^1. \tag{16-2}$$

By the same sort of arguments as before, all these constraints will be binding, and the solution will be

$$c_1^1 = \alpha(1 + m_1^0/p^2) \qquad m_2^1 = m_1^0$$

$$c_1^2 = \beta(1 + m_1^0/p^2) \qquad y_1^2 = m_1^0/p^2.$$

Now we consider whether these supergood sets have an intersection—the question of agreement. First consider agreement between players 1 and 2. Since in the supergood set for player 1, $m_2^1 = m_1^0 > 0$, case C cannot obtain for player 2. Thus a necessary condition for a nonempty intersection of the supergood sets is that either case A or case B obtain for player 2; that is:

$$(1/p^3) - (1/p^2) \geq 0. \tag{19}$$

If (19) holds, the intersection of the supergood sets of players 1 and 2 is characterized by:

$$m_3^2 = m_2^1 = m_1^0$$
$$y_1^2 = m_1^0/p^2$$
$$y_2^3 = m_1^0/p^3$$

and the associated amounts of consumption.

Agreement among players 1, 2 and 3 then requires that either case A or case B obtain for player 3, since agreement between player 1 and 2 requires $m_3^2 = m_1^0 > 0$. Thus a necessary condition is $1/p^4 - 1/p^3 \geq 0$. Combining this with (19):

$$1/p^2 \leq 1/p^3 \leq 1/p^4. \tag{20}$$

If (20) holds the intersection of the first three players' supergood sets is characterized by:

$$m_4^3 = m_3^2 = m_2^1 = m_1^0$$
$$y_1^2 = m_1^0/p^2, \quad y_2^3 = m_1^0/p^3, \quad y_3^4 = m_1^0/p^4$$

and the associated amounts of consumption. Note that (20) requires

$$y_1^2 \leq y_2^3 \leq y_3^4.$$

It is easy to see that we can continue in this fashion indefinitely. If we do, the necessary condition for all the supergood sets to have an intersection is

$$1/p^2 \leq 1/p^3 \leq 1/p^4 \leq \ldots \leq 1/p^t \leq \ldots$$

or

$$p^t \geq p^{t+1} \qquad \forall t \geq 2 \tag{21}$$

and that intersection is characterized by

$$m_t^{t-1} = m_1^0 \qquad \forall t \geq 2 \tag{22a}$$

$$y_{t-1}^t = m_1^0/p^t \qquad \forall t \geq 2 \tag{22b}$$

$$y_{t-1}^t \leq y_t^{t+1} \qquad \forall t \geq 2. \tag{22c}$$

This intersection is an equilibrium iff it is an NE. We used all the constraints that characterize an NE in developing this intersection except (12) and (12-1) hence we know without checking that the intersection is an NE iff (12) and (12-1) are satisfied. Are they?

First let us check (12):

$$c_1^1 \leq 1 \quad \text{or} \quad \alpha(1 + (m_1^0/p^2)) \leq 1 \tag{12-1}$$

i.e.,

$$p^2 \geq \alpha(m_1^0/\beta). \tag{23-1}$$

So (23-1) is a necessary condition for this supergoodness approach to yield the equilibrium we are considering. Similarly for $t \geq 2$

$$y_{t-1}^t + c_t^t \leq 1 \tag{12}$$

or

$$\frac{m_1^0}{p^t} + \alpha\left(1 + \frac{m_1^0}{p^{t+1}} - \frac{m_1^0}{p^t}\right) \leq 1$$

i.e.,

$$\frac{\beta}{p^t} + \frac{\alpha}{p^{t+1}} \leq \frac{\beta}{m_1^0}.$$

From (21) we have

$$\frac{1}{p^t} \leq \frac{1}{p^{t+1}}$$

hence

$$\frac{1}{p^t} \leq \frac{\beta}{p^t} + \frac{\alpha}{p^{t+1}} \leq \frac{1}{p^{t+1}} .$$

From this it follows that

$$\frac{1}{p^{t+1}} \leq \frac{\beta}{m_1^0}$$

or

$$p^{t+1} \geq \frac{m_1^0}{\beta}$$

is a sufficient condition for (12) to be satisfied for t, while

$$\frac{1}{p^t} \leq \frac{\beta}{m_1^0}$$

or

$$p^t \geq \frac{m_1^0}{\beta}$$

is a necessary condition. By similar reasoning for $(t-1)$,

$$p^t \geq \frac{m_1^0}{\beta}$$

is a sufficient condition for (12) to be satisfied for $(t-1)$. Hence

$$\begin{aligned} p^2 &\geq \alpha \frac{m_1^0}{\beta} \\ p^t &\geq \frac{m_1^0}{\beta} \qquad \forall t > 2 \end{aligned} \tag{23}$$

is necessary and sufficient for (12) and (12-1) to be satisfied.

By (21), then, $(p^2, p^3, \ldots, p^t, \ldots)$ is a weakly monotonically decreasing series. By (23), it is bounded from below. The Bolzano-Weierstrass Theorem states that a bounded monotonic series must converge. Hence (p^t) must converge; i.e.:

$$\lim_{t \to \infty} p^t = \bar{p} \geq \frac{m_1^0}{\beta} .$$

By Cauchy's Theorem

$$\lim_{t\to\infty} (p^t - p^{t+1}) = 0.$$

Thus

$$\lim_{t\to\infty} \left(\frac{1}{p^{t+1}} - \frac{1}{p^t}\right) = \lim_{t\to\infty} \left(\frac{p^t - p^{t+1}}{p^t\, p^{t+1}}\right) = 0,$$

since $(p^t p^{t+1})$ is bounded away from zero by (23). It follows that

$$\lim_{t\to\infty} c_t^t = \alpha$$

$$\lim_{t\to\infty} c_t^{t+1} = \beta.$$

Thus in the long run, people are no better off than self-sufficient. In the short run, however, (that is, for small t) money and trade can make some players better off. Player 1 is sure to benefit if, through (15c), he can pretend that he is unwilling to part with something—paper money—which in fact is absolutely worthless. But after him such advantages become problematic and eventually must disappear.

The equilibrium with a naked trade commitment pattern is in many respects similar. Such a commitment pattern would be

$$\begin{aligned} g_1^N(\cdot) &= f_1(\cdot) && \text{if } m_2^1 > 0 && \text{and } y_1^2 < \bar{\bar{y}}_1^2 \\ & && \text{or if } y_1^2 \geq \bar{\bar{y}}_1^2 && \text{and } m_2^1 \neq \bar{\bar{m}}_2^1 \\ &= 0 && \text{otherwise} \\ g_t^N(\cdot) &= f_t(\cdot) && \text{if } y_{t-1}^t < \bar{y}_{t-1}^t && \text{and } m_t^{t-1} \geq \bar{m}_t^{t-1} \\ & && \text{or if } m_{t+1}^t > 0 && \text{and } y_t^{t+1} < \bar{\bar{y}}_t^{t+1} \\ & && \text{or if } m_{t+1}^t \neq \bar{\bar{m}}_{t+1}^t && \text{and } y_t^{t+1} \geq \bar{\bar{y}}_t^{t+1} \\ &= 0 && \text{otherwise, for } t \geq 2. \end{aligned}$$

Single bar and double bar variables are parameters of the commitment pattern; double bar variables appear only in enforcement constraints.

Necessary conditions for a commitment pattern of this type to be associated with an equilibrium with trade are:

$$\begin{aligned} &\bar{m}_t^{t-1} > 0 && (\forall t) \\ &\bar{\bar{m}}_t^{t-1} \geq \bar{m}_t^{t-1} && (\forall t \geq 2) \\ &\bar{y}_{t-1}^t = \bar{\bar{y}}_{t-1}^t && (\forall t \geq 2) \\ &\bar{\bar{m}}_{t+1}^t \geq \bar{\bar{m}}_{t+2}^{t+1} && (\forall t) \\ &m_1^0 \geq \sup_t (\bar{\bar{m}}_t^{t-1}, \bar{m}_t^{t-1}) \\ &\bar{y}_t^{t+1} > \bar{y}_{t-1}^t \qquad \bar{y}_t^{t+1} \leq \beta && (\forall t \geq 2). \end{aligned} \tag{24}$$

If these conditions hold, an equilibrium is given by

$$y_{t-1}^{t} = \bar{y}_{t-1}^{t} = \bar{\bar{y}}_{t-1}^{t} \qquad (\forall t \geq 2)$$
$$m_{t+1}^{t} = \bar{\bar{m}}_{t+1}^{t} \qquad (\forall t)$$
$$m_1^0 \geq m_2^1 \geq m_3^2 \geq \ldots \geq m_{t-1}^{t-2} \geq m_t^{t-1} \geq m_{t+1}^{t} \geq \bar{m}_{t+1}^{t} \quad (\forall t). \tag{25}$$

$$\text{Let} \quad \bar{m}^* \triangleq \inf_t (\bar{m}_{t+1}^t) > 0.$$

From (25) (m_{t+1}^t) is a weakly monotonically decreasing series bounded from below by $\bar{m}^*$. By the Bolzano-Weierstrass Theorem it must converge to some m^* with

$$m_1^0 \geq m^* \geq \bar{m}^*.$$

By (25), similarly, (y_t^{t+1}) must converge to $\bar{y}^* \leq \beta$. By Cauchy's Theorem, then, $(y_t^{t+1} - y_{t-1}^t)$ must converge to zero. Thus, as in the price commitment pattern case:

$$\lim_{t\to\infty} c_t^t = \lim_{t\to\infty} \alpha(1 - y_{t-1}^t + y_t^{t+1}) = \alpha$$
$$\lim_{t\to\infty} c_t^{t+1} = \lim_{t\to\infty} \beta(1 - y_{t-1}^t + y_t^{t+1}) = \beta$$

so that in the limit people are no better off than self-sufficient.

Now define π^t as the variable that would look like price to an outside observer who did not know how the players in fact bargained:

$$\pi^t \triangleq \frac{m_t^{t-1}}{y_{t-1}^t}.$$

Then from (24) and (25), (π^t) must be monotonically decreasing, since y_{t-1}^t is increasing and m_t^{t-1} is decreasing. Recall that (p^t) was also monotonically decreasing in the price commitment pattern. (π^t) is bounded from below by $(m^*/\bar{y}^*)$; thus by the Bolzano-Weierstrass Theorem it converges to π^* with

$$\bar{p} \geq \frac{m_1^0}{\beta} \geq \pi^* \geq \frac{m^*}{\bar{y}^*}.$$

The "prices" that the observer would see in the naked trade case are uniformly not higher than those he or she would see in the true price case, but they would behave in the same way. Since the observer would generally not have independent information on the value of β (which is, after all, a utility function parameter) he or she would be unable to tell by looking at actual behavior what type of commitment pattern was being used.

III

Our ability to deal with time makes it possible now to discuss economies with production, and the most interesting production economies are those in which trade must be roundabout. Leijonhufvud in particular has emphasized the significance of roundaboutness in a production economy: "The individual steel producer cannot pay a newly-hired worker by handing over to him his physical product (nor will the worker try to feed his family on a ton-and-a-half of cold-rolled sheet a week)" (1968, p. 90). For this reason we will refer to the model in this section as the "L-economy." We will consider two types of commitment patterns. First we will use a standard price system—and end up, of course, with the Walrasian equilibrium. Then we will modify this price system slightly to allow a bit of prudential rationing; an equilibrium with involuntary employment will result.

Since in this section money will not be our primary concern, our treatment of it will be opportunistic and somewhat schizoid. Since we have only finite time paper money cannot be used. It is much more convenient, though, to include expenditure constraints as technology rather than as conditionals in commitments—but if we do so without money at the beginning trade will be impossible. Our escape from this dilemma is to use checking accounts which must balance only at the end of the game, and to consider the balance constraints as technological. This approach does not particularly make sense; it is harmless, though, and convenient.

In the L-economy, then, there are four players, two workers and two employers, and two goods, x and y. Those who make x like to consume y and those who make y like to consume x. We will take the game to consist of two stages. At stage 1, the workers, players 1 and 2, choose amounts of labor l_1 and l_2 respectively, subject to

$$l_1 \leq 1 \tag{26}$$

$$l_2 \leq 1, \tag{27}$$

and the employers, players 3 and 4, choose money payments m_1^3 and m_2^4, respectively, to workers 1 and 2, respectively. We may imagine production as taking place at stage 1, with player 1's labor combining with player 3's existing capital to produce good y, and player 2's labor combining with player 4's existing capital to produce good x.

Distribution, trade, and consumption take place at stage 2. Players 1 and 2 choose payments m_4^1 and m_3^2, respectively, to players 4 and 3, respectively, subject to

$$m_4^1 \leq m_1^3 \tag{28}$$

$$m_3^2 \leq m_2^4. \tag{29}$$

Player 3 chooses amounts y_2^3 and y_4^3 of good y to give to players 2 and 4, respectively, subject to

$$y_2^3 + y_4^3 \leq l_1 - \tfrac{1}{2} l_1^2 \tag{30}$$

and also chooses payment m_4^3 to player 4 subject to

$$m_1^3 + m_4^3 \leq m_3^2 + m_3^4. \tag{31}$$

Similarly player 4 chooses amounts x_1^4 and x_3^4 of good x to give to players 1 and 3, respectively, subject to:

$$x_1^4 + x_3^4 \leq l_2 - \tfrac{1}{2} l_2^2 \tag{32}$$

and also chooses payment m_3^4 to player 3 subject to:

$$m_2^4 + m_3^4 \leq m_4^1 + m_4^3. \tag{33}$$

Players 1 and 2 have Cobb-Douglas utility functions in consumption and leisure, while players 3 and 4 care only about consumption:

$$\begin{aligned} \ln u_1 &= \alpha \ln x_1^4 + \beta \ln(1 - l_1) \\ \ln u_2 &= \alpha \ln y_2^3 + \beta \ln(1 - l_2) \\ u_3 &= \zeta_3(x_3^4) \\ u_4 &= \zeta_4(y_4^3) \end{aligned}$$

where ζ_3 and ζ_4 are arbitrary monotonically increasing functions.

For any technologically feasible situation we have, from (33), (28), (31), and (29)

$$m_2^4 + m_3^4 \leq m_4^1 + m_4^3 \leq m_1^3 + m_4^3 \leq m_3^2 + m_3^4 \leq m_2^4 + m_3^4$$

so that equality holds at every point in the above expression, as well as (33), (28), (31), and (29). Thus we may write

$$\begin{aligned} m_4^1 &= m_1^3 \triangleq m_1 \\ m_3^2 &= m_2^4 \triangleq m_2 \\ m_1^3 + m_4^3 &= m_3^2 + m_3^4 = m_2^4 + m_3^4 = m_4^1 + m_4^3 \triangleq m \\ m_3^4 &= m - m_2 \\ m_4^3 &= m - m_1 \end{aligned}$$

at any feasible situation and ignore (33), (28), (31) and (29).

Let us consider a standard price commitment pattern:

$$\begin{aligned} g_1(\cdot) &= f_1(\cdot) \qquad \text{if} \quad w_1 l_1 < m_1 \qquad \text{or if } \bar{p}_1^4 x_1^4 < m_1 \\ &= 0 \qquad \text{otherwise} \end{aligned} \tag{34a}$$

$$g_2(\cdot) = f_2(\cdot) \quad \text{if} \quad w_2 l_2 < m_2 \quad \text{or if } \bar{p}_2^3 y_2^3 < m_2 \tag{34b}$$
$$= 0 \quad \text{otherwise}$$

$$g_3(\cdot) = f_3(\cdot) \quad \text{if} \quad p^3 y_2^3 \neq m_2 \quad \text{or if } p^3 y_4^3 \neq m - m_2 \tag{34c}$$

$$\text{or if} \quad \bar{p}_3^4 x_3^4 < m - m_1 \tag{34d}$$

$$\text{or if} \quad \bar{w}_1 l_1 < m_1 \tag{34e}$$

$$= 0 \quad \text{otherwise}$$

$$g_4(\cdot) = f_4(\cdot) \quad \text{if} \quad p^4 x_1^4 \neq m_1 \quad \text{or if } p^4 x_3^4 \neq m - m_1 \tag{34f}$$

$$\text{or if} \quad \bar{p}_4^3 y_4^3 < m - m_2 \tag{34g}$$

$$\text{or if} \quad \bar{w}_2 l_2 < m_2 \tag{34h}$$

$$= 0 \quad \text{otherwise.}$$

Note that in (34c) and (34f) we force employers to sell output at the same price to all buyers. This again is laziness, for an equal price is what would result from arbitrage if we permitted another stage at which a second round of trading could take place. Rather than complicate the problem with an arbitrage stage, we have merely grafted onto it the result that that stage would produce. Without either an equal selling price assumption or an arbitrage stage, the problem would be one of four goods with joint production—not the simple two-good problem we wish to consider. We do not, however, require that different buyers commit themselves to the same buying price.

We may find the expressions characterizing acceptable situations in the usual manner. For player 1, acceptable situations must satisfy:

$$m_1 \leq \bar{p}_1^4 x_1^4 \tag{35}$$

$$w_1 l_1 = m_1 . \tag{36}$$

Similarly for player 2:

$$m_2 \leq \bar{p}_2^3 y_2^3 \tag{37}$$

$$w_2 l_2 = m_2 . \tag{38}$$

For players 3 and 4, since nothing that they do affects their own utilities directly, any situation in which they do not violate their commitments is acceptable. Thus in acceptable situations for player 3:

$$p^3 y_2^3 = m_2 \tag{39}$$

$$p^3 y_4^3 = m - m_2 \tag{40}$$

$$m - m_1 \leq \bar{p}_3^4 x_3^4 \tag{41}$$

$$\bar{w}_1 l_1 \geq m_1 \tag{42}$$

and in acceptable situations for player 4:

$$p^4 x_1^4 = m_1 \tag{43}$$

$$p^4 x_3^4 = m - m_1 \tag{44}$$

$$m - m_2 \leq \bar{p}_4^3 y_4^3 \tag{45}$$

$$\bar{w}_2 l_2 \geq m_2. \tag{46}$$

Situations that satisfy acceptability conditions (35)—(46) and feasibility conditions (26), (27), (30), and (32) are NEs.

The good situations for player 1 are those that maximize his utility subject to the feasibility conditions and acceptability conditions (37)–(46). We will follow an essentially (though not entirely) Walrasian supergoodness approach and ignore all these constraints except for (38), (40), (42), and (43). Hence the supergoodness problem for player 1 is:

$$\max_{\text{(all variables)}} \quad \alpha \ln x_1^4 + \beta \ln (1 - l_1) \quad \text{s.t.}$$

$$w_2 l_2 = m_2 \tag{38}$$

$$p^3 y_4^3 = m - m_2 \tag{40}$$

$$\bar{w}_1 l_1 \geq m_1 \tag{42}$$

$$p^4 x_1^4 = m_1. \tag{43}$$

It is easy to see that (42) will be binding. Substituting (42) into (43), solving for x_1^4 and substituting in the maximand, we have

$$\max_{l_1, l_2, m_2} \alpha \ln((\bar{w}_1 l_1)/(p^4)) + \beta \ln(1 - l_1) \quad \text{s.t.}$$

$$w_2 l_2 = m_2 \tag{38}$$

$$p^3 y_4^3 = m - m_2. \tag{40}$$

Hence player 1's supergood set has:

$$w_2 l_2 = m_2 \tag{38}$$

$$\bar{w}_1 \alpha = m_1 \tag{47}$$

$$l_1 = \alpha \tag{48}$$

$$x_1^4 = \alpha \bar{w}_1 / p^4 \tag{49}$$

$$p^3 y_4^3 = m - m_2. \tag{40}$$

By following a similar approach we can derive player 2's supergood set:

$$w_1 l_1 = m_1 \tag{36}$$

$$\bar{w}_2 \alpha = m_2 \tag{50}$$

$$l_2 = \alpha \tag{51}$$

$$y_2^3 = \alpha \bar{w}_2 / p^3 \tag{52}$$

$$p^4 x_3^4 = m - m_1 . \tag{44}$$

Comparing (38) with (50) and (51), we see that the intersection of the two supergood sets will always be empty unless

$$\bar{w}_2 = w_2 . \tag{53}$$

Similarly, comparing (36) with (47) and (48), the intersection will be empty unless

$$\bar{w}_1 = w_1 . \tag{54}$$

Since the supergoodness approach will yield an equilibrium only if the intersection of all supergood sets is nonempty, we will assume henceforth that (53) and (54) hold.

For player 3 the goodness problem is to maximize x_3^4 subject to the feasibility conditions, (35)–(38), and (43)–(46). From (44)

$$x_3^4 = \frac{m - m_1}{p^4} .$$

Since p^4 is a parameter of the commitment pattern, the goodness problem may be taken as maximizing $(m - m_1)$. By supergoodness we will ignore all constraints except (30), (36), (37), and (45). Thus player 3's supergoodness problem is:

$$\max_{m, m_1, m_2, y_2^3, y_4^3, x_1^4, x_3^4} \quad m - m_1 \quad \text{s.t.}$$

$$y_2^3 + y_4^3 \leq l_1 - {}^1\!/_2 l_1^2 \tag{30}$$

$$w_1 l_1 = m_1 \tag{36}$$

$$m_2 \leq \bar{p}_2^3 y_2^3 \tag{37}$$

$$m - m_2 \leq \bar{p}_4^3 y_4^3 . \tag{45}$$

Use (36) to substitute for m_1 in the maximand. (30), (37) and (45) imply:

$$\frac{m_2}{\bar{p}_2^3} + \frac{m - m_2}{\bar{p}_4^3} \leq y_2^3 + y_4^3 \leq l_1 - {}^1\!/_2 l_1^2$$

Consider, then, the problem:

$$\max_{m_0, m_2, l_1} m - w_1 l_1 \text{ s.t.}$$

$$\frac{m_2}{\bar{p}_2^3} + \frac{m - m_2}{\bar{p}_4^3} \leq l_1 - \tfrac{1}{2} l_1^2. \tag{30^1}$$

First order conditions for a maximum include:

$$\frac{\partial \mathcal{L}}{\partial m} = 1 + \frac{\lambda}{\bar{p}_4^3} \leq 0, \qquad m \frac{\partial \mathcal{L}}{\partial m} = 0.$$

Thus $\lambda < 0$ is a necessary condition for a maximum. By complementary slackness, (30^1) is binding at a maximum. If (30^1) is binding, then so must be (30), (37), and (45) in the previous maximization problem. If (37) and (45) are binding, then in every situation of player 3's supergood set $m_2 = \bar{p}_2^3 y_2^3$ and $m - m_2 = \bar{p}_4^3 y_4^3$. But for every situation in player 2's supergood set we have $m_2 = p^3 y_2^3$ (from (52) and (50)) and for every situation in player 1's supergood set we have

$$m - m_2 = p^3 y_4^3. \tag{40}$$

Thus the intersection of the three players' supergood sets will be empty unless

$$\bar{p}_2^3 = \bar{p}_4^3 = p^3 \tag{55}$$

which we henceforth assume.

Substituting (55) in (30^1) we find:

$$\frac{m_2}{\bar{p}_2^3} + \frac{m - m_2}{\bar{p}_4^3} = \frac{m_2}{p^3} + \frac{m - m_2}{p^3} = \frac{m}{p^3}$$

so player 3's supergoodness problem finally becomes

$$\max_{m, l_1} m - w_1 l_1 \text{ s.t.}$$

$$\frac{m}{p^3} = l_1 - \tfrac{1}{2} l_1^2 . \tag{30^{11}}$$

The solution to this problem is

$$l_1 = 1 - \frac{w_1}{p^3} \tag{56}$$

$$m = p^3 (l_1 - \tfrac{1}{2} l_1^2) = \tfrac{1}{2} p^3 \left(1 - \left(\frac{w_1}{p^3}\right)^2\right). \tag{57}$$

Player 4's supergoodness problem is symmetrical with player 3's. Hence its solution is:

$$l_2 = 1 - \frac{w_2}{p^4} \tag{58}$$

$$m = p^4(l_2 - \tfrac{1}{2} l_2^2) = \tfrac{1}{2}p^4 \left(1 - \left(\frac{w_2}{p^4}\right)^2\right). \tag{59}$$

We must now determine whether and under what conditions the four supergood sets will have a nonempty intersection. It will be sufficient to have agreement on l_1, l_2, and m, because it can be verified that agreement on these three variables will lead to agreement on all other variables. (The Walrasian analogue of this statement is that if the markets for both types of labor and one type of good clear, then the remaining market must clear by Walras's law.)

For l_1 then, agreement between players 1 and 3 implies that (48) and (56) must both hold: $l_1 = \alpha = 1 - (w_1/p^3)$ hence

$$w_1/p^3 = \beta \tag{60}$$

is a necessary condition for an equilibrium to exist with this supergoodness approach. Similarly for l_2 agreement between players 2 and 4 requires from (51) and (58) that:

$$w_2/p^4 = \beta. \tag{61}$$

Finally, since by (48) and (51) $l_1 = l_2 = \alpha$, agreement between players 3 and 4 on m requires from (57) and (59) that:

$$m = p^3(l_1 - \tfrac{1}{2} l_1^2) = p^4(l_2 - \tfrac{1}{2} l_2^2)$$

or

$$p^3(\alpha - \tfrac{1}{2}\alpha^2) = p^4(\alpha - \tfrac{1}{2}\alpha^2)$$

that is:

$$p^3 = p^4 \triangleq p \tag{62}$$

which implies in (60) and (61):

$$w_1 = w_2 = \beta p. \tag{63}$$

The necessary conditions for an equilibrium with the type of commitment pattern in (34), then, are the agreement-between-sellers-and-buyers conditions (53), (54), (55), and the analogue of (55) for player 4, and conditions (62) and (63), for any $p > 0$. It is easy to show that the situations in the intersection of the four supergood sets are NEs, because every NE constraint except (26) and (27) was used in developing them, and (26) and (27) hold. Thus we have found an equilibrium, and one that corresponds to Walrasian equilibrium.

There is nothing sacred, however, about the purely price commitment pattern of (34). In many instances it is clearly not a very good representation of how people bargain with each other. It would seem to represent well the process that occurs, for instance, when I go to a store, ask for two newspapers, and plunk down 4 dimes on the counter. For if I were to receive no newspapers or only one I would feel angry and cheated, and if I confronted the storekeeper with my dissatisfaction, the response would not be:

"I will give you however many newspapers I please. These are my newspapers and I will do what I want with them. Thank you for your gift of 40 cents."

But rather:

"You can't count. You only gave me 2 dimes. I gave you one newspaper. We're even. Get outtahere before I call the cops."

On the other hand, if I were to go to the same store, plunk down 4 million dimes, and ask for 2 million newspapers, I do not expect that I would receive them either, but the dialogue would be qualitatively different. On ascertaining that it was in fact 4 million dimes I had plunked down on the counter and finding himself unable to supply me with 2 million newspapers, the storekeeper almost certainly would not thereupon commit harakiri in accordance with a price commitment pattern. He or she would not even, I suspect, show any remorse (pity, maybe, but not remorse). If I were to remonstrate,

"Your sign says newspapers are 20 cents each. Here's my 4 million dimes. You owe me 2 million newspapers," the most kindly response I could expect would be:

"The sign doesn't mean what it says. What it means is newspapers are 20 cents each until we run out."

In this manner we would learn that the storekeeper's commitment is not in fact a bare price commitment, but rather a commitment that includes some quantity constraints. Similarly, if the storekeeper had put 2 million unrequested newspapers on my doorstep and asked for 4 million dimes, we would have learned that my commitment also included quantity constraints. Indeed, if quantity constraints by buyers are not the normal practice, why do people comment that medicine is odd because physicians as sellers do not consider themselves affected by quantity constraints?

We should not think, then, that commitment patterns with quantity constraints are in any sense weird or unusual. A commitment pattern is a commitment pattern, and a pure price commitment pattern is just a very special type of commitment pattern—one which, in fact, as the newspaper store story suggests, is probably not very important empirically. Let us modify (34), then, to add some quantity constraints and thereby make it more realistic.

There is no solid reason why we should not put quantity constraints on every line of (34). I do not know anyone who would commit herself to work 25 hours per day for the right amount of money or deliver an arbitrarily large number of pizzas tonight for an arbitrarily large amount of money, but these are the sorts of commitments the L-economy players are making in (34). Nevertheless, putting quantity constraints on every line in (34) would make finding an equilibrium situation computationally difficult.

So we will only put quantity constraints on the purchase of labor. We will do this by considering a new commitment pattern called (34^1) that is exactly like (34) except in the lines (34e) and (34h). We replace these lines by

$$g_3(\cdot) = f_3(\cdot) \quad \text{if} \quad \bar{w}_1 l_1 < m_1 \quad \text{or if} \quad \bar{w}_1 \bar{l}_1 < m_1 \tag{34^1e}$$

and

$$g_4(\cdot) = f_4(\cdot) \quad \text{if} \quad \bar{w}_2 l_2 < m_2 \quad \text{or if} \quad \bar{w}_2 \bar{l}_2 < m_2 \tag{34^1h}$$

respectively. What (34^1e) and (34^1h) say is that employers will not pay for more than $\bar{l}_i$, $i = 1, 2$, "hours" of labor even if workers work more than that. One should not be surprised to see capitalists making such commitments, because they must decide on how much money to give workers in stage 1, before they have received any payments for products in stage 2. It is entirely reasonable to expect employers to want some control over how much they pay workers and how much is produced; commitment pattern (34) puts these determinations solely in the hands of labor, but (34^1) does not. Employers in (34) say "Whoever shows up will be paid at a rate not to exceed $\bar{w}$ no matter how much work is done and how much output is produced," while employers in (34^1) say, "Whoever shows up will be paid at a rate not to exceed $\bar{w}$ but once $\bar{l}$ is done everyone can go home." (34^1) thus seems to correspond more closely to the type of commitments we see in actual labor markets: most employers determine the amount of work they want done, and will pay for no more than that amount. After all, if (34) were the case rather than (34^1), disgruntled employees would try to harm employers by working extravagant amounts of overtime, rather than by withholding labor.

Let us see then what sort of equilibria result with commitment patterns like (34^1). Acceptable situations for players 1 and 2 remain the same with (34^1) as they were with (34). For player 3, (42) must be replaced by

$$\bar{w}_1 l_1 \geq m_1 \quad \text{if} \quad l_1 < \bar{l}_1 \tag{64}$$

$$\bar{w}_1 \bar{l}_1 \geq m_1 \quad \text{if} \quad l_1 \geq \bar{l}_1 \tag{65}$$

so that player 3's acceptable situations are characterized by (39), (40), (41), (64), and (65). Similarly for player 4, (46) must be replaced by

$$\bar{w}_2 l_2 \geq m_2 \quad \text{if} \quad l_2 < \bar{l}_2 \tag{66}$$

$$\bar{w}_2 \bar{l}_2 \geq m_2 \quad \text{if} \quad l_2 \geq \bar{l}_2 \tag{67}$$

and player 4's acceptable situations are characterized by (43), (44), (45), (66), and (67).

The changes we must make in supergood sets are somewhat the opposite of the changes in acceptable sets. For players 3 and 4 the supergood sets will remain the same, since neither used either (42) or (46). For players 1 and 2, however, we must find new supergood sets.

For player 1, we will maximize utility subject to (38), (40), (43), (64), and (65):

$$\max_{\substack{x_1^4,\, l_1,\, l_2,\, m_2 \\ m,\, y_4^3\, m_1}} \quad \alpha \ln x_1^4 + \beta \ln (1 - l_1) \ \text{ s.t.}$$

$$w_2 l_2 = m_2 \tag{38}$$

$$p^3 y_4^3 = m - m_2 \tag{40}$$

$$p^4 x_1^4 = m_1 \tag{43}$$

$$\bar{w}_1 l_1 \geq m_1 \quad \text{if} \quad l_1 < \bar{l}_1 \tag{64}$$

$$\bar{w}_1 \bar{l}_1 \geq m_1 \quad \text{if} \quad l_1 \geq \bar{l}_1 . \tag{65}$$

First suppose that $\alpha \leq \bar{l}_1$. Then we can solve in the same way we did before and obtain:

$$w_2 l_2 = m_2 \tag{38}$$

$$p^3 y_4^3 = m - m_2 \tag{40}$$

$$\alpha \bar{w}_1 = m_1 \tag{47}$$

$$l_1 = \alpha \tag{48}$$

$$x_1^4 = \alpha (\bar{w}_1 / p^4) \tag{49}$$

for any situation in player 1's supergood set, and (65) is obviously satisfied.

If, on the other hand, $\alpha > \bar{l}_1$, (65) becomes a problem. Then player 1's supergood set is given by:

$$w_2 l_2 = m_2 \tag{38}$$

$$p^3 y_4^3 = m - m_2 \tag{40}$$

$$\bar{l}_1 w_1 = m_1 \tag{66}$$

$$\bar{l}_1 = l_1 \tag{67}$$

$$x_1^4 = \bar{l}_1 (w_1 / p^4). \tag{68}$$

Similarly, if $\alpha \leq \bar{l}_2$, player 2's supergood set is characterized by:

$$w_1 l_1 = m_1 \tag{36}$$

$$p^4 x_3^4 = m - m_1 \tag{44}$$

$$\bar{w}_2 \alpha = m_2 \tag{50}$$

$$l_2 = \alpha \tag{51}$$

$$y_2^3 = (\bar{w}_2 \alpha) / p^3 \tag{52}$$

and if $\alpha > \bar{l}_2$, it is characterized by:

$$w_1 l_1 = m_1 \tag{36}$$

$$p^4 x_3^4 = m - m_1 \tag{44}$$

$$\bar{l}_2 w_2 = m_2 \tag{69}$$

$$\bar{l}_2 = l_2 \tag{70}$$

$$y_2^3 = \bar{l}_2 (\bar{w}_2 / p^3). \tag{71}$$

It is easy to verify that these supergood sets require for a nonempty intersection the usual equalities of selling and buying price, i.e., (53), (54), (55), and the analog of (55) for player 4.

In looking for agreement, we realize that there are four different subfamilies of the family of commitment patterns given by (34^1). In each of these families there are different requirements for equilibrium.

Subfamily 1. If $\alpha \leq \bar{l}_1$ and $\alpha \leq \bar{l}_2$ then the results are exactly the same as they were for the pure price commitment pattern (34).

Subfamily 2. If $\alpha > \bar{l}_1$, $\alpha \leq \bar{l}_2$, the quantity constraint is binding in the "market" for player 1's labor. For agreement between players 1 and 3 on l_1, (67) and (56) require: $\bar{l}_1 = 1 - (w_1 / p^3)$ or

$$w_1 / p^3 = 1 - \bar{l}_1. \tag{72}$$

Since $\bar{l}_1 < \alpha$, (w_1 / p^3), player 1's wage in terms of output, is greater than β, its value under (34).

The market for player 2's labor in this case is unaffected by any quantity constraint, and so acts in the same way it did under (34)

$$l_2 = \alpha$$

$$w_2 / p^4 = \beta. \tag{73}$$

Finally agreement between players 3 and 4 on m means:

$$p^4 \alpha(1 - \tfrac{1}{2}\alpha) = p^3 \bar{l}_1 (1 - \tfrac{1}{2}\bar{l}_1)$$

or

$$\frac{p^4}{p^3} = \frac{\bar{l}_1 (1 - \tfrac{1}{2}\bar{l}_1)}{\alpha(1 - \tfrac{1}{2}\alpha)} < 1. \tag{74}$$

From (74) we can substitute into (72) and (73) to find the prices and wages that are necessary for an equilibrium given any p^3:

$$p^4 = \frac{\bar{l}_1 (1 - \tfrac{1}{2}\bar{l}_1)}{\alpha(1 - \tfrac{1}{2}\alpha)} p^3 < p^3 \tag{75}$$

$$w_2 = \beta p^3 \frac{l_1 (1 - \tfrac{1}{2}l_1)}{\alpha(1 - \tfrac{1}{2}\alpha)} < \beta p^3 \tag{76}$$

$$w_1 = (1 - \bar{l}_1) p^3 > \beta p^3. \tag{77}$$

The situations that are supergood for all players when the commitment pattern satisfies these conditions may easily be verified to be NEs, and hence we have an equilibrium.

Let us spend some time comparing this unemployment equilibrium with the full employment equilibrium of (34) or subfamily 1. Notice first that we no longer have $p^3 = p^4$ and $w_1 = w_2$, despite the fact that technology and demand in both sectors remain identical. An immediate consequence is that we lose the equality between the "production real wage," w_1/p^3 or w_2/p^4 and the "consumption real wage," w_1/p^4 or w_2/p^3. Thus if we talk about "real wages" we must specify whether we are talking about wages relative to the price of the good being produced or wages relative to the price of the good being consumed. This distinction between wage in terms of product and wage in terms of consumption, it should be noted, is crucial to Keynes's definition of involuntary unemployment in the second chapter of the *General Theory* (1936). Readers familiar with that chapter will also note that what Keynes called the first and second postulates of the classical theory survive this model in precisely the manner he predicted. The first postulate—the equality of wage and marginal product—is always valid, while the second postulate—the equality of wage and marginal disutility of labor—holds only with full employment.

These distinctions are quite helpful in assessing whether players are better off in this subfamily or in the full employment equilibrium. Since player 2's hours of labor are the same in either case, player 2 is better off or worse off according as his real wage in terms of consumption, w_2/p^3 is greater or lesser. Now

$$\frac{w_2}{p^3} = \frac{w_2}{p^4} \cdot \frac{p^4}{p^3}.$$

So that player 2 is worse off in the unemployment equilibrium, since his real wage in terms of product, w_2/p^4, is the same in both subfamilies, while from (74)

$$p^4/p^3 < 1$$

when there is unemployment, but by (62), $p^4 = p^3$ when there is not.

For player 1 we must consider both the change in the real wage in terms of consumption and the change in the amount of labor. Player 1's real wage in terms of consumption increases with unemployment, since

$$\frac{w_1}{p^4} = \frac{w_1}{p^3} \cdot \frac{p^3}{p^4} = (1 - \bar{l}_1)\ \frac{p^3}{p^4}$$

and $1 - \bar{l}_1 > 1 - \alpha$ and $p^3/p^4 > 1$. (Cf. Keynes's discussion in the *General Theory*, chapter 2, section V.) On the other hand, consumption x_1^4 might be reduced because hours of work are less with unemployment. But the increase in the real wage in terms of consumption turns out to be more important.

$$x_1^4 = l_1\ \frac{w_1}{p^4} = \bar{l}_1(1 - \bar{l}_1)\ \frac{\alpha(1 - \tfrac{1}{2}\alpha)}{\bar{l}_1\,(1 - \tfrac{1}{2}\bar{l}_1)} = (1 - \bar{l}_1)\ \frac{\alpha(1 - \tfrac{1}{2}\alpha)}{(1 - \tfrac{1}{2}\bar{l}_1)}$$

$$= \alpha\beta\ \frac{1 - \bar{l}_1}{1 - \alpha} \cdot \frac{1 - \tfrac{1}{2}\alpha}{1 - \tfrac{1}{2}\bar{l}_1} > \alpha\beta$$

where $\alpha\beta$ is the value of x_1^4 under full employment. The second effect of reduced work is increased leisure, which increases player 1's utility. Since both arguments of his utility function, consumption and leisure, are greater with unemployment than with full employment, player 1 is better off in the unemployment equilibrium. It follows almost immediately that player 3 is worse off in the unemployment equilibrium. This is because player 3's utility is proportional to x_3^4, the difference between total output of x and x_1^4. The output of x is not affected by unemployment in this case, while we have just seen that x_1^4 increases. Thus x_3^4 decreases.

How can we say that the unemployment case is an equilibrium when the player who "causes" it, player 3, becomes worse off? Because he cannot find any actions or commitments that will make him better off, given the actions and commitments of the other players. Does not the existence of a commitment pattern like (34) that appears to differ from (34[1]) only for player 3 belie this claim? No, since (34) or (34[1], subfamily 1) only *appear* to be the same as (34[1], subfamily 2) for the other players. In fact, for the versions of these commitment patterns for which equilibria exist, the parameters differ in the different cases, so that the other players are making different commitments, even if those commitments have the same form. If players 1, 2, 3 are making commitments with p^4, w_1, and w_2 given by (75), (76), and (77), then player 3 can do no better than to ration employment. It is by no means contradictory, surprising or even interesting that if they were making other commitments—e.g., those given by (62) and (63), and (34)—player 3 could be better off. (Similarly our conclusion that player 1 is better off at the unemployment equilibrium than at the full employment equilibrium does not imply that unemployment is good for workers. Player 1 would be even better off if the other players' commitments satisfied (75), (76), and (77) and there were no quantity constraint, but this would not be an equilibrium.)

Finally, we can also show that player 4 is worse off in the unemployment equilibrium. In the full employment equilibrium we had:

$$y_4^3 = (1/p^3)(m - w_2 l_2) = \alpha(1 - \tfrac{1}{2}\alpha) - \alpha\beta$$

with unemployment we now have:

$$y_4^3 = \frac{1}{p^3}(m - w_2 l_2) = \frac{m}{p^4} \cdot \frac{p^4}{p^3} - \frac{w_2}{p^4} l_2 \cdot \frac{p^4}{p^3}$$

$$= \frac{p^4}{p^3}\left(\frac{m}{p^4} - \alpha\beta\right) = \frac{p^4}{p^3}(\alpha(1 - \tfrac{1}{2}\alpha) - \alpha\beta) < \alpha(1 - \tfrac{1}{2}\alpha) - \alpha\beta$$

so player 4 is worse off.

Subfamily 3. If $\alpha > \bar{l}_1$, $\alpha < \bar{l}_2$, we have a problem that is exactly symmetrical with that of case 2. Player 2 will be better off than in the full employment equilibrium, and players 1, 3, and 4 will be worse off.

Subfamily 4. If $\alpha > \bar{l}_1$, $\alpha > \bar{l}_2$, we have unemployment in both sectors. By our usual method, necessary conditions for an equilibrium to exist in this case are:

$$p^4 = \frac{\bar{l}_1(1 - \tfrac{1}{2}\bar{l}_1)}{\bar{l}_2(1 - \tfrac{1}{2}\bar{l}_2)} p^3$$

$$w_2 = (1 - \bar{l}_2)\frac{\bar{l}_1(1 - \tfrac{1}{2}\bar{l}_1)}{\bar{l}_2(1 - \tfrac{1}{2}\bar{l}_2)} p^3$$

$$w_1 = (1 - \bar{l}_1)\, p^3$$

and if these conditions are fulfilled it is easy to verify that with the corresponding NE there is an equilibrium.

This equilibrium is a combination of the equilibria of subfamilies 2 and 3. Players 3 and 4 are worse off in both subfamilies 2 and 3 than they were in subfamily 1; they are also worse off in subfamily 4 than they were in subfamily 1. For players 1 and 2 the comparison is not so easy.

We will deal with player 1; symmetry will extend the results to player 2. If $\bar{l}_2$ is quite close to α and $\bar{l}_1$ is quite far from α, then we will be quite close to subfamily 2 and player 1 will be better off than in the full employment equilibrium. Similarly if $\bar{l}_2$ is quite far from α and $\bar{l}_1$ is quite close to it, player 1 will be worse off.

But what if we are somewhere in the middle between subfamilies 2 and 3? To make matters simple let us consider what happens at the exact middle:

$$\bar{l}_1 = \bar{l}_2 \triangleq \bar{l} < \alpha. \tag{78}$$

When there is no unemployment, player 1's utility is

$$\ln u_1 = \alpha \ln \alpha\beta + \beta \ln \beta = \alpha \ln \alpha + \ln \beta.$$

When (78) obtains we have:

$$\begin{aligned}\ln u_1 &= \alpha \ln \left[\frac{\dfrac{(1-\bar{l})p^3\bar{l}}{\bar{l}(1-\frac{1}{2}\bar{l})}}{\bar{l}(1-\frac{1}{2}\bar{l})} p^3 \right] + \beta \ln(1-\bar{l}) \\ &= \alpha \ln (1-\bar{l})\bar{l} + \beta \ln (1-\bar{l}) \\ &= \alpha \ln \bar{l} + \ln (1-\bar{l}).\end{aligned}$$

We will call this last expression $h(\bar{l})$:

$$h(\bar{l}) \triangleq \alpha \ln \bar{l} + \ln(1-\bar{l}).$$

The question can then be phrased as: for what (if any) $\bar{l} < \alpha$ is $h(\bar{l}) > h(\alpha)$?

Obviously such a question calls for an examination of the shape of $h(\cdot)$. This function is twice continuously differentiable on [0, 1] with

$$h'(\bar{l}) = \frac{\alpha}{\bar{l}} - \frac{1}{1-\bar{l}}$$

$$h''(\bar{l}) = -\frac{\alpha}{\bar{l}^2} + \frac{1}{(1-\bar{l})^2}.$$

The only stationary point occurs at $\bar{l} = \alpha/(1+\alpha)$ since $h'[\alpha/(1+\alpha)] = 0$. This is a maximum because

$$h''[\alpha/(1+\alpha)] = (1+\alpha)^2 [(1-(1/\alpha)] < 0.$$

Since $\alpha/(1+\alpha) < \alpha$, $h(\cdot)$ is decreasing in the interval $(\alpha/(1+\alpha), \alpha)$. Thus if $\alpha/(1+\alpha) < \bar{l} < \alpha$, $h(\bar{l}) > h(\alpha)$, and player 1 is better off under (78) than under the full employment equilibrium. If $\bar{l} < \alpha/(1+\alpha)$, the matter is not clear-cut. If $\bar{l}$ is in the upper part of this range, $h(\bar{l}) > h(\alpha)$, but if $\bar{l}$ is close to zero, the opposite is true. There is no explicit expression for the dividing line. Player 1, then, will be better off under (78) than under the full employment equilibrium unless unemployment is rather substantial.

Thus we see that in three of the four possible kinds of equilibrium with (34^1) there is involuntary unemployment. The key question is then what determines which type of equilibrium will prevail. The answer is simple: nothing. An unemployment equilibrium is every bit as much an equilibrium as a full employment equilibrium; no equilibrium is any better than any other; every equilibrium is consistent with the technology and the utility functions.

The commitment pattern (34^1) has essentially six parameters: w_1, w_2, p^3, p^4, $\bar{l}_1$, and $\bar{l}_2$. Necessary conditions for an equilibrium (e.g., (75), (76), (77) or (62), (63)) are three equalities. Hence a commitment pattern for which there is an equilibrium has three undetermined, "free" parameters. Based on our motivational discussion of how employers operate, and convenience, we have taken the free parameters to be p^3, $\bar{l}_1$, and $\bar{l}_2$. Often economists take w_1, w_2, and p^3 to be free and proceed to talk about "sticky wages." It does not matter: free parameters are free, and equilibrium is equilibrium. Some triplets of free parameters are associated with full employment equilibria, and some are associated with unemployment equilibria, but every (positive) triplet of free parameters is associated with some equilibrium, and hence no triplet is any better or any more special than any other. Unemployment equilibria are neither fictions nor anomalies.

These findings, of course, are in many ways derivative from the "macroeconomic disequilibrium" tradition of Clower (1965), Leijonhufvud (1968), Drèze (1975), Benassy (1975), and Malinvaud (1977), inter alia (surveyed in Drazen [1980]). This tradition, however, has been criticized for not giving a convincing explanation for its fundamental assumption: that agents will at times pass up transactions that yield Pareto improvements. Game theory provides a very quick and satisfying explanation: just as we saw in prisoners' dilemma, there exist commitment patterns with which there are equilibria only in unattractive situations.

IV

Unemployment equilibria cannot exist unless labor market commitments include quantity constraints, but when they do we can use quantity constraints in the output market as well to illustrate the role of "aggregate demand."

To be definite, consider a commitment pattern (34^{II}) that differs from (34^{I}) in that $\bar{l}_1 > \alpha$ so that player 1 is fully employed at equilibrium, and in that (34^{I}a) and (34^{I}d) are replaced by

$$\begin{aligned} g_1(\cdot) = f_1(\cdot) \quad & \text{if} \quad w_1 l_1 < m_1 \\ & \text{or if} \quad \bar{p}_1^4 x_1^4 < m_1 \\ & \text{or if} \quad \bar{p}_1^4 \bar{x}_1^4 < m_1 \end{aligned} \tag{34^{II}a}$$

and

$$\begin{aligned} g_3(\cdot) = f_3(\cdot) \quad & \text{if} \quad \bar{p}_3^4 x_3^4 < m - m_1 \\ & \text{or if} \quad \bar{p}_3^4 \bar{x}_3^4 < m - m_1 \end{aligned} \tag{34^{II}d}$$

respectively. Also, let player 4 charge different prices to players 1 and 3. In the new commitment pattern, player 1 refuses to pay for more than $\bar{x}_1^4$ of good x, and player 3 refuses to pay for more than $\bar{x}_3^4$ of it. We can imagine that players 1 and 3 believe that their incomes will not permit them to purchase more than these amounts, and do not want to go into debt, or cannot do so.

If we assume that

$$\bar{x}_1^4 + \bar{x}_3^4 < \alpha - \tfrac{1}{2}\alpha^2$$

then an equilibrium will exist with (34^{II}) iff:

$$\bar{x}_1^4 + \bar{x}_3^4 = \bar{l}_2 - \tfrac{1}{2}\bar{l}_2^2$$

$$p_1^4 = (\alpha\beta p^3)/(\bar{x}_1^4)$$

$$\beta = w_1/p^3$$

$$w_2 < p_1^4 (1 - \bar{x}_1^4 - \bar{x}_3^4)^{1/2}$$

$$w_2 < p_3^4 (1 - \bar{x}_1^4 - \bar{x}_3^4)^{1/2}$$

for some positive p^3.

How accurate, then, will be the fears of players 1 and 3 that they will not be able to afford more than $\bar{x}_1^4$ and $\bar{x}_3^4$ respectively? Completely accurate, no matter what the level of aggregate demand ($\bar{x}_1^4 + \bar{x}_3^4$). For, substituting from the equilibrium values, we find that player 1's income, $w_1\ l_1$, will always equal $p_1^4\,\bar{x}_1^4$, and player 3's income, $m - m_1$, will always equal $p_3^4\,\bar{x}_3^4$.

This is the sort of equilibrium that Malinvaud (1977) deals with at length, and what lies behind the IS analysis and Keynesian cross of standard macroeconomics. Notice in particular that reducing w_2 has no effect on employment: "sticky wages" cannot be singled out as "the cause" of unemployment.

8 ▪ Multitudes

A people is but the attempt of many
To rise to the completer life of one;
And those who live as models for the mass
Are singly of more value than they all.
ROBERT BROWNING, *Luria*, act 5.

The best known result of game theoretic investigations of economics has been that the core converges to the Walrasian equilibrium allocation as the number of agents in the economy becomes very large. Edgeworth (1881) first argued that this was the case, and his work was brought to the attention of a modern audience and translated into modern terminology by Shubik (1959). Edgeworth dealt with an exchange economy with two goods and two types of agents which grew large by replication. Debreu (1962) generalized this result to the case of a finite number of commodities and types, while Debreu and Scarf (1963) simplified Debreu's proof and added the possibility of production. A different approach was taken by Nishino (1970), Hildenbrand (1970) and Arrow and Hahn (1971, ch. 8), who consider a sequence of economies with successively greater numbers of participants. Aumann (1964), on the other hand, showed the equivalence of the core and the Walrasian equilibrium in economies where agents are plentiful enough to form a continuum; Hildenbrand (1974) and others elaborated on Aumann's finding. Finally, Aumann and Shapley (1974), showed that value is also equivalent to Walrasian equilibrium in economies with a continuum of agents.

The obvious question, then, is whether the non-Walrasian results we have found in the last two chapters will similarly disappear when we consider large economies. Large economy questions are also important in their own right, since most real economies have more agents than you can count on your fingers and toes. This chapter will look briefly at the large economy question, and find that the answer is no. The non-Walrasian results are robust. Commitment equilibrium is built on noncooperative (*bellum omnium contra omnes*) game theory in which it does not fundamentally matter to a player the number of the *omnes* against which he is warring. Unlike solution concepts based on effortless, all-encompassing, mysterious, and magical coalition formation, commitment equilibrium does not degenerate in the presence of large numbers.

This does not mean, of course, that large games do not provide new and interesting phenomena to be studied with commitment equilibrium, or that a properly detailed study of the relationship of Robinson Crusoe and Friday can tell us all that we need to know about how the world economy will evolve over the next fifty years or what the price of green neckties will be in Philadelphia in June 1997. Some of these new phenomena, especially in the labor market, are examined in the latter part of this chapter.

I

Let us quickly put to rest any suspicion that commitment equilibrium necessarily converges to Walrasianism with a very simple counterexample. Recall from chapter 6 the two-person, two-good economy—the one whose possibilities could be summarized so easily with an Edgeworth box. We showed there that the only commitment equilibrium with a price commitment pattern coincided with Walrasian equilibrium, but that any point at all in the Edgeworth box could be associated with a commitment equilibrium with a naked trade commitment pattern. (When endowment was not a corner of the Edgeworth box, this was revised to state that any point weakly Pareto-superior to the endowment point could be associated with a commitment equilibrium.)

Now let us see what happens when we expand this economy to a size of $2n$ agents, where we allow n to be arbitrarily large. Let n of these agents be type 1 agents, with an endowment of one unit of the first good and none of the second; we denote these type 1 agents by $i = 1, 2, \ldots, n$. The other n agents will be type 2 agents, with an endowment of zero units of the first good and one unit of the second; we will denote these type 2 agents by $j = 1, 2, \ldots, n$. As before, a type 1 agent's utility will be given by

$$\ln u_i = \alpha \ln(1 - \sum_j x_j^i) + \beta \ln \sum_j y_i^j$$

where x_j^i denotes the amount of the first good that type 1 agent i gives type 2 agent j and y_i^j the amount of the second good that type 2 agent j gives to type 1 agent i. Similarly a type 2 agent's utility is

$$\ln u_j = \alpha \ln \sum x_j^i + \beta \ln(1 - \sum_i y_i^j).$$

Thus a strategy for a type 1 player i is an n-vector (x_j^i), $j = 1, \ldots, n$ with

$$\sum_j x_j^i \leq 1;$$

and a strategy for player 2 is an n-vector (y_i^j), $i = 1, \ldots, n$ with

$$\sum_i y_i^j \leq 1.$$

This game is the n-fold replica of the game we studied in chapter 6.

Now consider the following naked trade commitment pattern:

$$\text{For all } i,\ g_i(\cdot) = f_i(\cdot) \quad \text{if } x_j^i < \bar{x}(i) \quad \text{and} \quad y_i^j \geq \bar{y}(i) \quad \text{for } j = i \qquad (1)$$
$$= 0 \quad \text{otherwise.}$$
$$\text{For all } j,\ g_j(\cdot) = f_j(\cdot) \quad \text{if } x_j^i \geq \bar{x}(i) \quad \text{and} \quad y_i^j < \bar{y}(i) \quad \text{for } i = j$$
$$= 0 \quad \text{otherwise.}$$

It is quite easy to verify that for any $2n$-vector $(\bar{x}(i), \bar{y}(i))$, all of whose elements are strictly between 0 and 1, g is a commitment equilibrium with the following situation:

Type 1 player i gives $\bar{x}(i)$ to the type 2 player j for whom $j = i$, and nothing to any other player. (2)

Type 2 player j gives $\bar{y}(i)$ to the type 1 player i for whom $i = j$, and nothing to any other player.

This holds for any n, and thus there is no tendency for convergence to the Walrasian equilibrium, either individually or in the aggregate.

Nor would modifying the game to allow an additional "arbitrage stage" for trading change this result. (1) would still be a commitment pattern in the modified game, with no commitments whatsoever being made about "arbitrage stage" moves. Then (2), with the additional proviso that no trade take place at the arbitrage stage, would be a commitment equilibrium with (1). There would still be no convergence.

II

Other phenomena far more interesting than convergence to Walrasian equilibrium occur with large economies. For instance, let us see what happens in the labor market of the L-economy when the number of workers increases.

Recall that in the L-economy of chapter 7 players 1 and 2 were workers, and players 3 and 4 employers. Player 1's labor was sold to player 3 to produce good x; player 2's to player 4 to produce good y. Player 1 consumed leisure and good y; player 2 consumed leisure and good x.

Now let there be n clones of player 1 called $(1,1), (1,2), \ldots, (1,i), \ldots, (1,n)$, and n clones of player 2 called $(2,1), (2,2), \ldots, (2,i), \ldots, (2,n)$. There are no clones of player 3 or player 4, but production functions have been changed to accommodate the possibility of additional labor (the production function of chapter 7 decreases when labor is greater than unity):

$$x_4^3 + \sum_i x_2^3(i) \leq \sum_i l_1(i) - \frac{1}{2n}\left(\sum_i l_1(i)\right)^2 \tag{3}$$

$$y_3^4 + \sum_i y_1^4(i) \leq \sum_i l_2(i) - \frac{1}{2n}\left(\sum_i l_2(i)\right)^2 \tag{4}$$

where $x_2^3(i)$ denotes the amount of good x that player 3 gives player $(2,i)$, $y_1^4(i)$ the amount of good y that player 4 gives player $(1,i)$, $l_1(i)$ the amount of labor that player $(1,i)$ supplies, and $l_2(i)$ the amount of labor that player $(2,i)$ supplies. Monetary constraints are, for player $(1,i)$,

$$m_4^1(i) \leq m_1^3(i), \qquad i = 1, \ldots, n \tag{5}$$

for player $(2,i)$

$$m_3^2(i) \leq m_2^4(i), \qquad i = 1, \ldots, n \tag{6}$$

for player 3:

$$m_4^3 + \sum_i m_1^3(i) \leq \sum_i m_3^2(i) + m_3^4 \tag{7}$$

and for player 4

$$m_3^4 + \sum_i m_2^4(i) \leq \sum_i m_4^1(i) + m_4^3 \tag{8}$$

where the notation should be self-explanatory. By the same argument we used in chapter 7 inequalities (5)–(8) imply that at any (feasible) situation:

$$\begin{aligned} m \triangleq m_4^3 + \sum_i m_1^3(i) &= \sum_i m_3^2(i) + m_3^4 = m_3^4 + \sum_i m_2^4(i) \\ &= \sum_i m_4^1(i) + m_4^3 \end{aligned}$$

$$m_1(i) \triangleq m_4^1(i) = m_1^3(i) \qquad i = 1, \ldots, n$$

$$m_2(i) \triangleq m_3^2(i) = m_2^4(i) \qquad i = 1, \ldots, n$$

$$m_4^3 = m - \sum_i m_1(i)$$

$$m_3^4 = m - \sum_i m_2(i).$$

First let us try a commitment pattern like the ones we used in chapter 7:

$$g_{1i}(\cdot) = f_{1i}(\cdot) \qquad \text{if} \quad w_1(i)\,l_1(i) < m_1(i) \tag{9a}$$

$$\text{or if} \quad \bar{p}^{\,4}_{1}(i)\,y^4_1(i) < m_1(i) \tag{9b}$$

$$= 0 \qquad \text{otherwise}$$

$$g_{2i}(\cdot) = f_{2i}(\cdot) \qquad \text{if} \quad w_2(i)\,l_2(i) < m_2(i) \tag{9c}$$

$$\text{or if} \quad \bar{p}^{\,3}_{2}(i)\,x^3_2(i) < m_2(i) \tag{9d}$$

$$= 0 \qquad \text{otherwise}$$

$$g_3(\cdot) = f_3(\cdot) \qquad \text{if} \quad \bar{w}_1(i)\,l_1(i) < m_1(i) \quad \text{and} \quad l_1(i) \le \bar{l}_1(i) \text{ for any } i \tag{9e}$$

$$\text{or if} \quad \bar{w}_1(i)\,\bar{l}_1(i) < m_1(i) \quad \text{and} \quad l_1(i) > \bar{l}_1(i) \text{ for any } i \tag{9f}$$

$$\text{or if} \quad p^3\,x^3_2(i) \neq m_2(i) \quad \text{for any } i \tag{9g}$$

$$\text{or if} \quad p^3\,x^3_4 \neq m - \sum_i m_2(i) \tag{9h}$$

$$\text{or if} \quad \bar{p}^{\,4}_{3}\,y^4_3 < m - \sum_i m_1(i) \tag{9i}$$

$$= 0 \qquad \text{otherwise}$$

$$g_4(\cdot) = f_4(\cdot) \qquad \text{if} \quad \bar{w}_2(i)\,l_2(i) < m_2(i) \quad \text{and} \quad l_2(i) \le \bar{l}_2(i) \text{ for any } i \tag{9j}$$

$$\text{or if} \quad \bar{w}_2(i)\,\bar{l}_2(i) < m_2(i) \quad \text{and} \quad l_2(i) > \bar{l}_2(i) \text{ for any } i \tag{9k}$$

$$\text{or if} \quad p^4\,y^4_1(i) \neq m_1(i) \quad \text{for any } i \tag{9l}$$

$$\text{or if} \quad p^4\,y^4_3 \neq m - \sum_i m_1(i) \tag{9m}$$

$$\text{or if} \quad \bar{p}^{\,3}_{4}\,x^3_4 < m - \sum_i m_2(i) \tag{9n}$$

$$= 0 \qquad \text{otherwise.}$$

Equilibrium in this economy is essentially no different from equilibrium in the chapter 7 L-economy. Let

$$N_1 \triangleq \{i \mid \bar{l}_1(i) < \beta\}$$

$$N_2 \triangleq \{i \mid \bar{l}_2(i) < \beta\}$$

$$n_1 \triangleq |N_1|$$

and

$$n_2 \triangleq |N_2|.$$

Then necessary conditions for there to be an equilibrium associated with a commitment pattern like (9) are:

$$w_1(i) = \bar{w}_1(i) \triangleq w_1 \qquad \{\forall i \mid \bar{l}_1(i) > 0\}$$

$$w_2(i) = \bar{w}_2(i) \triangleq w_2 \qquad \{\forall i \mid \bar{l}_2(i) > 0\}$$

$$\bar{p}_1^4(i) = p^4 \qquad \{\forall i \mid \bar{l}_1(i) > 0\}$$

$$\bar{p}_2^3(i) = p^3 \qquad \{\forall i \mid \bar{l}_2(i) > 0\}$$

$$p^4 = p^3 \left\{ \frac{(n - n_1)\beta + \sum_{N_1} \bar{l}_1(i) - \tfrac{1}{2}[(n - n_1)\beta + \sum_{N_1} \bar{l}_1(i)]^2}{(n - n_2)\beta + \sum_{N_2} \bar{l}_2(i) - \tfrac{1}{2}[(n - n_2)\beta + \sum_{N_2} \bar{l}_2(i)]^2} \right\}$$

$$w_1 = p^3 \{1 - (1/n)[(n - n_1)\beta + \sum_{N_1} \bar{l}_1(i)]\}$$

$$= p^3 \{\alpha + (1/n)[n_1\beta - \sum_{N_1} \bar{l}_1(i)]\}$$

$$w_2 = p^4 \{\alpha + (1/n)[n_2\beta - \sum_{N_2} \bar{l}_2(i)]\}$$

$$p^3 > 0.$$

In the situation associated with any such commitment pattern

$$l_1(i) = \beta \qquad \text{if} \quad i \notin N_1$$

$$l_1(i) = \bar{l}_1(i) \qquad \text{if} \quad i \in N_1$$

$$l_2(i) = \beta \qquad \text{if} \quad i \notin N_2$$

$$l_2(i) = \bar{l}_2(i) \qquad \text{if} \quad i \in N_2$$

and all acceptability constraints, as well as (3) and (4), are binding.

A couple of extreme cases best illustrate how little change there is from chapter 7. First suppose

$$N_1 = N_2 = \emptyset$$

i.e., full employment. Then

$$p^3 = p^4$$

$$w_1 = w_2 = \alpha p^3$$

$$p^3 > 0$$

$$l_1(i) = l_2(i) = \beta \qquad (\forall i)$$

just as in the full employment case. Indeed, it may be checked in (3) and (4) that output of each good is exactly n times as great as it was in the single worker economy, each worker consumes the same amount that his progenitor did in the single worker economy, and each capitalist's consumption is n times as great.

Now let $N_2 = \emptyset$, to simplify matters, and for all $i \in N_1$

$$\bar{l}_1(i) = 0$$

i.e., workers are either fully employed or fully (and involuntarily) unemployed; there is no involuntary part-time employment. If

$$u \triangleq n_1/n$$

is the unemployment rate, we have

$$p^4 = \left\{1 - u + \tfrac{1}{2}u \frac{1-u}{1-\tfrac{1}{2}\beta}\right\} p^3 < p^3$$

$$w_1 = (\alpha + u\beta)p^3$$

$$w_2 = \alpha p^3\left[1 - u + \tfrac{1}{2}u \frac{1-u}{1-\tfrac{1}{2}\beta}\right]$$

$$p^3 > 0$$

$$l_1(i) = \beta \qquad \text{if} \quad i \notin N_1$$

$$l_1(i) = 0 \qquad \text{if} \quad i \in N_1$$

$$l_2(i) = \beta \qquad (\forall i).$$

As in chapter 7, unemployment in the first labor market results in an equilibrium worse than the full employment one for player 2's clones, player 3, and player 4. Employed clones of player 1 are better off, but unemployed clones are worse off. At any rate, equilibria with involuntary unemployment are just as possible with many workers as with only one.

III

Note that $\bar{l}_1(i) = 0$ means that player 3 is making no commitment whatsoever to player $(1, i)$ in (9). As a result, player $(1, i)$ must end up unemployed in equilibrium. Cultural differences and communications problems can thus cause unemployment—if player 3 is unwilling or unable to make a commitment to $(1, i)$, or vice versa, $(1, i)$ will never go to work, no matter how low a wage he volunteers to accept.

IV

Expanding the work force also lets us consider organized labor. After all, labor unions are not spectacularly interesting organizations when there is only one worker.

Labor unions do not work in the context of pure price commitment patterns (since labor unions do exist this gives us another reason to suspect that not every commitment in the real world is purely price). Indeed, the standard explanation in economics for how unions work—workers get together and agree to withhold all their labor unless the employer agrees to increase all their wages—is faulty.

To understand why this scenario fails, consider how a union organization of this kind would affect a typical worker's commitment. For simplicity, we will consider only a union of player 1's clones, and assume that all these clones have joined a union and have formulated a wage demand $w_1(i)$, $i = 1, \ldots, n$ on which they have come to complete agreement. This means that the commitment (9a) must be modified to (9'a):

$$g_{1i}(\cdot) = f_{1i}(\cdot) \quad \text{if} \quad l_i > 0 \quad \text{and} \quad (\exists j)\, w_1(j) > \frac{m_1(j)}{l_1(j)} \qquad (9'\text{a})$$

$$\text{or if} \quad w_1(i) l_1(i) < m_1(i) \quad \text{and} \quad (\forall j)\, w_1(j) \leq \frac{m_1(j)}{l_1(j)}$$

and the rest of (9) remains the same. This change affects the constraints defining only one super-possible set, that of player 3, and what it does to those constraints does not affect the supergood set at all. With (9), the labor market constraints in player 3's supergoodness problem were:

$$(\forall i) \;\; w_1(i) l_1(i) = m_1(i). \qquad (10)$$

With (9') they become

$$(\forall i) \;\; w_1(i) l_1(i) = m_1(i) \quad \text{if} \quad (\forall j) \;\; w_1(j) l_1(j) \leq m_1(j) \qquad (11)$$
$$l_1(i) = 0 \qquad \text{otherwise.}$$

Clearly the only new addition to player 3's super-possible set that (11) makes are those situations where $l_1(i) = 0$, for all i, and $m_1(i) > 0$ for some i. Since these situations are by no means maximal for player 3 in his super-possible set, they are not supergood for him. Since no player's supergood set changes, there is no change in the equilibrium situation. Labor unions like this cannot help their members.

A proper understanding of unions requires that we consider commitment patterns with quantities as well as prices. The simplest such commitment pattern is naked trade. Let player 3's commitment then become:

$$g_3(\cdot) = f_3(\cdot) \quad \text{if} \quad m_1(i) \neq \bar{w}_1(i)\bar{l}_1(i) \quad \text{and} \quad l_1(i) \geq \bar{l}_1(i) > 0 \quad \text{for any } i \tag{9^{11}e}$$

$$\text{or if} \quad m_1(i) > 0 \quad \text{and} \quad l_1(i) < \bar{l}_1(i) \quad \text{for any } i \tag{9^{11}f}$$

and nothing else changes from (9). Player 3's commitment is thus a "take it or leave it," "all or nothing" offer to each worker. Workers must "take it" since the alternative is starvation:

$$l_1(i) = \bar{l}_1(i)$$

$$m_1(i) = \bar{w}_1(i)\bar{l}_1(i)$$

in the supergood set of each worker $(1, i)$. Equilibrium then requires:

$$\begin{aligned}
\bar{w}_1(i) &= w_1(i) = w_1 \\
\bar{w}_2(i) &= w_2(i) = w_2 \\
p^4 &= p^3 \left\{ \frac{\sum_i \bar{l}_i - \frac{1}{2n}\left(\sum_i \bar{l}_i\right)^2}{n\beta\left(1 - \tfrac{1}{2}\beta\right)} \right\} \\
w_2 &= \alpha p^4 \\
w_1 &= p^3 \left\{ 1 - \frac{\sum_i \bar{l}_1(i)}{n} \right\} \\
p^3 &> 0 \\
l_1(i) &= \bar{l}_1(i) \\
l_2(i) &= \beta
\end{aligned} \tag{11}$$

where we have assumed full employment in the other sector of the economy. Notice that increasing $(\Sigma_i \bar{l}_1(i))$ hurts player 1's clones twice: by increasing p^4, the price they must pay for their consumption good, and by decreasing their wage w_1. If $\bar{l}_1(i) \geq \beta$, moreover, increasing $l_1(i)$ hurts player i directly by depriving him of leisure that he wants. The historical importance to the labor movement of the demand for a shorter work week leads one to suspect that employers' commitments are in fact naked like those of (9^{11}); the emphasis placed on this demand is hardly explicable in a Walrasian system.

Workers will not be able to improve their lot merely by switching to naked trade commitments. Individually, of course, no worker can improve his lot by changing his commitment—this is the definition of a commitment equilibrium. Nor can a coordinated movement to naked trade commitments help. On the contrary. For let (9^{III}) be the same as (9^{II}) except that for every i we revise (9a) to:

$$g_{1i}(\cdot) = f_{1i}(\cdot) \quad \text{if} \quad m_1(i) \geq w_1(i)\hat{l}_1(i) \quad \text{and} \quad \hat{l}_1(i) > l_1(i). \qquad (9^{III}\text{a})$$

Then player 3's supergoodness problem can be written (with the usual substitutions:

$$\max_{(\epsilon)} \; p^3 \sum_i \hat{l}_1(i)\epsilon_i - \frac{p^3}{2n}\left(\sum_i \hat{l}_1(i)\epsilon_i\right)^2 - \sum_i w_1(i)\hat{l}_1(i)\epsilon_i \qquad (12)$$

s.t. $\quad \epsilon_i \in \{0, 1\} \quad$ for all i.

This is a quadratic combinatorial programming problem; player 3 either employs player $(1, i)$ for $\hat{l}_1(i)$ hours and pays him $w_1(i)\hat{l}_1(i)$—in which case $\epsilon_i = 1$—or does nothing at all with him—in which case $\epsilon_i = 0$.

Now whatever the solution to this problem there will be no agreement between player 3 and player $(1, i)$ unless $\epsilon_i = 1$, because $l_1(i) > 0$ in player $(1, i)$'s supergood set. Thus a necessary condition for equilibrium is that a solution to problem (12) be $\epsilon_i = 1$ for all i. This will be the case only if for every $j = 1, \ldots, n$ the maximand in (12) does not decrease when ϵ_j changes from 0 to 1, holding $\epsilon_i = 1$, for all $i \neq j$. That is, a necessary condition is

$$p^3 \sum_i \hat{l}_1(i) - \frac{p^3}{2n}\left(\sum_i \hat{l}_1(i)\right)^2 - \sum_i w_1(i)\hat{l}_1(i)$$

$$\geq p^3 \sum_{i \neq j} \hat{l}_1(i) - \frac{p^3}{2n}\left(\sum_{i \neq j} \hat{l}_1(i)\right)^2 - \sum_{i \neq j} w_1(i)\hat{l}_1(i)$$

or, after suitable manipulation,

$$w_1(j) + \frac{\hat{l}_1(j)}{2n} \leq p^3\left(1 - \frac{\sum_i \bar{l}_1(i)}{n}\right) \qquad (\forall j). \qquad (13)$$

Since

$$\hat{l}_1(j) = \bar{l}_1(j) \qquad (\forall j)$$

is also clearly a necessary condition for equilibrium, we can compare (11) and (13) and see that worker $(1, j)$'s wage rate cannot exceed what it was when workers made price commitments, and the length of work is the same. Although the minimum penalty in wages for using naked trade commitments

$$\frac{\hat{l}_1(j)}{2n}$$

vanishes when $n \to \infty$, there is still no gain. It would be foolish for unions to act as coordinators of naked trade commitments.

For unions to have some purpose, then, they must be able to make to the employer a single all-or-nothing naked trade offer, just as the employer makes a single all-or-nothing naked trade offer to each worker. If a union can do this, it creates essentially a bilateral naked trade commitment pattern, with which, as we have seen, any situation not Pareto-inferior to autarky is an equilibrium. The obvious candidate for the commitments needed to accomplish this end is (9*a), where it is assumed that all workers have agreed on the demand $(w_1(i), \hat{l}_1(i))$, $i = 1, \ldots, n$:

$$\begin{aligned} g_{1i}(\cdot) = f_{1i}(\cdot) \qquad & \text{if} \quad l_1(i) > 0 \quad \text{and} \quad (\exists j) l_1(j) > \hat{l}_1(j) \\ & \text{or} \quad m_1(j) < w_1(j)\hat{l}_1(j) \\ & \text{or if} \quad l_1(i) < \hat{l}_1(i) \quad \text{and} \quad m_1(i) \geq w_1(i)\hat{l}_1(i). \end{aligned} \tag{9*a}$$

Then the labor market conditions for acceptability to player (1,i) are

$$\begin{aligned} l_1(i) = \hat{l}_1(i) \quad & \text{if} \quad m_1(i) \geq w_1(i)\hat{l}_1(i) \quad \text{and} \quad (\forall j)\, l_1(j) \leq \hat{l}_1(j) \\ & \text{and} \quad m_1(j) \geq w_1(j)\hat{l}_1(j) \\ l_1(i) = 0 \quad & \text{otherwise} \end{aligned}$$

so that player 3's supergoodness problem becomes:

$$\max_{(l_1(i),\, m_1(i))} \quad p^3 \sum l_1(i) - (p^3/2n)\Big(\sum_i l_1(i)\Big)^2 - \sum_i m_1(i) \quad \text{s.t.} \tag{14}$$

$$\begin{aligned} (\forall i) \quad l_1(i) = \hat{l}_1(i) \quad & \text{if} \quad m_1(i) \geq w_1(i)\hat{l}_1(i) \\ & \text{and} \quad (\forall j) \quad l_1(j) \leq \hat{l}_1(j) \\ & \text{and} \quad m_1(j) \geq w_1(j)\hat{l}_1(j) \\ = 0 \quad & \text{otherwise,} \end{aligned}$$

the solution to which is (provided profits (14) are positive):

$$l_1(i) = \hat{l}_1(i)$$

$$m_1 = w_1(i)\, l_1(i)$$

for all i. (Note that the wage part of (9*a),

$$m_1(j) < w_1(j)\hat{l}_1(j)$$

is in fact redundant.) Then for equilibrium we have

$$l_1(i) = \hat{l}_1(i) = \bar{l}_1(i) \qquad (\forall i)$$

$$l_2(i) = \beta \qquad (\forall i)$$

$$w_1(i) = \bar{w}_1(i) \qquad (\forall i)$$

$$w_2(i) = \bar{w}_2(i) = w_2 \qquad (\forall i)$$

$$p^4 = p^3 \left\{ \frac{\sum_i \hat{l}_1(i) - \frac{1}{2n} (\sum_i \hat{l}_1(i))^2}{n\beta (1 - \frac{1}{2}\beta)} \right\}$$

$$w_2 = \alpha p^4$$

$$p^3 > 0.$$

Thus (9*) works as promised; given positive profits it turns the determination of wages and hours into a matter for bargaining between labor and management—a matter largely undetermined by so-called "market forces."

V

The commitments (9*a) work in part because they command the unanimous consent of all workers. What if they don't command unanimous consent? A way to look at this question is to study a case of discrimination.

For suppose that player $(1, n)$ is not very well liked by his clone colleagues. Accordingly they set very low values of $\hat{l}_1(n)$ and $w_1(n)$. Player $(1, n)$ disagrees. Thus while for $i = 1, \ldots, n - 1$ commitment (9*a) holds for $i = n$ we have

$$g_{1n}(\cdot) = f_{1n}(\cdot) \quad \text{if } l_1(n) < \tilde{l}_1(n) \quad \text{and } m_1(n) \geq \tilde{w}_1(n)\tilde{l}_1(n). \qquad (9^{**}a)$$

Then player 3's supergoodness problem essentially becomes a choice between two alternatives (assuming both produce positive profit). The first alternative is to go along with players $(1, 1) \ldots (1, n - 1)$. Then player 3's supergood set has

$$l_1(i) = \hat{l}_1(i) \qquad i = 1, \ldots, n \qquad (15)$$

and his maximand has value

$$p^3 \sum_i \hat{l}_1(i) - (1/2n) p^3 \left(\sum_i \hat{l}_1(i)\right)^2 - \sum_i w_1(i)\hat{l}_1(i). \qquad (16)$$

The other alternative is to go along with player n. Then player 3's super-good set has

$$l_1(i) = 0 \qquad i = 1, \ldots, n-1 \tag{17a}$$

$$l_1(n) = \tilde{l}_1(n) \tag{17b}$$

and his maximand has value

$$p^3 \tilde{l}_1(n) - (1/2n) p^3 (\tilde{l}_1(n))^2 - \tilde{w}_1(n) \tilde{l}_1(n). \tag{18}$$

If (16) is greater than (18), then player 3 chooses the first alternative. For agreement we need as with (9*a)

$$l_1(i) = \hat{l}_1(i) = \bar{l}_1(i) \quad (\forall i)$$

and in particular

$$l_1(n) = \hat{l}_1(n) = \bar{l}_1(n)$$

i.e., player 3 must agree with players $(1, 1), \ldots (1, n-1)$ that n should be discriminated against. But this situation can be part of an equilibrium only if it is an NE, and it is an NE only if it is acceptable to player $(1, n)$. A situation is acceptable to player $(1, n)$ only if $l_1(n)$ equals either $\tilde{l}_1(n)$ or 0. Since in this case $l_1(n) \neq \tilde{l}_1(n)$ *ex hypothesi*

$$l_1(n) = \hat{l}_1(n) = \bar{l}_1(n) = 0$$

is a necessary condition for this sort of equilibrium.

If (16) is less than (18), the same sort of argument will show that necessary conditions for equilibrium include:

$$l_1(i) = \bar{l}_1(i) = 0 \qquad i = 1, \ldots, n-1$$

$$l_1(n) = \tilde{l}_1(n).$$

If (16) equals (18) either equilibrium is possible, but not both or any convex combination.

We can draw two conclusions from this model by drawing on the two different motivations for this section:

1. For the study of discrimination, we see that discrimination by workers requires employer concurrence (not necessarily vice versa), and will result in the complete exclusion of one group or another. The latter conclusion would be better confirmed empirically if we had developed a more complex model with a number of different kinds of jobs within the one industry. Then we could have seen exclusion from particular types of jobs, even in the very long run, since we are describing an equilibrium.

Long run discriminatory results are extremely hard to come by, if not impossible, in Walrasian models.

2. For the study of labor organization, we see that to the extent to which union membership is equivalent to concurrence in bargaining demands, some sort of union shop or closed shop arrangement is a necessary condition for equilibrium in an organized labor market, quite apart from arguments about public goods.

9 ■ Booms and Busts

Fortuna vitrea est; tum cum splendet, frangitur.

PUBILIUS SYRUS

Production and consumption are not the only activities that go on in a modern economy; saving and investment, technological change, birth, death, and speculation happen as well. Reasonable macroeconomic models ought, and are expected, to include room for all (at least) of these phenomena.

This chapter will develop one such model. Models are useful only to the extent that they are incomplete, since simplicity is achieved only by chopping away realism, and so the many unrealistic simplifying assumptions that have gone into this model call for no abject apology. On the other hand, there is no reason to suspect that the model cannot be improved upon.

The world we will consider has embodied clay-clay technological change, no depreciation, uncertainty, and lasts forever. As in standard macroeconomic models, there are two inputs (labor and capital), one output, and two types of nongovernment agent: the household, which sells labor and buys bonds and output, and the firm, which buys labor and sells bonds and output. (Our firm also buys and sells capital.) The distinction, however, among "long-run," "medium-run," and "short-run," is absent from (and alien to) our model, as is, of course, the idea of expectations. Everything is built up from the tradition of rationality.

I

Keynes emphasized the importance of uncertainty in economic affairs, and a model in which the future held no mystery might miss many significant macroeconomic phenomena. The economic games that we have discussed so far, however, all had equilibria in pure strategies: there was never any doubt about what anyone would do in equilibrium. For a game to have an equilibrium in mixed strategies, it is necessary that at least one player finds it optimal to choose a mixed rather than a pure strategy. With the convex payoff functions that generally characterize economic games and the type of perturbation that everything resembling a price or a price-and-quantity commitment pattern makes in those payoff functions, mixed strategy equilibria are impossible (even with "price-like" commitments in mixed strategy space).

There are two ways that mixed strategy equilibria can appear. One way is to introduce nonconvex technology and payoff functions (that is why simple finite games often have mixed strategy equilibria); the other way is to introduce a player—Mother Nature, as we discussed in chapter 5—who is indifferent among all situations but makes a commitment to engage in a particular mixed strategy. This latter course is the one we will follow. Mother Nature's job will be to determine the rate of technological change. The other players will turn out to choose pure strategies in equilibrium, but local strategies in these pure strategies will be contingent on what Mother Nature does; thus Mother Nature's participation will make the whole system stochastic.

II

Besides Mother Nature, the players in the game we will be studying are a Federal Reserve Bank, a sequence of households, and a sequence of firms. Like Mother Nature, the Federal Reserve Bank in this chapter will be indifferent among all situations, and will have made an essentially arbitrary commitment. The other players can thus treat it like a vending machine whose owners have departed to Mars. In the next chapter we will discuss macroeconomic policy more interestingly.

A new household Ht and a new firm Ft are born at the start of period t; both live for two periods.

Firm t begins life by choosing a quantity $\hat{b}(t)$ of bonds to give to the old household $H(t-1)$; the household gives the firm a quantity of money $m(H(t-1), F(t), b)$. We will see later just what these bonds are; think of them now as just pieces of paper. The new firm then chooses a quantity of money $m(F(t), F(t-1))$ to give to the old firm; the old firm then gives the new firm a collection of machines $(K(t, v))$. $K(t, v)$ stands for the quantity of machines that were made at time $v \leq t-1$ ("vintage v") that firm $(t-1)$ gives to firm t.

Firm t also gives money $m(Ft, Ht, t)$ to household t and receives a vector of labor $(l(t, v))$ from that household. $l(t, v)$ denotes the amount of labor applied to vintage v machines.

Firm t uses these machines and labor to produce all-purpose output $Y(t)$. The production function is

$$Y(t) = \sum_{v=1}^{t-1} \alpha(v) \min[K(t,v),\ l(t,v)] \tag{1}$$

where $\alpha(v)$ is a technological parameter that is generally growing as v increases, but we need not insist on strict monotonicity (sometimes technology screws up). Note that (1) does *not* require that technical progress be Hicks-neutral; it requires only that a unit of vintage v capital be defined as that amount that requires one unit of labor to work with it. The Leontief production function is, however, a substantive restriction.

Next, firm t chooses amounts $y_H(t)$ and $y_F(t)$ of output to give to household $(t-1)$ and firm $(t-1)$, respectively. This is for consumption. These players give firm t money amounts $m(H(t-1), Ft, y)$ and $m(F(t-1), Ft)$ respectively.

The final event in period t is Mother Nature's move: she picks a technological parameter $\alpha(t)$ to determine how much output a unit of vintage t capital—that is, a unit of period t output used for manufacturing purposes—will be able to produce in the future (given adequate labor). We let the set A with typical element a denote the possible values that Mother Nature can assign to $\alpha(t)$. We assume that ϕ_a is the probability that Mother Nature has committed herself to for assigning value a to $\alpha(t)$. The set A and the probability assignment ϕ vary with time—otherwise we would not have technical progress in general—but we will suppress the "t" subscript to save notation.

In period $(t+1)$, firm t gives firm $(t+1)$ a vector $(K(a, t+1, v))$ of machines and receives a quantity of money $m(a, F(t+1), Ft)$. The argument a indicates that both players' actions may be contingent on Mother Nature's action in period t (just as all actions in period t were in fact contingent on Mother Nature's actions in all previous periods—but notation is something that should be economized). Firm t can give its successor every vintage of machine its predecessor gave it, and can also give machines of vintage t, Mother Nature having determined their productivity.

Then firm t pays money $m(a, Ft, Ht, t+1)$ and $m(a, Ft, FRB)$ to household t and the Federal Reserve Bank respectively (we will recognize these payments later as debt service), and money amount $m(a, Ft, F(t+1))$ to firm $(t+1)$. Firm $(t+1)$ gives firm t an amount $y_F(a, t+1)$ of period $(t+1)$ output. This completes firm t's life.

Its payoff function is the expected value of its consumption,

$$\sum_a \phi_a\, y_F(a, t+1)$$

and its choice of variables is subject to constraints forbidding paying more money than is received

$$m(Ft, F(t-1)) + m(Ft, Ht, t) \leq m(H(t-1), Ft, b)$$

$$\begin{aligned} &m(Ft, F(t-1)) + m(Ft, Ht, t) + m(a, Ft, Ht, t+1) \\ &\quad + m(a, Ft, FRB) + m(a, Ft, F(t+1)) \leq m(H(t-1), Ft, b) \\ &\quad + m(H(t-1), Ft, y) + m(H(t-1), Ft) \qquad \text{for all } a \in A, \end{aligned}$$

constraints forbidding giving away more output than is produced;

$$y_H(t) + y_F(t) + K(a, t+1, t) \leq Y(t)$$

and constraints forbidding giving away more used machines than were received:

$$K(a, t+1, v) \leq K(t, v) \qquad \text{for all} \quad a \in A \qquad \text{and} \qquad v \leq t-1.$$

The account of firm t's life has already revealed much about household t's life. We have already seen that in period t household t chooses labor vector $l(t, v)$ and receives money amount $m(Ft, Ht)$. Household t then chooses a money payment $m(Ht, H(t-1))$ to make to household $(t-1)$ and receives an amount of bonds $b(t)$ from that household.

In period $(t+1)$, after Mother Nature has picked a, household t receives a money amount $m(a, FRB, Ht)$ from the Federal Reserve, and gives the Federal Reserve a money amount $m(a, Ht, FRB)$. The Federal Reserve gives household t $b^*(a, t)$ bonds, where we allow $b^*(a, t)$ to be negative to reflect a payment from the household to the bank. In fact, it is only the net of these transactions that will concern us.

Also in period $(t+1)$, household t gives firm $(t+1)$ money amount $m(a, Ht, Ft+1, b)$ and receives $\hat{b}(a, t+1)$ bonds. Household t receives the money amount $m(a, Ft, Ht, t+1)$ from firm t as debt service. Then household t gives household $(t+1)$ $b(a, t+1)$ bonds and receives $m(a, H(t+1), Ht)$ money. Finally, household t gives firm $(t+1)$ the money amount $m(a, Ht, F(t+1), y)$, receives $y_H(a, t+1)$ output, and expires.

Household t's payoff function is the expected value of its consumption

$$\sum_a \phi_a y_H(a, t+1)$$

and its constraints forbid it from giving away more money than it has:

$$\begin{aligned} &m(Ht, H(t-1)) + m(a, Ht, FRB) - m(a, FRB, Ht) \\ &\quad + m(a, Ht, F(t+1), b) \leq m(Ft, Ht) \qquad \text{for all } a \in A \end{aligned}$$

$$\begin{aligned} &m(Ht, H(t-1)) + m(a, Ht, FRB) - m(a, FRB, Ht) \\ &\quad + m(a, Ht, F(t+1), b) + m(a, Ht, F(t+1), y) \leq m(Ft, Ht) \\ &\quad + m(a, H(t+1), Ht) + m(a, Ft, Ht, t+1) \qquad \text{for all } a \in A, \end{aligned}$$

$H(t-1)$	$H(t)$	$F(t-1)$	$F(t)$	FRB	MN
$m \to FRB$				$b^* \to H(t-1)$	
$b^* \to FRB$				$m \to H(t-1)$	
$m \to Ft$			$\hat{b} \to H(t-1)$		
		$K \to F(t)$	$m \to F(t-1)$		
	$l \to F(t)$		$m \to H(t)$		
		$m \to H(t-1)$, FRB			
$b \to H(t-1)$	$m \to H(t-1)$				
$m \to F(t)$		$m \to F(t)$	$y \to H(t-1)$, $F(t-1)$		
					a

Figure 5

from supplying more than one unit of labor

$$\sum_v l(t, v) \leq 1$$

and from giving away more bonds than it has received

$$b(t) + b^*(a, t) + \hat{b}(a, t+1) \geq b(a, t+1) \qquad \text{for all} \quad a \in A.$$

The assumptions of risk neutrality and no consumption until old age are quite restrictive, but make the computations tractable.

Figure 5 provides a useful summary of what goes on in a typical period t.

III

We will consider commitment patterns of what Malinvaud (1977) calls the "Keynesian unemployment" family. In these commitment patterns households are quantity-constrained in the amount of labor they can supply and firms are quantity-constrained in the amount of output they can sell; otherwise commitments are of the pure price variety. Malinvaud's other "regimes" (classical unemployment, repressed inflation, and Walrasian full employment) can also be studied in this game, but Keynesian unemployment has historically received the greatest attention, and, we will see, has considerable explanatory power.

We define

$$D(t-1) = D(t-2) + \hat{b}(t-1)$$

the debt that has been accumulated at the beginning of period t.

The commitment patterns we will be interested in have the following form

$$g_{Ht}(\cdot) = f_{Ht}(\cdot) \quad \text{if} \quad w(t)\, \Sigma_{v=1}^{t-1} l(t,v) \neq m(Ft, Ht) \tag{2-1}$$

$$\text{or if} \quad u(t)b(t) < m(Ht, H(t-1)) \tag{2-2}$$

$$\text{or if} \quad u(t)b^*(a,t) < m(a, Ht, FRB) - m(a, FRB, Ht) \quad \text{for any } a \tag{2-3}$$

$$\text{or if} \quad \hat{u}(a,t+1)\hat{b}(a,t+1) < m(a, Ht, F(t+1), b) \quad \text{for any } a \tag{2-4}$$

$$\text{or if} \quad u(a,t+1)b(a,t+1) \neq m(a, H(t+1), Ht) \quad \text{for any } a \tag{2-5}$$

$$\text{or if} \quad p(a,t+1)y_H(a,t+1) < m(a, Ht, F(t+1), y) \quad \text{and} \quad y_H(a,t+1) \leq \bar{y}_H(a,t+1) \quad \text{for any } a \tag{2-6}$$

$$\text{or if} \quad p(a,t+1)\bar{y}_H(a,t+1) < m(a, Ht, F(t+1), y) \quad \text{and} \quad y_H(a,t+1) > \bar{y}_H(a,t+1) \quad \text{for any } a \tag{2-7}$$

$$\text{or if} \quad m(a, Ft, Ht, t+1) < b(t) + b^*(a,t) \quad \text{for any } a \tag{2-8}$$

$$= 0 \quad \text{otherwise}$$

$$g_{Ft}(\cdot) = f_{Ft}(\cdot) \quad \text{if} \quad \hat{u}(t)\hat{b}(t) \neq m(H(t-1), Ft, b) \tag{2-9}$$

$$\text{or if} \quad \Sigma_{v=1}^{t-1} q(t,v)K(t,v) - \hat{u}(t)D(t-1) < m(Ft, F(t-1)) \quad \text{and} \quad K(t,t-1) \leq \bar{K}(t-1) \tag{2-10}$$

$$\text{or if} \quad \Sigma_{v=1}^{t-2} q(t,v)K(t,v) + q(t,t-1)\bar{K}(t-1) - \hat{u}(t)\mathrm{D}(t-1) < m(Ft, F(t-1)) \quad \text{and} \quad K(t,t-1) > \bar{K}(t-1) \tag{2-11}$$

$$\text{or if} \quad \Sigma_{v=1}^{t-1} l(t,v)w(t) \neq m(Ft, Ht) \quad \text{and} \quad \Sigma_{v=1}^{t-1} l(t,v) \leq \bar{l}(t) \tag{2-12}$$

$$\text{or if} \quad \bar{l}(t)w(t) \neq m(Ft, Ht) \quad \text{and} \quad \Sigma_{v=1}^{t-1} l(t,v) > \bar{l}(t) \tag{2-13}$$

$$\text{or if} \quad p(t)y_H(t) \neq m(H(t-1), Ft, y) \tag{2-14}$$

$$\text{or if} \quad p(t)y_F(t) \neq m(F(t-1), Ft) \tag{2-15}$$

$$\text{or if} \quad \Sigma_{v=1}^{t} q(a,t+1,v)K(a,t+1,v) - \hat{u}(a,t+1)D(t) \neq m(a, F(t+1), Ft) \quad \text{for any } a, \text{ where } q(a,t+1,t) = p(t) \quad \text{for all } a \tag{2-16}$$

$$\text{or if} \quad m(a, Ft, Ht, t+1) \neq b(t) + b^*(a,t) \quad \text{for any } a \tag{2-17}$$

$$\text{or if} \quad m(a,Ft,FRB) \neq D(t-1)+\hat{b}(t)-b(t)-b^*(a,t) \quad \text{for any } a \tag{2-18}$$

$$\text{or if} \quad p(a,t+1)y_F(a,t+1) < m(a,Ft,F(t+1)) \quad \text{and} \quad y_F(a,t+1) \leq \bar{y}(a,t+1) - \bar{y}_H(a,t+1) \quad \text{for any } a \tag{2-19}$$

$$\text{or if} \quad p(a,t+1)[\bar{y}(a,t+1) - \bar{y}_H(a,t+1)] < m(a,Ft,F(t+1)) \quad \text{and} \quad y_F(a,t+1) > \bar{y}(a,t+1) - \bar{y}_H(a,t+1) \quad \text{for any } a \tag{2-20}$$

$$= 0 \qquad \text{otherwise}$$

$$g_{FRB}(\cdot) = f_{FRB}(\cdot) \quad \text{if} \quad u(t)\, b^*(a,t) \neq M(t) - M(a,t+1) \quad \text{for any } (a,t) \tag{2-21}$$

$$\text{or if} \quad u(t)b^*(a,t) \neq m(a,Ht,FRB) - m(a,FRB,Ht) \quad \text{for any } (a,t) \tag{2-22}$$

$$\text{or if} \quad m(a,Ft,FRB) < D(t-1) + \hat{b}(t) - b(t) - b^*(a,t) \quad \text{for any } (a,t) \tag{2-23}$$

$$= 0 \qquad \text{otherwise.}$$

In (2-1) Ht promises to sell labor to Ft at wage $w(t)$, in (2-2) and (2-3) it promises to buy bonds from $H(t-1)$ and the FRB at price $u(t)$, and, in (2-4), from $F(t+1)$ at price $\hat{u}(a,t+1)$. It promises to sell bonds to its successor at price $u(a,t+1)$ in (2-5) and to buy output from $F(t+1)$ at price $p(a,t+1)$ in (2-6) and (2-7). However, Ht will pay for no more than $\bar{y}_H(a,t+1)$ output.

From (2-8), (2-17), (2-18), and (2-23) we see what bonds are: a bond is a promise that its holder will be paid one unit of money every period (starting the period after it is issued), no matter what Mother Nature does. In (2-17) and (2-18), Ft promises to pay current bondholders what they are due, and in (2-8) and (2-23) the current bondholders—Ht and the FRB—require that payment. Notice that we make no provision for bankruptcy; conceptually it would be easy to modify these lines to do so, but the computational burden would be considerable.

In (2-9), Ft promises to sell bonds to $H(t-1)$ at price $\hat{u}(t)$. In (2-10) and (2-11), Ft promises to buy machines from $F(t-1)$ at prices $q(t,v)$. Buying the machines carries with it the responsibility for servicing the existing debt $D(t-1)$, and so the cost of the machines is reduced by the cost of this debt $\hat{u}(t)\, D(t-1)$. In addition, Ft will pay for no more than

$\bar{K}(t-1)$ of the newest vintage of machines, that is, those that come from $(t-1)$'s output. (In common macro parlance, $K(t, t-1)$ is investment.)

In (2-12) and (2-13), *Ft* promises to buy labor at wage $w(t)$, but no more than $\bar{l}(t)$ of it. To make rationing interesting, we assume $\bar{l}(t) < 1$. In (2-14) and (2-15), it sells its output to consumers at price $p(t)$, and in (2-16) it sells its output (as investment good $K(a, t+1, t)$), its used machines and the responsibility for servicing the debt to its successor firm. In (2-19) and (2-20), *Ft* promises to buy output from the successor firm at price $p(a, t+1)$, but no more than $\bar{y}(a, t+1) - \bar{y}_H(a, t+1)$ of it.

In (2-22), the FRB promises always to buy and sell bonds at the going secondary market price $u(t)$. By buying bonds, it increases the money supply; by selling them it decreases the supply. In (2-21), we state that the Federal Reserve has committed itself to a particular arbitrary path of money supply $M(t)$. This path is a parameter of the commitment pattern.

IV

Virtually every situation where one of its own commitments is not being violated is acceptable to every player, and every situation acceptable to the other players is good for Mother Nature and the Federal Reserve Bank.

Household t's supergoodness problem becomes, after suitable substitutions

$$\max_{l,b,b^*,\hat{b}} \sum_a \frac{\phi_a}{p(a,t+1)} \{w(t)\sum_v l(t,v) + [u(a,t+1)+1-u(t)] \times$$

$$[b(t)+b^*(a,t)]+[u(a,t+1)-\hat{u}(a,t+1)]\hat{b}(a,t+1)\}, \text{ s.t.}$$

$$u(t)[b(t)+b^*(a,t)]+\hat{u}(a,t+1)\,\hat{b}(a,t+1) \leq w(t)\sum_v l(t,v) \qquad (\forall a)$$

$$\sum_v l(t,v) \leq \bar{l}(t).$$

Obviously

$$\sum_v l(t,v) = \bar{l}(t) \tag{3}$$

in *Ht*'s supergood set. If

$$\sum_a \frac{\phi_a}{p(a,t+1)} \frac{u(a,t+1)+1}{u(t)} > \sum_a \frac{\phi_a}{p(a,t+1)} \frac{u(a,t+1)}{\hat{u}(a,t+1)} \tag{4}$$

household t would invest all its money in $b(t)$ and $b^*(a,t)$; there would be nothing left for buying newly issued bonds $\hat{b}(a, t+1)$. Firm $(t+1)$

could not operate and would not agree with Ht's refusal to lend it money. Thus there can be no equilibrium involving a commitment pattern in which (4) held. On the other hand, if the inequality in (4) were reversed, household t would buy bonds from neither its predecessor nor the Federal Reserve, and there would be a similar failure of agreement. Thus

$$\sum_a \left[\frac{u(a,t+1)+1}{u(t)} - \frac{u(a,t+1)}{\hat{u}(a,t+1)}\right] \frac{\phi_a}{p(a,t+1)} = 0 \tag{5}$$

is a necessary condition for a commitment pattern to have an equilibrium. We call (5) the sensible behavior condition for household t. Given (5) any feasible portfolio is acceptable to Ht.

After similar substitutions, firm t's supergoodness problem becomes

$$\max \sum_a \frac{\phi_a}{p(a,t+1)} \{p(t)y(t) + p(t)K(a,t+1,t)$$
$$- \sum_{v=1}^{t-1} [(q(t,v) - q(a,t+1,v))K(t,v) + w(t)l(t,v)]$$
$$- [\hat{b}(t) + D(t-1)][\hat{u}(a,t+1) + 1 - \hat{u}(t)]\}, \quad \text{s.t.}$$

$$\sum_{v=1}^{t-1} [q(t,v)K(t,v) + w(t)l(t,v)] \leq \hat{u}(t)[D(t-1) + \hat{b}(t)]$$

$$y(t) \leq \bar{y}(t)$$

$$K(a,t+1,t) \leq \bar{K}(a,t) \qquad (\forall a)$$

$$y(t)\ K(a,t+1,t) \leq \sum_v Y(t,v)\alpha(v) \qquad (\forall a)$$

$$Y(t,v) \leq K(t,v) \qquad (\forall v)$$

$$Y(t,v) \leq l(t,v) \qquad (\forall v)$$

where $Y(t,v)\,\alpha(v)$ is the output produced from the process using vintage v machines, and $y(t)$ is the total output sold to consumers (the old firm and the old household). We have already taken advantage of the obvious relationship that

$$K(a,t+1,v) = K(t,v) \quad \text{if} \quad q(a,t+1,v) > 0$$

for all vintages of capital that Ft acquires: the firm wants to sell whatever used machines command a positive price.

Next, note that unless

$$\sum_a \frac{\phi_a}{p(a,t+1)}\, q(a,t+1,v) \leq q(t,v) \sum_a \frac{\phi_a}{p(a,t+1)} \cdot \frac{\hat{u}(a,t+1)+1}{\hat{u}(t)} \tag{6}$$

firm t will be able to expect a real profit on each unit of vintage v capital it buys, simply by holding onto it. Then it would want an infinite amount of vintage v capital and agreement would be impossible. Thus (6) must hold for all v or there is no equilibrium. On the other hand, if

$$\sum_a \frac{\phi_a}{p(a,t+1)} q(a,t+1,v) = q(t,v) \sum_a \frac{\phi_a}{p(a,t+1)} \cdot \frac{\hat{u}(a,t+1)+1}{\hat{u}(t)} \tag{7}$$

any amount of $K(t, v)$ being held for purely speculative purposes without producing any output is supergood for firm t. We will denote by $V_2(t)$ the set of vintages v for which (7) holds.

If we let $V_1(t)$ denote the set of vintages for which output is positive, we have the following supergoodness conditions:

$$\begin{aligned} &D(t-1) = \text{anything} \\ &I(t,v) = Y(t,v) \geq 0 && \text{if} \quad v \in V_1(t) \\ &I(t,v) = 0 && \text{if} \quad v \notin V_1(t) \\ &I(t,v) = K(t,v) && \text{if} \quad v \notin V_2(t) \end{aligned}$$

$$y(t) = \bar{y}(t) \tag{8}$$

$$\alpha(v)p(t)\left[\sum_{a\in\bar{R}} \frac{\phi_a}{p(a,t+1)}\right] - \sum_A \frac{\phi_a}{p(a,t+1)} \{[q(t,v) + w(t)] \times \frac{\hat{u}(a,t+1)+1}{\hat{u}(t)} - q(a,t+1,v)\} = 0 \quad \text{for all } v \in V_1(t) \tag{9}$$

$$\alpha(v)p(t)\left[\sum_{a\in\bar{R}} \frac{\phi_a}{p(a,t+1)}\right] - \sum_A \frac{\phi_a}{p(a,t+1)} \{[q(t,v) + w(t)] \times \frac{\hat{u}(a,t+1)+1}{\hat{u}(t)} - q(a,t+1,v)\} < 0 \quad \text{for all } v \notin V_1(t) \tag{10}$$

where $\bar{R}$ is the set of a where $\bar{K}(a, t)$ is large enough that all output can be sold:

$$\bar{R} = \{a \mid \bar{K}(a,t) > \sum_{V_3} \alpha(v)\, Y(t,v) - \bar{y}(t)\}.$$

Equation (8) follows because, with the assumed equality of price for consumption and investment purposes, output withheld from sale for consumption will not necessarily be sold.

Subtracting (6) from (9), we see:

$$\alpha(v)p(t)\left[\sum_{a\in\bar{R}} \frac{\phi_a}{p(a,t+1)}\right] \geq w(t) \sum_A \frac{\phi_a}{p(a,t+1)} \cdot \frac{\hat{u}(a,t+1)+1}{\hat{u}(t)} \tag{11}$$

for all $v \in V_1(t)$. Since there will be equality in (11) for at most one value of $\alpha(v)$, the intersection of $V_1(t)$ and $V_2(t)$ will have at most one value of $\alpha(v)$. For convenience we will assume this intersection empty.

Subtracting (7) from (10):

$$\alpha(v)p(t)\left[\sum_{a\in\bar{R}} \frac{\phi_a}{p(a,t+1)}\right] < w(t) \sum_{A} \frac{\phi_a}{p(a,t+1)} \cdot \frac{\hat{u}(a,t+1)+1}{\hat{u}(t)} \tag{12}$$

for all v in $V_2(t)$ and not in $V_1(t)$. From (11) and (12) we see that $\alpha(v)$ for $v \in V_1(t)$ is always greater than $\alpha(v)$ for $v \notin V_1(t)$ and in $V_2(t)$: every vintage that is producing is always more productive (newer) than every vintage that is being held idle.

V

Now we can consider the conditions that are necessary for agreement. A commitment pattern whose parameters do not meet these conditions cannot support an equilibrium. We will suppose that all parameters with arguments of $(t-1)$ or earlier have somehow been determined, as well as $q(t, v)$ (for all $v \leq t-1$), $u(t)$ and $\hat{u}(t)$; the problem becomes finding requirements for the rest of the parameters for period t and those for subsequent periods.

In the period t used machine markets, firm $(t-1)$ wants to give firm t precisely what it received from firm $(t-2)$, for every vintage v with positive price. Thus for $v \leq t-2$, what firm $(t-1)$ wants $K(t, v)$ to be is determined by history. We will assume that the same is true for vintage $(t-1)$. On the other hand, firm t wants a positive quantity of vintage v capital only if $v \in V_1(t)$ or $v \in V_2(t)$; if either is the case, any quantity is supergood for Ft. Thus if $V_3(t-1)$ denotes the set of vintages v for which $q(t, v)$ is positive, a necessary condition for agreement is

$$V_1(t) \cup V_2(t) \supset V_3(t-1).$$

Consider for a moment the vintages that are not in $V_3(t-1)$; that is, the vintages with $q(t, v) = 0$. By (6), these vintages must be in $V_2(t)$, and by our assumption that $V_1(t)$ and $V_2(t)$ are disjoint they cannot be in $V_1(t)$. Thus every vintage $v \leq t-1$ is in either $V_1(t)$ or $V_2(t)$, and hence, every vintage in $V_1(t)$ is more productive than every vintage not in $V_1(t)$.

In the labor market, firm t's supergoodness condition is

$$\sum_{V_1(t)} K(t, v) = \sum_{v} l(t, v)$$

while household t's supergoodness condition is

$$\sum_{v} l(t, v) = \bar{l}(t).$$

Thus for agreement we need

$$\sum_{V_1(t)} K(t, v) = \bar{l}(t).$$

Since the $K(t, v)$ are determined historically, this sets up a relationship between $V_1(t)$ and $\bar{l}(t)$. In fact, if we let $\alpha(V_1(t))$ denote the smallest $\alpha(v)$ for v in $V_1(t)$, $\alpha(V_1(t))$ will be determined uniquely by $\bar{l}(t)$.

In the market for debt, any value of $D(t-1)$ is supergood for firm t, while

$$D(t-1) = D(t-2) + \hat{b}(t-1)$$

is supergood for firm $(t-1)$. This determines $D(t-1)$.

In the market for new bonds, firm t's supergoodness condition is

$$\begin{aligned}\hat{u}(t)\hat{b}(t) &= \sum_{V_1(t)} [w(t)l(t, v) + q(t, v)K(t, v)] \\ &\quad + \sum_{V_2(t)} q(t, v)K(t, v) - \hat{u}(t)D(t-1) \\ &= w(t)\bar{l}(t) + \sum_{v=1}^{t-1} q(t, v)K(t, v) - \hat{u}(t)D(t-1).\end{aligned}$$

For household $(t-1)$ it is supergood to lend firm t whatever money it has. Whatever money it has is the total amount of money held by the nonbank public, $M(t)$, less the amount of money that $F(t-1)$ is holding. Since all of what $F(t-1)$ borrowed at the start of period t has been used to buy labor and machines, the amount of money that $F(t-1)$ is holding at the beginning of period t is precisely its receipts from consumer sales

$$p(t-1)[y_F(t-1) + y_H(t-1)].$$

Thus

$$\hat{u}(t)\hat{b}(t) = M(t) - p(t-1)[y_F(t-1) + y_H(t-1)]$$

is supergood for household $(t-1)$. Agreement, then, requires that

$$\begin{aligned}M(t) - p(t-1)[y_F(t-1) + y_H(t-1)] &= w(t)\bar{l}(t) \\ &\quad + \sum_{v=1}^{t-1} q(t, v)K(t, v) - \hat{u}(t)D(t-1).\end{aligned}$$

This expression can tell us what $w(t)$ has to be in terms of predetermined parameters and $\bar{l}(t)$:

$$w(t) = \frac{1}{\bar{l}(t)} \{M(t) - p(t-1)[y_F(t-1) + y_H(t-1)] \tag{13}$$

$$-\sum_{v=1}^{t-1} q(t,v)K(t,v) + \hat{u}(t)D(t-1)\},$$

or, letting $X(t)$ stand for the expression in curly brackets,

$$w(t) = X(t)/\bar{l}(t).$$

In the market for consumption goods, firm t wants to sell $y(t)$. Household $(t-1)$ wants to use all its money, $u(t)\,b(t)$, to buy these, and so does $F(t-1)$ which has $\pi(t-1)$, its profit, in money. Thus

$$p(t) = \frac{u(t)b(t)+\pi(t-1)}{\bar{y}(t)} \tag{14}$$

gives the value that $p(t)$ must have, where

$$\begin{aligned} b(t) &= b(t-1) + \frac{X(t-1)-u(t-1)b(t-1)-M(t-1)+M(t)}{\hat{u}(t)} \\ &= \frac{1}{\hat{u}(t)}\{X(t-1)+[\hat{u}(t)-u(t-1)]b(t-1)-M(t-1)+M(t)\} \end{aligned}$$

and

$$\begin{aligned} \pi(t-1) = \sum_{V_1(t-1)} & K(t,v)\left\{p(t-1)\alpha(v)+q(t,v)\right. \\ & \left.-[w(t-1)+q(t-1,v)]\frac{\hat{u}(t)}{\hat{u}(t-1)}\right\} \\ & + \sum_{V_2(t-1)} K(t-1,v)\left\{q(t,v)-q(t-1,v)\frac{\hat{u}(t)}{\hat{u}(t-1)}\right\}. \end{aligned}$$

In the $(t+1)$ output markets, we can find similar expressions:

$$p(a,t+1) = \frac{u(a,t+1)b(a,t+1)+\pi(a,t)}{\bar{y}(a,t)} \tag{15}$$

where

$$\begin{aligned} b(a,t+1) = \frac{1}{\hat{u}(a,t+1)} & \{X(t)+[\hat{u}(a,t+1)-u(t)]\,b(t) \\ & -M(t)+M(t+1)\} \end{aligned}$$

and

$$\pi(a,t) = \sum_{V_1(t)} K(t,v)\left\{p(t)\alpha(v)+q(a,t+1,v)\right.$$

$$-[w(t)+q(t,v)]\ \frac{\hat{u}(a,t+1)}{\hat{u}(t)}\Bigg\}$$

$$+\sum_{V_2(t)} K(t,v)\ \Bigg\{q(a,t+1,v)-q(t,v)\ \frac{\hat{u}(a,t+1)}{\hat{u}(t)}\Bigg\}$$

if $a \in \bar{R}$,

$$\pi(a,t) = p(t)[\bar{y}(t)+\bar{K}(a,t)] - \sum_{V_1(t)} K(t,v)\{[w(t)+q(t,v)] \times \frac{\hat{u}(a,t+1)}{\hat{u}(t)} - q(a,t+1,v)\}$$

$$+\sum_{V_2(t)} \left[q(a,t+1,v)-q(t,v)\ \frac{\hat{u}(a,t+1)}{\hat{u}(t)}\right] K(t,v)$$

if $a \notin \bar{R}$. Expression (15), however, differs from (14), in that it depends upon $u(a,t+1)$, $\hat{u}(a,t+1)$, and $q(a,t+1,v)$, which have not yet been determined. This situation can be partially rectified by considering the sensible behavior condition (5), the *Ft* supergoodness conditions (7) and (9), and a new condition needed to keep firm t from wanting to enter the secondary bond market:

$$\{u(a,t+1)+1-u(t)\} = 0 \tag{16}$$

Then (15), (5), (7) and (9) together, and (16) make four sets of equations in four sets of unknowns: $u(\cdot,t+1)$, $\hat{u}(\cdot,t+1)$, $q(\cdot,t+1,v)$ and $p(\cdot,t+1)$. But the number of unknowns is $(t+2)|A|$ and the number of equations is only $|A| + t+1$. This disparity results solely from a lack of contingent claims markets and has nothing to do with our Keynesian rather than Walrasian approach. With $|A| = 1$—if there is no uncertainty—there is no problem.

The requirements of agreement, then, do not determine uniquely what the parameters of the commitment pattern have to be. Putting additional requirements on the commitment pattern could determine the parameters uniquely, but we have little interest in doing so. Equations (7) and (9), for instance, tell us about the mathematical expectation of period $(t+1)$ real stock prices; I do not think we are entitled to ask for more. Economic theory, in this case, can talk only about statistical properties.

We will, however, take advantage of the indeterminacy by adding one requirement for the sake of computational ease. This requirement is that $p(a,t+1) = p(t+1)$ for all $a \in A$: next period prices do not respond to Mother Nature.

VI

So far we have described what equilibrium must be like—or what its statistical properties must be—given the quantity constraints $\bar{l}(t)$—which determines $V_1(t)$ and $V_2(t)$—$\bar{y}(t)$ and $\bar{K}(a, t)$. The question that remains is how the quantity constraints are related to each other.

The key to resolving this question lies in inequalities (11) and (12). Let us rewrite these using (13), (14), (16) and the assumed constancy of $p(t+1)$ with respect to Mother Nature:

$$\Phi(\bar{R}) \geq \frac{\bar{y}(t)}{\bar{l}(t)\alpha(v)}\left\{X(t)\,\frac{u(t)-1}{\hat{u}(t)}\cdot\frac{1}{u(t)\,b(t)+\pi(t-1)}\right\} \tag{11*}$$

for all $v \in V_1(t)$, and

$$\Phi(\bar{R}) < \frac{\bar{y}(t)}{\bar{l}(t)\alpha(v)}\left\{X(t)\,\frac{u(t)-1}{\hat{u}(t)}\cdot\frac{1}{u(t)\,b(t)+\pi(t-1)}\right\} \tag{12*}$$

for all $v \notin V_1(t)$, where

$$\Phi(\bar{R}) = \sum_{a\in\bar{R}} \phi_a,$$

the probability that the sale of output is not rationed. Let us consider $\bar{y}(t) > 0$ and $(\bar{K}(a,t))$ as exogenously determined. This is, in fact, the Keynesian tradition, especially with regard to investment, where $\bar{y}(t)$ comes from stable prices and $(\bar{K}(a, t))$ from "animal spirits."

Then $\Phi(\bar{R})$ depends only on total output, which, since only the most productive capital is used, depends only on $\bar{l}(t)$. When $\bar{l} = 0$, $\Phi(\bar{R}(\bar{l})) = 1$, since there is no output and hence no chance that output will be more than people will buy. As $\bar{l}$ increases, $\Phi(\cdot)$ stays the same or goes down, as the more output there is, the greater the chance it will be rationed. The step function Φ in figure 6 illustrates what this relationship might look like.

On the right-hand side of (11*) and (12*), the situation is more complicated. Let Z denote the expression in curly brackets there, and label the various vintages $v_1, v_2, \ldots, v_{t-1}$ in such a manner that $\alpha(v_1) \geq \alpha(v_2) \geq \ldots \geq \alpha(v_{t-1})$. (If scientific progress is monotonic, this will be in order of increasing age.) Let $L(v_i)$ denote the amount of labor that must be employed if all vintages at least as productive as v_i are being used:

$$L(v_i) = \sum_{j\leq i} K(t, v_j).$$

Let $\psi(v_i, \bar{l})$ denote the value of the RHS for vintages v_i when $\bar{l}$ labor is used

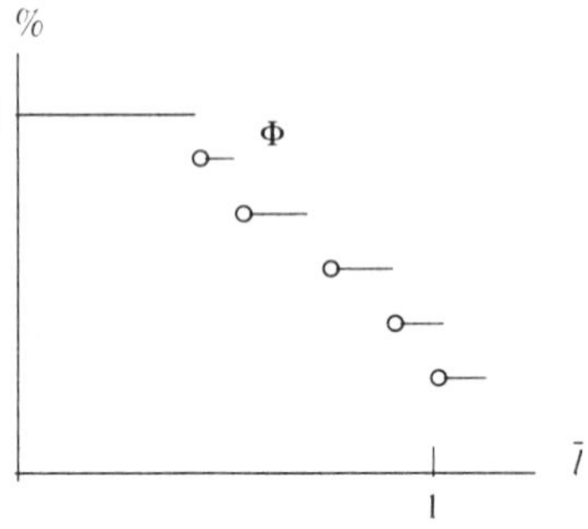

Figure 6

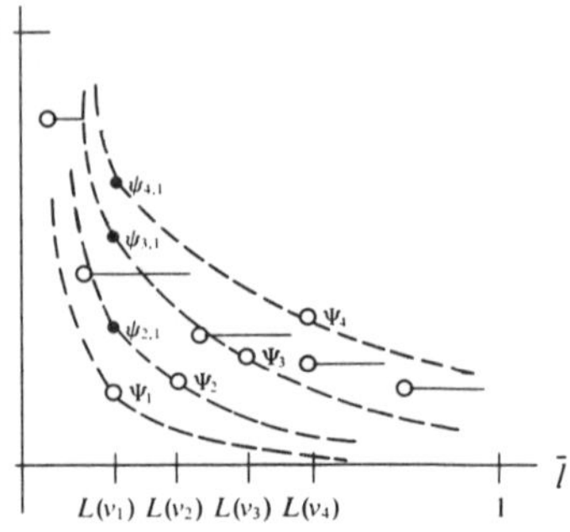

Figure 7

$$\psi(v_i, \bar{l}) = (\bar{y}(t)\, Z) \,/\, (\bar{l}\, \alpha(v_i)).$$

The family of functions $\psi(v_i, \bar{l})$ is graphed in figure 7; for every v_i, of course, $\psi(v_i, \cdot)$ is a right hyperbola. What matters for equilibrium is whether that $\psi(v_i, \bar{l})$ for which $\bar{l} = L(v_i)$ is the largest $\psi(v_i, \bar{l})$ less than $\Phi(\bar{R}(\bar{l}))$; for if it is, then (11*) and (12*) are satisfied and $\bar{l}$ is a level of employment which, with $\bar{y}(t)$ and $(\bar{K}(a, t))$, can support an equilibrium. Define, therefore, $\Psi(\bar{l}) = \psi(L^{-1}(\bar{l}), \bar{l})$ and restrict the range of $\Psi(\cdot)$ so that $L^{-1}(\cdot)$ is always defined. The circled dots in figure 7 show how $\Psi(\cdot)$ might look.

If $\Psi(\bar{l}) \leq \Phi(R(\bar{l}))$ and there is no v_i with $\Psi(\bar{l}) < \psi(v_i, \bar{l}) \leq \Phi(\bar{R}(\bar{l}))$, then $\bar{l}$ is an equilibrium employment level. If $\Psi(\cdot)$ is always below $\Phi(\cdot)$, but either full employment uses every vintage or there is no v_i with $\psi(v_i, 1)$ between $\Psi(1)$ and $\Phi(\bar{R}(1))$, then full employment need not imply that rationing is impossible; it need only imply that $\bar{y}(t)$ and $(\bar{K}(a,t))$ are large enough that rationing is a sufficiently rare occurrence relative to the efficiency of the oldest capital used at full employment. (If, however, Ψ is far enough below Φ at full employment that some $\psi(v_i, 1)$ can intervene, there will be no Keynesian equilibrium.) If $\Psi(\cdot)$ is always above $\Phi(\cdot)$, no employment is the only equilibrium: even the most productive machinery is not productive enough to pay wages.

When $\Psi(\cdot)$ is monotonically increasing and cuts through $\Phi(\cdot)$ from below, as in figure 7, equilibrium can be only at the last $L(v_i)$ before the cut, $L(v_3)$ in figure 7. In figure 7, $L(v_3)$ is in fact an equilibrium employment level, since

$$\psi(v_4, L(v_3)) > \Phi(\bar{R}(L(v_3))).$$

But the last $L(v_i)$ before the cut need not be an equilibrium, as figure 8 illustrates. In this case $L(v_3)$ is not an equilibrium because $\psi(v_4, L(v_3)) < \Phi(\bar{R}(L(v_3)))$, and neither is $L(v_4)$, since $\Psi(L(v_4)) > \Phi(\bar{R}(L(v_4)))$. The commitment pattern in figure 8 has no equilibrium although a small in-

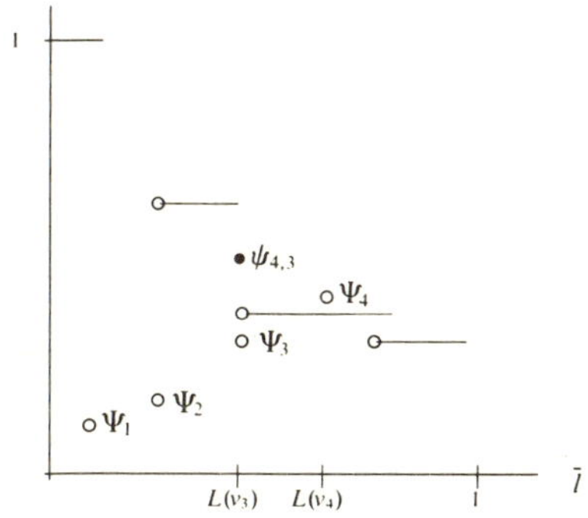

Figure 8

crease in $\bar{y}(t)$ could result in an equilibrium at $L(v_3)$. This difficulty can be obviated, though, if the amount of capital of each vintage is relatively small enough, and $|A|$ is large enough that Ψ and Φ can be treated as continuous functions. With continuity there will be an equilibrium wherever Ψ touches Φ; thus $(\bar{y}(t), \bar{K}(a,t))$ will always be associated with a Keynesian equilibrium unless they are so large that Ψ is everywhere above Φ including at full employment. (Even without continuity it is easy to prove that for every $\bar{l}$ with

$$\underline{\alpha}(\bar{l})\, X(t)\, y(t,\bar{l}) \geq \bar{l}\,[\min_A \phi_a]\, \frac{\hat{u}(t)}{u(t)-1}\, [u(t)\, b(t) + \pi(t-1)]$$

there is at least one $(\bar{y}(t), (\bar{K}(a,t)))$ such that $\bar{l}$ is associated with $(\bar{y}(t), (\bar{K}(a,t)))$ in a commitment equilibrium; thus unemployment equilibria exist.)

A more serious difficulty with the Ψ function is that it need not always slope upward. It slopes upward if and only if the elasticity of $\underline{\alpha}(\bar{l})$ is greater than unity; thus the slope of Ψ depends upon the economy's history of both science and investment. Multiple equilibria, including equilibria where Ψ cuts Φ from above, are possible, as in figure 9a.

Equilibria where Ψ cuts Φ from above, however, do not have the "comparative statics" properties we have come to expect in macroeconomics; we shall see this in the next section and next chapter. We will call such equilibria "abnormal." Fortunately, we have reason to believe that abnormal equilibria will be rare, especially in economies where most labor is employed. If, for instance, the $\bar{K}(a,t)$ are not widely dispersed in the neighborhood of the equilibrium, Φ will fall very rapidly, making it difficult for Ψ to fall even more rapidly. Moreover, the slope of Ψ will tend to increase as $\bar{l}$ increases, because equal absolute changes in $\bar{l}$ will bring about smaller percentage changes in $\bar{l}$, and, if investment grew at about the rate of the

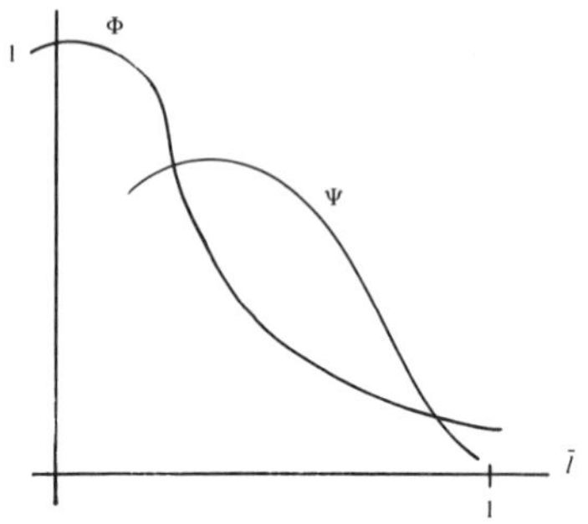

Figure 9a

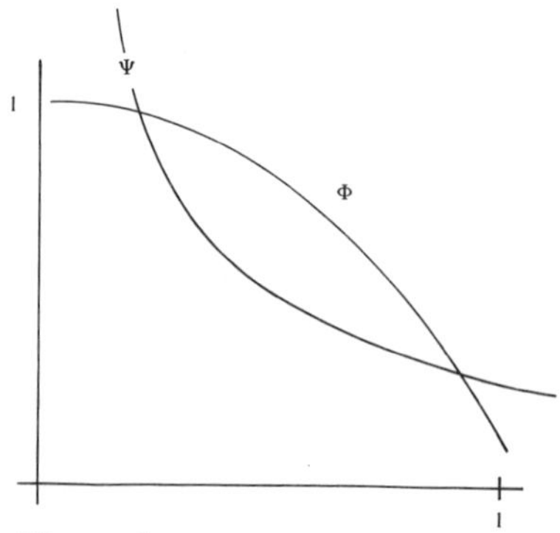

Figure 9b

economy in the past, more changes of vintage. Even if $\alpha(v)$ is a constant, the larger equilibrium will be normal if, for instance, Φ is weakly concave downward, as in figure 9b. We will confine our attention, therefore, to equilibria that are not abnormal, but we should bear in mind that any results contingent on normality may be reversed, especially in an equilibrium of mass unemployment.

VII

The last section's analysis lets us see what influences the level of employment. Increasing $X(t)$, for instance, shifts the Ψ function upward, and assuming normality decreases the level of employment required for given $(\bar{y}(t), \bar{K}(a,t))$ (precisely, it does not increase the level). Decreasing $p(t)$ has the same effect; thus there is a presumption for a Phillips' curve relationship.

Note that wages are not in any sense sticky. Given $X(t)$, higher employment means lower wages, and vice versa.

Note also that (5) and (16) keep the real rate of return on investment at zero in mathematical expectation. This is to be expected in a world of risk neutrality where households save all their income. An expanded, more complex model would be needed to study the rate of interest; key to understanding it will be the interplay of household and firm risk aversion.

We can use these ideas to see how the system evolves over time, and in particular, why we might often experience oscillations in employment. Let us look, therefore, at the equilibrium in period $(t+1)$.

The first determinant of $(t+1)$ period employment, given a, is $X(a,t+1)$:

$$X(a,t+1) = M(a,t+1) - p(t)[y_F(t) + y_H(t)] - \sum_{v=1}^{t} q(a,t+1,v)\, K(a,t+1,v) + \hat{u}(a,t+1)\, D(t).$$

We know, however:

$$q(a,t+1,t) = p(t) \qquad (\forall a)$$

$$K(a,t+1,v) = K(t,v) \qquad (\forall a) \quad (\forall v)$$

$$D(t) = D(t-1) + \hat{b}(t)$$

$$\hat{b}(t) = (1/\hat{u}(t))[X(t) + \sum_{v=1}^{t-1} q(t,v)\,K(t,v)] - D(t-1)$$

and hence

$$D(t) = (1/\hat{u}(t))[X(t) + \sum_{v=1}^{t-1} q(t,v)\,K(t,v)].$$

Substituting we obtain:

$$\begin{aligned} X(a,t+1) = {} & \mathrm{M}(a,t+1) + \frac{\hat{u}(a,t+1)}{\hat{u}(t)}\,X(t) \\ & - p(t)[y_F(t) + y_H(t) + K(a,t+1,t)] \\ & + \sum_{v=l}^{t-1} K(t,v) \left\{ \frac{\hat{u}(a,t+1)}{\hat{u}(t)}\,q(t,v) - q(a,t+1,v) \right\}. \end{aligned}$$

Substantial random movements are thus possible in $X(\cdot)$; quite aside from any considerations of economic theory we have no way of taming it. Since we have (7) and (9), though, and we know that sales are equal to production when $a \in \bar{R}$, we can make a definite statement about the mathematical expectation of $X(\cdot, t+1)$:

$$\begin{aligned} EX(\cdot,t+1) = {} & EM(\cdot,t+1) - p(t) \sum_{a \notin \bar{R}} \phi_a[\bar{y}(t) + \bar{K}(a,t)] \\ & - (1/\hat{u}(t))[X(t) + \sum_{v=l}^{t-1} q(t,v)\,K(t,v)], \end{aligned} \tag{17}$$

where E is the mathematical expectation operator.

From this we see, first, that a large $X(t)$ tends to make for a small $X(t+1)$, and vice versa. Everything else somehow being equal, $X(\cdot)$ will tend to oscillate, and unemployment with it.

On the other hand, the higher employment is in period t, given $\bar{y}(t)$ and $(\bar{K}(a,t))$, the more states will be rationed and the higher will be the values of $[\bar{y}(t) + \bar{K}(a,t)]$ in those states. This will decrease $EX(\cdot, t+1)$, increase employment in period $(t+1)$ and accentuate the cycle. This story of unusually high employment cumulating holds, however, only if employment is unusually high in period $(t+1)$ because costs are abnormally low or productivity abnormally high. If period t employment is high because $(\bar{y}(t),$

$(\bar{K}(a,t)))$ is unusually high, few states will be rationed and the stimulus to period $(t+1)$ will be less.

But $X(\cdot)$ is not the only thing that changes systematically between periods; technology does, too. A new vintage of machine is available in period $(t+1)$—vintage t—and since the almost inexorable march of progress means that vintage t machines will be among the most productive around, there will be a new relationship between employment and output, and a new relationship between employment and marginal productivity. The first change will increase the amount of output for any amount of labor (as long as there is enough labor to use the new vintage), and thus decreases the probability of not being rationed. This shifts the Φ function down, and increases unemployment (as bewailers of technological unemployment, from the Luddites on down, have been quick to point out). The marginal productivity effect operates by shifting out on $\psi(v_i,\cdot)$ curves. Assume, for simplicity, vintage t capital is more productive than any other vintage. Then in period $(t+1)$

$$L_{t+1,a}(v_i) = \sum_{j\neq i} K(t,v_j) + K(a,t+1,t) = L(v_i) + K(a,t+1,t)$$

and

$$\Psi_{t+1,a}(\bar{l}) = \psi(L^{-1}_{t+1,a}(\bar{l}),\bar{l}).$$

Since $L^{-1}_{t+1,a}(\bar{l})$ is a more productive vintage than $L^{-1}(\bar{l})$ was (the presence of a new vintage means that a given quantity of labor can be concentrated on a larger set of more productive vintages and not be used with some less productive ones),

$$\psi(L^{-1}_{t+1,a}(\bar{l}),\bar{l}) \leq \psi(L^{-1}(\bar{l}),\bar{l})$$

and

$$\Psi_{t+1,a}(\bar{l}) \leq \Psi(\bar{l}) \quad \text{for all } \bar{l}.$$

Thus the Ψ curve shifts down and employment increases. Which technological effect will be stronger is indeterminate.

The final determinant of period $(t+1)$ employment is $p(t+1)$. Remembering that

$$p(a,t+1) = \frac{u(a,t+1)b(a,t+1)+\pi(a,t)}{\bar{y}(a,t+1)}$$

we might want to say that the higher the numerator, the higher the level of employment, since we might want to adjust $\bar{y}(a,t+1)$ to hit a predetermined price. Then the higher the numerator, the higher $\bar{y}(a,t+1)$, and thus the higher the curve. If price is fixed, in other words, the Φ curve will move to increase employment when the numerator rises; if $\bar{y}(a, t+1)$ is fixed, the Ψ curve will fall to increase employment; thus our concern is how the numerator

$$u(a, t+1)\, b(a, t+1) + \pi(a, t)$$

behaves.

The first term is the amount of money household t can spend on consumption. This is largely determined by $X(t)$. Thus we have another reason for oscillation: a large $X(t)$ decreases employment in a period t, and increases it in period $(t+1)$. Period t profits $\pi(a, t)$, the amount of money firm t can spend on consumption, depend on luck, but (7) and (9) can give us a mathematical expectation:

$$E(\pi(\cdot, t)) = p(t) \sum_{a \notin \bar{R}} \phi_a[\bar{y}(t) + \bar{K}(a, t)]$$

the second expression in (17). The more rationing in period t, the greater the mathematical expectation of profits, and the higher the level of employment is likely to be in period $(t+1)$.

Thus, on net, the oscillatory factors predominate. The macroeconomic world that this model gives us is characterized by cycles, a Phillips' curve, and noise. That is not a bad description of reality.

10 ▪ Macroeconomic Policy

MacLugaċ, says Fionn, ...

Without a fault of his,
Beat not thy hound; . . . .
In battle meddle not with a buffoon,
For, O MacLugaċ, he is but a fool. . . .
Two-thirds of thy gentleness be shewn
To women and to creepers on the floor, . . .
And be not violent to the common people . . .
Utter not swaggering speech,
Nor say that thou wilt not render the thing that is right;
For a shameful thing it is to speak too swiftly
Unless it be feasible to carry out thy words . . .
Neither for gold nor for other earthly valuables
Abandon thou thy guarantee. . . .
Stick to thy raiment,
Hold fast to thine armature;
Yet follow after gentleness, MacLugaċ.

Agallaṁ na Senoraċ ("Colloquy of the Ancients")

Whenever Fionn MacCuṁail, the ancient Irish hero, put his thumb into his mouth and sang, whatever he was ignorant of was revealed to him. This was because he had accidentally burned his thumb while cooking the salmon of Fec's pool—the salmon of knowledge—and had put it into his mouth. Fionn used this ability to detect his enemies and slay them; it also helped when he gave advice to his ne'er-do-well grandson MacLugaċ.

More recently, economists have taken to solving systems of equations instead of sucking on their thumbs to gain Knowledge, and advising governments instead of grandsons. Just as the salmon of Fec's pool that Fionn was cooking was not originally intended for his consumption (it belonged to the poet Finneces, who had caught it after a seven-year wait), so too are the methods that economists use to acquire the wherewithal to slay and advise borrowed from their rightful owners.

Economics has borrowed its method of advising from physics. Consider, for example, how physics would go about advising a cannoneer about the amount of powder and the muzzle angle that should be used in firing a particular ball from a particular cannon. A physicist would use the laws of physics and the dimensions of the cannon and ball to derive a system of equations in which the amount of powder and the muzzle angle would be unspecified parameters. Solving these equations would associate a unique trajectory (or, in more sophisticated versions, a unique probability distribution over trajectories) with each pair of muzzle angle and amount of powder. The physicist could then make predictions to the cannoneer: "If you use this much powder and that muzzle angle, then the cannonball will go thus-and-so." Presumably the cannoneer would know the trajectory he wanted the cannonball to follow; thus when he had listened to the physicist's predictions he could choose the muzzle angle and powder amount that would jointly yield a trajectory as close as possible to the desired one. The cannoneer would consider the physicist's predictions useful advice.

Traditionally, economists have tried to come up with useful advice for governments the same way that the physicist came up with useful advice for the cannoneer: by deriving systems of equations in which the variables the government was seen as controlling (tax rates and money supply, for instance) were unspecified parameters, and then solving these systems to associate a unique equilibrium or disequilibrium path with each set of government-controlled variables. The goal has been to make predictions like, "If you raise the tax on turnips by a nickel, the price of onions will double"; for, when such predictions have been made, the government, knowing which equilibria or disequilibrium paths were most desirable to it, would choose the government variables that would yield the most desirable outcome. In this manner, it has been thought, economists would be providing useful advice.

There are two difficulties with this approach, both noted in the literature. The first is that economic theory may not yield unique predictions. This difficulty is especially prevalent in rational expectations models (see, e.g., Azariadis [1981]), but it afflicts, to a lesser extent, the standard Walrasian system as well (Arrow and Hahn [1971], chapter 9). The second and more fundamental difficulty, which has been pointed up by Kydland and Prescott (1977) and Kydland (1977), is that the government is not the only conscious actor in the economics world. The cannonballs (or Mother Nature) do not care what the cannoneer does, but the nongovernment actors do care about what the government does. The physicist is trying to advise a creature truly exogenous to the system he or she is studying, but the economist is advising an entity whose actions are considered by the actors under study, an entity that is not a junior demiurge like the physicist's advisee, but rather just another player in the game.

The difficulty is analogous to Robinson Crusoe's problem in chapter 5. Crusoe can be secular and listen to physicists when it is Mother Nature that puts coconuts in palm trees, because she does not care what he does. But when Friday puts coconuts in palm trees, Crusoe must participate in a game in which Friday cares what he does and he cares what Friday does. Since it is clever, caring Fridays that put coconuts in the government's palm trees and not icy indifferent Mother Natures, the government does not need a secular adviser like a physicist.

But if the salmon of physics cannot allow economists to suck on their thumbs to slay enemies and advise governments, what useful advice can economists give to governments, or anyone else? What they can do is to describe commitment equilibria, and this is the most useful advice imaginable. For in describing a commitment equilibrium one tells each player—and in particular, one's advisee—precisely what threats and actions will yield her or him the greatest reward, given the threats and actions of the other players (over which, of course, there is no control). What better advice could there be?

This chapter, then, is about giving this type of helpful advice to governments. The governments we will be concerned with are altruistic but can produce nothing of intrinsic value to anyone; this is the tradition of macroeconomic policy (public finance is the branch of economics having to do with governments that can produce intrinsically valuable items). The way to give this advice, we see, is to describe commitment equilibria in games that involve such governments as players. In this chapter we will describe some of the commitment equilibria of a game like the one we studied in the last chapter, but modified to make government more interesting. Along the way we will pause for some observations on the nature of altruism.

I

Let us suppose that there is a government in each period t that has all the responsibilities of the Federal Reserve Bank of the period, as well as the ability to raise taxes and buy output. Provisionally we will assume that in the period t government Gt seeks to maximize household $(t+1)$'s utility.

Specifically, a typical period will now look like the table we have set forth as figure 10. Government t and household $(t-1)$ exchange money and bonds in the same sort of Federal Reserve transaction we had in the

$H(t-1)$	$H(t)$	$F(t-1)$	$F(t)$	$G(t-1)$	$G(t)$	MN	
$m \to Gt$					$b^* \to Ht-1$		*
$b^* \to Gt$					$m \to Ht-1$		*
$m \to Ft$			$\hat{b} \to Ht-1$				
$m \to Gt-1$				$\hat{b}_G \to Ht-1$			
		$K \to Ft$	$m \to Ft-1$				
		$y \to Gt-1$		$m \to Ft-1$			
	$l \to Ft$			$m \to Ht$			
		$m \to Ht-1$			$m \to Ht-1$		
		$m \to Gt$					*
$b, b_G \to Ht$	$m \to Ht-1$						
$m \to Ft$		$m \to Ft$	$y \to Ft-1,\ Ft-1$				
$m \to Gt$		$m \to Gt$			z_H, z_F		
						a	

*Denotes *FRB* transaction

Figure 10

last chapter. Household $(t-1)$ and firm $(t-1)$, however, make payments $m(H(t-1), Gt)$ and $m(F(t-1), Gt)$ respectively to government Gt after they have paid Ft for output. The government then chooses $\{0, 1\}$ variables $z_H(t)$ and $z_F(t)$, of which more will be said later. In the next period, Gt gives government bonds $\hat{b}_G(t+1)$ to Ht, and receives money $m(a, Ht, Gt)$. It gives money $m(a, Gt, Ft)$ to firm t and receives output $y_G(a, t+1)$. Finally it makes payment $m(a, Gt, Ht)$ to household t.

The government's fiscal operations are subject to a budget constraint, which we will take to be binding:

$$m(a, Gt, Ft) + m(a, Gt, Ht) \le m(H(t-1), Gt) + m(F(t-1), Gt) \\ + m(a, Ht, Gt) \quad \text{for all } a \in A.$$

The government—aside from Federal Reserve operations—cannot give away more money than it receives. The other players' budget constraints must also be modified, in the obvious manner, to account for the new payments to and from the government. (Notice that we confine Federal Reserve transactions to commercial bonds, and government spending to investment goods; both of these restrictions are inessential.)

Let

$$D_G(t) = D_G(t-1) + \hat{b}_G(t)$$

denote government debt. Then we will consider the following form of commitment by government Gt:

$$g_{Gt}(\cdot) = f_{Gt}(\cdot) \quad \text{if} \quad u(t-1)\,b^*(t-1) \neq M(t-1) - M(t) \qquad (1\text{-}1)$$

$$\text{or if} \quad u(t-1)\,b^*(t-1) \neq M(H(t-1), Gt) - m(Gt, H(t-1)) \qquad (1\text{-}2)$$

$$\text{or if} \quad m(a, Ft, Gt) < D(t-1) + \hat{b}(t) - b(t) - b^*(a,t) \quad \text{for any } a \qquad (1\text{-}3)$$

$$\text{or if} \quad m(H(t-1), Gt) < \tau(t)\,m(H(t-1), Ft, y) \text{ and } z_H(t) = 0 \qquad (1\text{-}4)$$

$$\text{or if} \quad m(F(t-1), Gt) < \tau(t)\,m(F(t-1), Ft) \text{ and } z_F(t) = 0 \qquad (1\text{-}5)$$

$$\text{or if} \quad m(H(t-1), Gt) \geq \tau(t)\,m(H(t-1), Ft, y) \text{ and } z_H(t) = 1 \qquad (1\text{-}6)$$

$$\text{or if} \quad m(F(t-1), Gt \geq \tau(t)\,m(F(t-1), Ft) \text{ and } z_F(t) = 1 \qquad (1\text{-}7)$$

$$\text{or if} \quad \hat{u}(a, t+1)\,\hat{b}_G(a, t+1) \neq m(a, Ht, Gt) \quad \text{for any } a \qquad (1\text{-}8)$$

$$\text{or if} \quad p(a, t+1)\,y_G(a, t+1) \neq m(a, Gt, Ft) \quad \text{for any } a \qquad (1\text{-}9)$$

$$\text{or if} \quad m(a, Gt, Ht) \neq D_G(t-1) \quad \text{for any } (1\text{-}10)$$

$$= 0 \quad \text{otherwise}$$

Lines (1-1) to (1-3) of this commitment are the same as the Federal Reserve commitment in the last chapter. In lines (1-4) through (1-7) the government promises to collect ad valorem consumption taxes at a rate of $\tau(t)$. The binary variables $z_H(\cdot)$ and $z_F(\cdot)$ represent the government's ability to use coercion. Let us rewrite the utility function for household t as

$$10{,}000\,[1 - z_H(t+1)] + \Sigma_{a \in A}\, \phi_a\, y_H(a, t+1)$$

and that for firm t as

$$10{,}000\,[1 - z_F(t+1)] + \Sigma_{a \in A}\, \phi_a\, y_F(a, t+1).$$

Then when the government chooses $z_H(t) = 1$ a very bad thing happens to household $(t-1)$; similarly for firm $(t-1)$. Lines (1-4) and (1-5) threaten this bad thing unless they pay their taxes; lines (1-6) and (1-7) promise to refrain from the bad thing if they pay their taxes. In line (1-8) the government promises to sell government bonds at the going price for new bonds, and in line (1-9) it promises to buy output at the going price. In line (1-10) it promises to service the debt incurred by its predecessors.

We have already seen that the nongovernment players' feasible sets and utility functions have had to be modified to account for the new type of government; we shall have to add some provisions to their commitments as well.

For household t, we add to the commitment in chapter 9 taxes, a promise to buy new government bonds, promises to buy and sell government bonds in the secondary market, and a demand for debt service:

$$
\begin{aligned}
g_{Ht}(\cdot) = f_{Ht}(\cdot) \quad & \text{if (chapter 9)} \\
& \text{or if} \quad \hat{u}(a, t+1)\,\hat{b}_G(a, t+1) \neq m(a, Ht, Gt) \quad \text{for any } a \\
& \text{or if} \quad m(a, Gt, Ht) \neq D_G(t-1) \quad \text{for any } a \\
& \text{or if} \quad u(t)\,b_G(t) < m(Ht, H(t-1), g) \\
& \text{or if} \quad u(a, t+1)\,b_G(a, t+1) \neq m(a, H(t+1), Ht, g) \\
& \qquad \text{for any } a \\
& \text{or if} \quad m(a, Ht, G(t+1)) \neq \tau(a, t+1)\,m(a, Ht, F(t+1), y) \\
& \qquad \text{for any } a \\
= 0 \quad & \text{otherwise.}
\end{aligned}
$$

Similarly, firm t also promises to pay its taxes

$$
\begin{aligned}
g_{Ft}(\cdot) = f_{Ft}(\cdot) \quad & \text{if (chapter 9)} \\
& \text{or if} \quad m(a, Ft, G(t+1)) \neq \tau(a, t+1)\,m(a, Ft, F(t+1)) \qquad (2) \\
& \qquad \text{for any } a. \\
= 0 \quad & \text{otherwise.}
\end{aligned}
$$

With these changes we can easily construct supergood sets for firms and households. For both, we will need to use $[1 + \tau(a, t+1)]p(a, t+1)$ instead of $p(a, t+1)$ in the expressions for sensible behavior and demand for output. For households, we will have to talk about the sum of commercial and government debt instead of just commercial debt. For firms, we will have a new use for output. These minor changes give us the supergood sets for firms and households.

II

Let us now consider the supergood set for government t, and recall our provisional assumption that government t seeks to maximize the utility of household $(t+1)$. To find government t's supergood set we maximize household $(t+1)$'s utility, subject to a series of feasibility and acceptability constraints, none of which can be among government t's acceptability constraints. It is easy to check, though, that in constructing a supergood set for household $(t+1)$ no acceptability constraints for government t are used. Constructing this supergood set means maximizing $H(t+1)$'s utility, subject to no Gt acceptability constraints. Thus finding $H(t+1)$'s supergood set is the same as finding Gt's supergood set, and the two supergood sets must be identical.

Because Gt's supergood set is identical with $H(t+1)$'s the intersection of all players' supergood sets is the intersection of the nongovernment players' supergood sets. If that intersection is feasible and acceptable to all players (including the government), then its members are equilibrium situations. One need never bother with government supergood sets.

How dependent is this handy result on our assumption that government t maximizes household $(t+1)$'s utility? Let us see what happens with alternative assumptions about the government's payoff function. Clearly there will be no change if government t maximizes firm $(t+1)$'s utility or household $(t+2)$'s, since no government acceptability constraints appear in those supergoodness problems.

For firms t and $(t-1)$ and households t and $(t-1)$ the argument is more complicated, but the result is the same. Consider firm t.

$$m(a, Ft, Gt) \geq D(t-1) + \hat{b}(t) - b(t) - b^*(a, t) \quad \text{for all } a \tag{3}$$

is a constraint in Ft's supergoodness problem: firm t's not paying interest on its commercial debt is not acceptable to government t. In Ft's supergood set (3) is binding. Inequality (3) is an acceptability condition for Gt, however; therefore (3) cannot be used as a constraint in Gt's supergoodness problem when it maximizes firm t's utility. The negation of (2), however, is an acceptability condition for Ft, therefore,

$$m(a, Ft, Gt) = D(t-1) + \hat{b}(t) - b(t) - b^*(a, t) \quad (\forall a) \tag{3'}$$

can be used as a constraint in Gt's supergoodness problem. Government t's supergoodness problem then can be the same as firm t's, except that it uses (3′) instead of (3). But since the answer will be the same no matter whether (3′) or (3) is used, Gt's supergood set must be the same as Ft's. (Note that all we require is that (3) or (3′) be an acceptability condition for some nongovernmental player—meddlesome neighbors are just as good as conscientious actors.) Similar arguments hold for $F(t-1)$, Ht, and $H(t-1)$.

Thus, no matter what nongovernment player's utility—past, present, or future—the altruistic government acts to maximize, the equilibrium situations are the same: the intersection (if it exists) of the nongovernment players' supergood sets and the set of NEs.

Most of the time, however, economists postulate that altruistic governments maximize some social welfare function that takes into account the utility of many players, not just a single one. Our result generalizes to fit this case as well. The way to generalize it is a theorem called Altruistic Contagion:

Theorem 10 (Altruistic Contagion). *Consider the game* $\Gamma = \langle I, S, f\rangle^*$ *where* $f_1(s) \equiv \zeta_1(f_2(s), f_3(s), \ldots, f_i(s), \ldots f_n(s))$ *and* ζ_1 *is an arbitrary function, nondecreasing in each of its arguments. Let* $h_1^i(s) \equiv f_i(s)$ *and* $h_j^i(s) = f_j(s)$ *for all* $i, j \geq 2$, *and let* Γ^i *denote* $\langle I, S, h^i\rangle^*$, $i \geq 2$. *Then* (g, s) *is an equilibrium of* Γ *if*

(a) *for all i,* (g, s) *is an equilibrium of* Γ^i, *and*

(b) *there is some* $j^* \geq 2$ *for whom* $A(1, g) = A^{j^*}(1, g)$.

Proof. Observe first that for all $k, j \geq 2$

$$A(j, g) = A^k(j, g) \tag{4}$$

since these payoff functions are the same in Γ^k as they are in Γ.

Now suppose (g, s) satisfies (a) and (b) but is not an equilibrium of Γ. We will show that $s \in B(i, g)$ for all players.

First suppose that $s \notin B(1, g)$. Then either

(α) there exists a $j > 1$ such that $s \notin A(j, g)$, or

(β) there exists an $s' \in P(1, g)$ such that

$$f_1(s') > f_1(s). \tag{5}$$

By (4), however, if (α), then $s \notin A^k(j, g)$ and (g, s) could not be an equilibrium of Γ^k, as required by (a). Thus (α) is impossible.

Then suppose (β). From (5) and the nondecreasing property of $\zeta_1(\cdot)$, there must be some $j > 1$ such that $f_j(s') > f_j(s)$ which implies

$$h_1^j(s') > h_1^j(s). \tag{6}$$

From $s' \in P(1, g)$ in (β) and (4),

$$s' \in P^j(1, g).$$

Together with (6), this implies that s is not good for 1 in Γ^j, whence (g, s) is not an equilibrium of Γ^j. Since this is a contradiction we conclude that $s \in B(1, g)$.

Next suppose that $s \notin B(i, g)$ for some $i > 1$. Then either:

(α) there exists a $j \neq i$ such that $s \notin A(j, g)$, or

(β) there exists an $s' \in P(i, g)$ such that

$$f_i(s') > f_i(s). \tag{7}$$

For the same reason we showed above for player 1, (α) is impossible. Thus suppose (β). In game Γ^{j*}, (7) implies

$$h_i^{j*}(s') > h_i^{j*}(s).$$

By (b) in the hypothesis and (4):

$$P(i, g) = P^{j*}(i, g)$$

so (β) implies

$$s' \in P^{j*}(i, g)$$

and s is not good for player i in Γ^{j*}; thus (g, s) is not an equilibrium of Γ^{j*}. Since this is a contradiction, we see that s is good in Γ for all players and (g, s) is an equilibrium of Γ. ∎

The Altruistic Contagion Theorem applies to games and commitment patterns like those we are concerned with in this chapter and the last. Thus no matter what altruistic social welfare function the government employs, equilibrium situations are found in the intersection of the nongovernment players' supergood sets and the set of NEs. To advise an altruistic government one need never find out its social welfare function. With this result, moreover, the assumption of one government per period becomes immaterial. With a commitment pattern family like the one we are using and altruism, it does not matter whether there is one government for all time or many; nor does it matter which government chooses which government variable.

These results also encourage speculation about the nature of altruism in general. Reread Fionn's advice to MacLugaċ. Fionn tells MacLugaċ to be upright and gentle, but provides him with no formula to weight different individuals' utilities. This absence of a social welfare function seems to be universal in pre-Newtonian social thought; Christianity, for instance, teaches that we should love one another, not that we should maximize a particular function. Those brought up in the predict-and-optimize school of economic advising have often, I believe, been secretly either puzzled or embarrassed by this phenomenon: that such a vast body of what almost everyone else has seen as wisdom should be seen by them as essentially useless rhetoric. Altruistic contagion shows us that when the proper approach to economic advising is taken—when we do not attempt to imitate physics—there is no reason for puzzlement or embarrassment. In tightly knit, contrapuntal commitment patterns, morality consists in the virtues of Fionn and the Gospels, and no social welfare function is required. The salmon of knowledge on which Fionn burned his thumb was by no means deficient.

III

What matters, then, is agreement among the nongovernment players. This chapter did not substantially change their supergood sets from those we had in the last chapter; thus the agreement conditions do not substantially change either. For the most part, we need only garnish the last chapter's conditions with some tax rates; we will not repeat those conditions here. We saw in the last chapter that the important concerns were the evolution of $X(t)$, the amount of money available to pay wages, and of $p(t)$, and the condition for the separation of vintages into $V_1(t)$ and $V_2(t)$. In this chapter's game those conditions become:

$$w(t)\bar{l}(t) = X(t) \tag{8}$$

$$\begin{aligned} X(t) = {} & M(t)-p(t-1)\{[1+\tau(t-1)]\bar{y}(t-1)+y_G(t-1)+K(t,t-1)\} \\ & - \frac{1}{\hat{u}(t-1)}\left[X_{t-1} + \sum^{t-2} q(t-1,v)\,K(t,v)\right] - D_G(t-1) \\ & + \phi(\bar{R}_{t-1})\,p(t-1)y(t-1) \end{aligned} \tag{9}$$

$$\begin{aligned} EX(\cdot,t+1) = {} & EM(\cdot,t+1)-p(t)\sum_{a\notin\bar{R}} \phi_a[\bar{y}(t)+y_G(a,t+1) \\ & +\bar{K}(a,t)] - \frac{1}{\hat{u}(t)}[X(t) + \sum^{t-1} q(t,v)\,K(t,v)] \\ & - D_G(t) - \tau(t)p(t)\bar{y}(t) \end{aligned} \tag{10}$$

$$\Phi(\bar{R}) \geq \frac{1}{\bar{l}(t)\alpha(v)}\left\{\frac{X(t)}{p(t)} \cdot \frac{u(t)-1}{\hat{u}(t)}\right\} \quad \text{for all} \quad v \in V_1(t) \tag{11}$$

$$\Phi(\bar{R}) < \frac{1}{\bar{l}(t)\alpha(v)}\left\{\frac{X(t)}{p(t)} \cdot \frac{u(t)-1}{\hat{u}(t)}\right\} \quad \text{for all} \quad v \in V_2(t) \tag{12}$$

$$p(t) = \frac{u(t)b(t)+\pi(t-1)}{\bar{y}(t)[1+\tau(t)]}, \tag{13}$$

where $\Phi(\bar{R}) = \sum_{a \in \bar{R}} \phi_a$ and $\bar{R} = \{a |\ Y(t) < \bar{y}(t) + \bar{K}(a,t) + y_G(a,t+1)\}$.

These conditions allow us to draw up a catalogue of equilibria that is our advice to the government. One way to arrange such a catalogue is to hold $(\bar{y}(t), (\bar{K}(a,t)))$ constant, as we did in the last chapter, and see how the equilibria differ as we allow the various government variables to differ.

First consider what happens when some $y_G(\hat{a}, t+1)$ increases. For some values of $\bar{l}(t)$, $\Phi(\bar{R})$, the probability of no rationing, will increase. For other values of $\bar{l}(t)$, there will be no change in $\Phi(\bar{R})$ either because output is so small at these values of $\bar{l}(t)$ that $\hat{a} \in \bar{R}$ before the increase, or because output is so large at these values of $\bar{l}(t)$ that $\hat{a} \notin \bar{R}$ both before and after the increase. At any rate, Φ will increase for some values of $\bar{l}(t)$ and decrease for none. Nothing will happen to $\Psi(\cdot)$, and so the new equilibrium will have higher employment, or no change.

Let us consider further effects. Higher employment drives down wages by (8). If employment does not change because $\hat{a} \notin \bar{R}$ both before and after, then from (10) the mathematical expectation of $X(\cdot, t+1)$ decreases; this shifts the Ψ curve down in period $t+1$, and increases employment then. If employment in period t does not change because $\hat{a} \notin \bar{R}$ both before and after, there is no effect on $EX(\cdot, t+1)$. If employment increases in period t, $\hat{a}$ switches into $\bar{R}$; thus $EX(\cdot, t+1)$ increases and employment in period $(t+1)$ declines.

When the tax rate $\tau(t)$ increases, $p(t)$ falls by (13). From (11) and (12), $\Psi(\cdot)$ shifts upward, period t employment falls, and wages rise. For period $(t+1)$, however, $EX(\cdot, t+1)$ falls, both directly from the last term in (10), and indirectly, from increased rationing. Thus period $(t+1)$ employment tends to rise. Increased taxes also reduce $D_G(\cdot, t+1)$ by reducing the amount of borrowing the government has to do. This reduction, coupled with the decrease in $EX(\cdot, t+1)$, increases $EX(\cdot, \cdot, t+2)$ and tends to increase period $(t+2)$ employment.

Finally, increasing $M(t)$ increases $X(t)$ and reduces period t employment. It raises $EX(\cdot, t+1)$, however, and $Ep(\cdot, t+1)$, and both of these effects increase period $(t+1)$ employment.

IV

Why does monetary policy (changing $M(t)$) seem to be so pusillanimous in this model? All it can do is decrease period t employment and increase period $(t+1)$ employment; but we have already seen that the model's oscillatory tendencies almost assure that any period t disaster can do as well.

The reason is that we have opted to compare equilibria in which ($\bar{y}(t)$, ($\bar{K}(a, t)$)) are the same. Suppose instead that we compare equilibria in which $w(t)$ are the same. Then (8) determines the level of employment and ($\bar{y}(t)$, ($\bar{K}(a, t)$)) must be found to make (11) and (12) hold. (This problem is easy to solve and has many solutions. The $\Psi(\cdot)$ curve is given. One just has to arrange $\bar{y}(t)$ and (K, (a,t)) so that the Φ curve cuts Ψ just above the $\bar{l}(t)$ from (8).) The higher $X(t)$, the greater the level of employment. Since $X(t)$ still oscillates, employment still oscillates.

From (9), increasing $M(t)$ increases employment in period t, from (10) it decreases employment in period $(t+1)$. Increasing $M(t)$ will also tend to increase period $(t+1)$ prices. Government purchases $\bar{y}_G(a, t+1)$, on the other hand, are impotent in period t, as the Ψ curve is determined by (8) and the Φ curve must accommodate the Ψ curve. To the extent, moreover, that government spending is financed by taxes or debt it decreases employment in subsequent periods. If $a \in \bar{R}$, increasing $y_G(a, t+1)$ decreases employment in period $(t+1)$ more or less directly through (10); otherwise its only effects are through taxes and debt. Increasing taxes decreases prices in period t and employment in period $(t+1)$.

A sticky-wage world thus seems quite different from an animal-spirits world; the gulf between monetarists and fiscalists seems wider than it is usually presented to be. Such a gulf, though, is illusory. The loose language of causality we have been using ("increase," "decrease," "effect") is only metaphorical and should not be taken seriously. It is no ground for giving advice like a physicist ("Increase money supply in order to decrease unemployment").

Remember that ours is an exercise in taxonomy, not causality. We are cataloguing equilibria. Monetarists propose putting all equilibria with the same wages together in the catalogue; fiscalists propose putting all equilibria with the same set of output constraints together. In either event, the contents of the catalogue will be the same.

V

Our advice to altruistic governments, then, is the same as our advice to altruistic individuals (indeed, the same as our advice to avaricious governments and individuals): the catalogue of equilibria. If this catalogue had only one card, our advice would be just like a physicist's, since our card would tell our advisee exactly what commitment to make and exactly what strategy to choose. Even if the catalogue had many equilibria (like macroeconomics) and our advisee arrived at the scene after all the other players had irreversibly made their commitments and chosen their strategies, we could still give unambiguous, physicist-like advice by finding the card in the catalogue that corresponded to what the others had already done.

But when our advisee comes on time and the catalogue has many cards, then the multiplicity of equilibria is as much a source of freedom as it is a source of confusion. For then we and our advisee can attempt to have others commit and act in ways that result in better equilibria for us, just as they attempt to have us commit and act in ways that have better results for them. And so all the players persuade and cajole, argue and convince, hesitate and growl, issue ultimata and retract them, joke and scream, spy and lie, pound on tables and refuse to return telephone calls, laugh and cry, and in general behave like human beings have always behaved, except in economics books. Nothing should be less surprising.

11 ▪ Conclusion

Is fearr críoċ ná gnó.
Irish proverb*

We have said a great deal now about game theory and macroeconomics. Let us see if we can make some sense of it, review what needs to be done, and look at a few of the broader implications of our methods.

I

Our goal has been to incorporate macroeconomics into the tradition of rationality that has been definitory of economics. There was no a priori reason for believing that such incorporation was possible, and only vague analogical reasons for believing it was desirable. Now we know that incorporation is possible, and our suspicions about desirability, if they have not been fully confirmed yet, at least have not yet been shown to be misplaced.

The first part of the book, the game theory part, served two purposes: it explicated the tradition of rationality and what that tradition entails, and it showed why certain approaches that have been taken in the past were incapable of providing the incorporation that we sought.

In chapter 2, for instance, we found that game theory, while firmly within the tradition of rationality, had not been developed sufficiently to be of much help for the problems we were interested in. Cooperative versions of game theory did not permit these problems to exist, while noncooperative versions could generate only autarky. Neither, moreover, recognized the strategic moves—commitments, promises, threats—that Schelling found so important.

Thus we developed the concept of "commitment equilibrium," which we found to correspond to the basic notion of rationality that underlies the tradition in which we intended to work. Essentially, commitment equilib-

* Generally translated, "Economy is better than business," but literally, "End is better than work."

rium extends the idea of Nash equilibrium to encompass strategic moves as well as strategies. At a commitment equilibrium, no player can improve his payoff by changing either his strategy or his strategic moves, given the strategies and strategic moves of the other players.

On the other hand, in chapter 5, we examined the methods that sought to link external events to numerical probabilities in players' heads. Keynes, Poincaré, Borel, and most explicitly, von Neumann and Morgenstern have all questioned the applicability of these methods to games of strategy. We found that Mother Nature's vast indifference and the accompanying secularity axioms allowed these methods to be useful for games against nature, but that their utility did not carry over to games of strategy. In games of strategy, only commitment equilibria can be rational. Expectations—mappings of external events to numerical probabilities—are used in temporary equilibrium models, but temporary equilibrium is not equilibrium; temporary equilibrium permits irrationality.

In the second part of the book, the economics part, we examined some particular commitment equilibria of some particular games. As with any economic investigation, we were especially interested in how our more general view of rationality related to the Walrasian view of rationality. Walrasian equilibria are the commitment equilibria that result when players' commitments are of the pure price variety: that is, when players promise always to supply goods in strict proportion to the amount of money (or other goods) they receive and to supply money in strict proportion to the amount of goods they happen to receive. There are, however, other equilibria that are associated with commitment patterns that are not of the pure price variety, and these equilibria include non-Walrasian phenomena like rationing and unemployment. There is nothing ad hoc, aprioristic, mystical, or unstable about these unemployment equilibria: they are full commitment equilibria just like the Walrasian equilibria are. They are equilibria the same way dual confession is an equilibrium in prisoners' dilemma. Nor do the non-Walrasian equilibria disappear in the face of large numbers of agents. These results contribute to the rehabilitation, begun by Clower (1965) and Leijonhufvud (1968), of Keynes as an economic theorist.

Our chief difference with the users of expectations in economics centers, then, around the relative priority of rationality and prices. Both of us are concerned with the inability of pure price commitment patterns to explain unemployment. Users of expectations react by keeping prices and modifying rationality by accepting temporary equilibria. Our approach is to keep rationality but modify price commitment patterns by accepting quantity constraints.

With this background we went on in chapters 9 and 10 to explore a complex model with banks, government, durable machines, stochastic embodied technological change, and several other features of real life. This model produced equilibria with business cycles, Phillips' curves, and noise—a decent description of reality. Holding output quantity constraints constant, increasing government spending or decreasing taxes increases employment; increasing money supply decreases employment. Holding wages constant, increasing money supply increases employment and prices; increasing government spending does nothing. Whether monetary or fiscal policy is more efficacious in combatting unemployment would then depend on whether wages or quantity constraints should be perceived as constant. Such is the interpretation, at any rate, if one considered the government a vending machine programmed by Martians eons ago.

The correct interpretation, however, is much more subtle. The government must be considered as just another player in the macroeconomic game—altruistic and powerful perhaps, but another player nonetheless. An important finding of chapter 10 is that altruism is such that, for sufficiently well-enforced families of commitment patterns like the one we used there, no explicit social welfare function is required for government, because equilibria are the same no matter what altruistic social welfare function is employed. (This result applies to altruism by individuals as well as altruism by governments.) The macroeconomic game with an altruistic government as a participant has many equilibria, some with full employment, some with unemployment. In each of these the government is doing the best it can, given the commitments and actions of the other players.

The best advice—and the only advice—that economists can give governments—or any other players—is simply a catalogue of commitment equilibria. This catalogue will tell each player how to do as well as possible, given the others' actions and commitments. One way to arrange this catalogue is to act as if quantity constraints were exogenous; another way is to act as if wages were fixed. In this way we can associate, say, equilibria with high unemployment and contractionary monetary policy, and we can outline some necessary conditions for, say, full employment, but there is no foundation for the traditional type of causal language that we started to use above. Causal language may be appropriate in physical systems where secularity holds but it is not appropriate in games.

The multiplicity of commitment equilibria, however, while it makes analysis difficult with a vocabulary developed for Newtonian endeavors, is what makes life interesting and what gives scope to free will. The trick is to cajole others into making commitments and choosing actions that will result in an equilibrium more favorable to one's objectives, be they avaricious or altruistic or both. This applies to both governments and individuals alike, and is another "meta-game-theoretic" reason why the catalogue of equilibria is useful.

II

Of course we have by no means exhausted all questions of macroeconomics and game theory. We looked seriously only at special functions, simple models, and severely restricted families of commitment patterns, and the worlds we considered were wholly imaginary.

The most pressing need, it seems to me, is for an econometric method to flesh out the skeleton of macroeconomic theory. Econometrics has always displayed tremendous ingenuity, and the work of Ito (1980), for instance, on the econometrics of "disequilibrium" (i.e., non-Walrasian) systems, may point to the way to the needed methods.

On a more theoretical level, more general commitment pattern families should be explored, and mixed strategies should receive more attention (a bit of work in this direction is presented in Appendices A and, especially, B).

Probably the most fertile area for theoretical advances is nonconvexity. It is well known that Walrasian rationality may be impossible when either payoff functions or strategy spaces are nonconvex, and Weitzman (1982) has recently argued that involuntary unemployment happens because of nonconvexity. The Nikaido-Isoda theorem, which we cited in chapter 2, leads one to suspect that nonconvexity is responsible for much of the uncertainty and speculation we observe in economic life (if people are not choosing mixed strategies why are their actions so unpredictable?). The Nikaidô-Isoda theorem and nonconvexity may in fact be related in a definite way to the phenomena Keynes was alluding to in chapter 12 of *The General Theory* when he maintained that "there is no such thing as liquidity of investment for the community as a whole" (p. 155).

III

There is no reason why the methods we have used should be confined to macroeconomics. Chapter 8, to be sure, was concerned with microeconomic topics primarily, and in Appendix A we show that the methods yield quite interesting results when applied to questions of crime and the social contract. We concentrated on macroeconomics in this book because of its importance and high degree of controversy. But clearly there are problems in microeconomics that would benefit from a similar treatment.

Indeed we have already seen in chapter 9 how labor union organization and racial discrimination can be easily and illuminatingly portrayed within this framework. In view of the result reported by Arrow (1973) and Freeman (1976) that Walrasian analysis cannot give a convincing explanation or description of discrimination, further work in this area would seem appropriate.

Another area that would seem ripe for application of these methods is housing. Houses are long-lived assets whose value now depends on what people think they will sell for later; thus there is an expectations morass from which conventional analysis cannot escape. In addition, there are nonmarket interactions through neighborhood effects, and a lumpiness problem because houses are typically sold through naked trade commitments, not in bits and pieces. For all these reasons a game-theoretic analysis seems to be the best approach here.

On a more theoretical level, the consideration we have given to strategic moves may shed some light on the questions raised by the Gibbard-Satterthwaite theorem. Gibbard (1973) and Satterthwaite (1975) independently showed that no basically acceptable deterministic social decision mechanism can always elicit true revelation of preferences; and Gibbard (1977, 1978) showed that random dictator and random duple mechanisms have certain distinct advantages over all deterministic mechanisms. Why then don't people use random dictator and random duple mechanisms? There are thousands of state, local, and national governments, and millions of clubs and associations: why do randomization devices play such a small role in their politics, and commitments and promises such a large one? Perhaps further study of strategic moves can lead to an answer to this question.

Unemployment and inflation, race, labor organization, housing, crime, the social contract, politics—these are not trivial matters, and we have seen that they are not matters that can be discussed adequately within a framework of secularity and Walrasian price commitment patterns. The grand tradition of rationality, however, may still be used. Commitment equilibrium shows one way of doing so.

APPENDIXES

A ▪ Hobbes, Cops, Robbers, and Mixed Strategies

Non, mihi si linguae centum sint oraque centum,
Ferrea vox, omnes scelerum comprendere formas,
Omnia poenarum percurrere nomina possim.
VIRGIL, *Aeneid*, book 6

This appendix began in my mind as a discussion of crime. Like Becker's (1968) seminal essay on the economics of crime, it was to have been essentially advice for police departments. Before providing useful advice, though, I had to answer two questions: why isn't everybody a criminal? why are some people criminals? These two questions are ethical, not technological like Becker's theory, and are quite difficult. Answering them, however, is a necessary preliminary to any serious discussion of the economics of crime and the subject of this appendix. We will start by examining the philosophically famous "state of nature."

I

Hobbes (1651, 112–115) first investigated the state of nature:

> Hereby it is manifest, that during the time men live without a common power to keep them all in awe, they are in that condition which is called war; and such a war, as is of every man, against every man. . . .
>
> Whatsoever therefore is consequent to a time of war, where every man is enemy to every man; the same is consequent to the time, wherein men live without other security, than what their own strength, and their own invention shall furnish them withal. In such condition, there is no place for industry; because the fruit thereof is uncertain: and consequently no culture of the earth; no navigation, nor use of the commodities that may be imported by the sea; no commodious building; no instruments of moving, and removing, such things as require much force; no knowledge of the face of the earth; no account

> of time; no arts; no letters; no society; and which is worst of all, continual fear, and danger of violent death; and the life of man, solitary, poor, nasty, brutish, and short. . . .
>
> It is consequent also to the same condition, that there be no propriety, no dominion, no *mine* and *thine* distinct; but only that to be every man's, that he can get; and for so long, as he can keep it.

There is a rich philosophical tradition of describing how society could evolve from the state of nature; Nozick's *Anarchy, State and Utopia* (1974) is the most recent well-known contribution to this tradition. Any such description answers our first question of why not all people are criminals. Obviously, game theory should have much to say about the state of nature, and Schotter (1981, pp. 45–51) has already tried to use cooperative game theory to derive a peaceable society from this state. We saw in chapter 2 that cooperative theory ignores many of the questions we want to address. However, we will use the framework of Schotter's "state-of-nature theft game" for our analysis.

In the state-of-nature theft game, then, there are n players, $i = 1, 2, \ldots n$. At the beginning of the game each player receives M units of manna. If another player attacks him successfully he loses all his manna. If he attacks another player successfully and alone, he receives all that player's manna. Attacking, though, has a psychic cost to him of $c < M$ units of manna. Each player also has an option of preparing—at a cost—a defense against an attack by any other set of players. If an attack is defended against, there is only a 50 percent probability it will succeed. Utility is linear in manna.

To be precise, a strategy for player i is a pair of vectors (A_i, D_i) where

$$A_i = (a_{ij}),\ j = 0, 1, 2, \ldots, i-1, i+1, \ldots, n$$

$$D_i = (d_{ij}),\ j = 1, 2, \ldots, i-1, i+1, \ldots, n$$

with

$$\sum_j a_{ij} = 1.$$

If $a_{ij} = 1$, $j = 1, \ldots, n$, then player i attacks player j; if $a_{io} = 1$, player i attacks no one. Player i is permitted to attack at most one player. Similarly, if $d_{ij} = 1$, $j = 1, \ldots, n$, player i prepares a defense against player j. The cost of attack for player i is

$$c \sum_{j=1}^{n} a_{ij} = (1 - a_{io})\, c,$$

and the cost of defense is

$$\delta(\sum_j d_{ij})$$

where $\delta(\cdot)$ is a real function of the nonnegative integers with

$$\delta(k+1) > \delta(k)$$

$$\delta(k+2) - \delta(k+1) \leq \delta(k+1) - \delta(k)$$

$$\delta(1) > c$$

for any nonnegative integer k. Preparing a defense against more attackers costs at least as much as preparing a defense against fewer, but marginal costs decrease.

Player i's gain from attacking player j depends both on player j's defense strategy D_j and the identities of the other players attacking player j. Let Δ_j denote the set of players against whom player j is defending, and let Ⓗ$_j$ denote the set of players who are attacking player j:

$$\Delta_j = \{k \mid d_{jk} = 1\}$$

$$Ⓗ_j = \{k \mid a_{kj} = 1\}.$$

If $\Delta_j \cap Ⓗ_j = \emptyset$, then the attackers in Ⓗ$_j$ meet no defense and split all of player j's manna among them. Each gains $M/|Ⓗ_j|$. When $\Delta_j \cap Ⓗ_j$ is nonnull, how much each attacking player receives depends on which players attack successfully. If player i is not being defended against, i.e., if $i \in Ⓗ_j - (\Delta_j \cap Ⓗ_j)$, then his expected gain is the expected value of

$$\frac{M}{|Ⓗ_j - (\Delta_j \cap Ⓗ_j)| + |(\Delta_j + Ⓗ_j)_s|}$$

where $|(\Delta_j + Ⓗ_j)_s|$ denotes the number of defended against attackers who succeed in their attack on j. This is a random variable, with

$$\text{Prob}\ \{|(\Delta_j \cap Ⓗ_j)| = l\} = (1/2)^{|\Delta_j \cap Ⓗ_j|} \binom{|\Delta_j \cap Ⓗ_j|}{l} \ ;$$

that is, $|(\Delta_j \cap Ⓗ_j)_s|$ has a binomial distribution with parameter ½. Thus for $i \in Ⓗ_j - (\Delta_j \cap Ⓗ_j)$, the expected gain is

$$M(1/2)^{|\Delta_j \cap Ⓗ_j|} \sum_{l=0}^{|\Delta_j \cap Ⓗ_j|} \frac{\binom{|\Delta_j \cap Ⓗ_j|}{l}}{|Ⓗ_j - (\Delta_j \cap Ⓗ_j)| + l} \ .$$

The expected gain for $i \in (\Delta_j \cap Ⓗ_j)$ is half as great, since there is only half the chance of his attack succeeding (but if successful he needs to consider only the other members of $(\Delta_j \cap \Theta_j)$). Thus we may write the payoff function for the state-of-nature theft game as:

$$f_i(A, D) = M - \{(1 - a_{io})\,c + \delta(\sum_{j=1}^{n} d_{ij})\}$$
$$+ \left\{ M \sum_{\substack{j \notin \Delta_i^{-1} \\ j \in V(A,D)}} (a_{ij}/|\Theta_j|) + M \sum_{\substack{j \notin \Delta_i^{-1} \\ j \notin V(A,D)}} a_{ij}(1/2)^{|\Delta_j \cap \Theta_j|} \times \right.$$
$$\sum_{l=0}^{|\Delta_j \cap \Theta_j|} \frac{\binom{|\Delta_j \cap \Theta_j|}{l}}{|\Theta_j - (\Delta_j \cap \Theta_j)| + l}$$
$$+ M \sum_{j \in \Delta_i^{-1}} a_{ij}(1/2)^{|\Delta_j \cap \Theta_j| + 1} \times$$
$$\left. \sum_{l=0}^{|\Delta_j \cap \Theta_j| - 1} \frac{\binom{|\Delta_j \cap \Theta_j| - 1}{l}}{|\Theta_j - (\Delta_j \cap \Theta_j)| + 1 + l} \right\}$$
$$- M\{1 - \prod_{j \in \Delta_i} (1 - \tfrac{1}{2} a_{ji}) \prod_{j \notin \Delta_i} (1 - a_{ji})\},$$

where

$$V(A, D) = \{j | \Delta_j \cap \Theta_j = \emptyset\} \quad \text{and}$$
$$\Delta_i^{-1} = \{j | d_{ji} = 1\}.$$

The first term in curly brackets is the cost to i of the strategy he adopts, the second term in curly brackets is his expected gain from attacking, and the third is his expected loss from being attacked.

As Hobbes reasoned, all NEs of this game involve general warfare. To see this, note first that a situation is not acceptable to player i if he is defending against a player who is not attacking him. For if $d_{ij} = 1$ and $a_{ji} = 0$, player i can reduce defense costs by setting $d_{ij} = 0$. Hence at all acceptable situations for i: $\Delta_i \subseteq \Theta_i$. Now suppose $\Delta_i \subset \Theta_i$, that is, there is some attacker against whom i is not defending. Then i's loss is total, no matter how many other players he is defending against. Thus if there is one attacker against whom i is not defending, it makes no sense for i to defend against any other attacker, since such defenses are costly but do not reduce his losses. Thus at any acceptable situation for i,

$$\text{Either } \Delta_i = \Theta_i, \quad \text{or}$$
$$\Delta_i = \emptyset.$$

Player i defends against all attackers or none.

Suppose now that at an NE both players j and k are attacking player i. There are $(n-2)$ players other than j and k; since each of these players can attack at most once, these players together can attack at most $(n-2)$ players other than i. But there are $(n-1)$ players other than i in the game. Thus at least one of these players (possibly j or k) is not being attacked. Let $l \neq i$ denote the player not being attacked, and assume $l \neq j$ w.l.o.g., since if $l = j$ we can interchange the names of players k and j. Player j's gain from attacking i is at most $M/2$, since player k is also attacking and i defends against both or neither (if i is defending, player j's gain is $M/4 < M/2$). Since j is not attacking l, $d_{lj} = 0$. Thus if j changes his strategy and attacks l instead of i, he will gain M instead of something not greater than $M/2$. Attacking i is not acceptable to j, and we have contradicted our supposition that we are at an NE.

Thus at an NE $|\textcircled{H}_i| \leq 1$ for all i, and the number of players being attacked is the same as the number of players attacking.

If $M/2 > \delta(1)$, all attacked players are defending against their attackers (and only their attackers) and receiving a final payoff of $M - c - \delta(1)$; if $M/2 < \delta(1)$, none are defending and their payoffs are $M - c$.

Once again, suppose we are at an NE with player i not attacking anyone ($a_{io} = 1$) and player $j \neq i$ not being attacked. Then $d_{ji} = 0$ and player i can improve his payoff by $M - c > 0$ by changing his strategy and attacking j. Thus such situations are not acceptable to i. We cannot have NEs where more than one person is not being attacked, we cannot have NEs where more than one person is not attacking, and we cannot have NEs where the person not attacking is different from the person not being attacked.

Suppose, however, that $M/2 > c$ and player i is neither being attacked nor attacking. Then $d_{ji} = 0$ for any $j \neq i$. Let k be attacking j, and let i contemplate attacking j as well. If $M/2 < \delta(1)$, then j is not defending against k, and attacking j will gain player i $M/2$ at a cost of c. Thus player i is better off attacking j. If $M/2 > \delta(1)$, player j is defending against k and attacking j will gain player i $\frac{3}{4}M > \frac{1}{2}M > c$. So in either case not attacking j is not acceptable to i.

Hence if $M/2 > c$ all players must attack and be attacked at an NE even though all would be better off in a state of peace; if $M/2 < c$, one player may be exempt from the carnage.

II

What peaceable commitment equilibria exist for the state-of-nature theft game? Answering this question is the same as finding out what types of social contract are viable. We will consider four types of commitment pattern in this section.

The first is an absolute renunciation of violence

$$(\forall i)\, g_i^A(\cdot) = f_i(\cdot) \quad \text{if} \quad a_{io} = 0$$
$$= 0 \quad \text{otherwise.}$$

No equilibrium can be associated with this commitment pattern. Player i's possible set with this commitment pattern consists of the situation where no one attacks anyone else ("peace") and the situations where i attacks one other player (with no other players attacking). If $M/2 > \delta(1)$ the attacked player in the latter situations is defending and player i's gain is $M/2 - c > M/2 - \delta(1) > 0$. If $M/2 < \delta(1)$, the attacked player is not defending and player i's gain is $M - c > 0$. In either event, the peaceable situation is never good; in all situations in player i's good set he is the only player attacking. Similarly, in all situations in player j's good set player j is attacking and player i is not. Thus there can be no agreement.

Next, consider the "Hammurabi commitment pattern":

$$(\forall i)\, g_i^H(\cdot) = f_i(\cdot) \quad \text{if } \exists j > 0 \quad \text{with } a_{ij} = 1 \quad \text{and } a_{ji} = 0$$
$$= 0 \quad \text{otherwise.}$$

"I won't attack you if you don't attack me," is what each player promises in this commitment pattern. For certain values of M, c, and $\delta(\cdot)$, peace is an equilibrium with this commitment pattern (thus we can say that for these values the Hammurabi pattern is a possible form of the social contract); otherwise there is no equilibrium.

To see this, consider player i's possible set, and divide it into three subsets. The first subset consists of all possible situations in which $a_{io} = 1$. In all these situations no one is attacking player i—because of the Hammurabi commitment pattern attacking a nonattacker is not acceptable to any player. In the situations in this subset where i's payoff is greatest he will not expend any energies on defense; thus

$$f_i = M \tag{1}$$

in these situations. Note that one of these situations is peace.

The next subset of possible situations is those with $a_{ij} = 1$ for some $j > 0$ and $a_{kj} = 0$ for all $k \neq i$. No $l \neq j$ attacks i in any of these situations since $a_{il} = 0$ and j attacks no $k \neq i$ since $a_{kj} = 0$. First, suppose $M/2 > \delta(1)$. Then j defends against i. Since $M/2 > \delta(1) > c$, j will attack i, even if i defends against j. Since $M/2 > \delta(1)$ the situations in the possible set where

i defends against j are better for i than those where he does not. Thus if $M/2 > \delta(1)$, player i's maximal payoff in this portion of his possible set is

$$f_i = M - c - \delta(1) + M/2 - M/2 = M - c - \delta(1) < M. \quad (2)$$

Next, suppose $c < M/2 < \delta(1)$. Then in the possible set j does not defend against i. Since $M/2 > c$, j will still attack i, even if i defends against him. Since $M/2 < \delta(1)$, the situations where i does not defend are better for him than the situations where he defends. Thus, player i's maximal payoff in this subset, given $c < M/2 < \delta(1)$, is

$$f_i = M - c + M - M = M - c < M. \quad (3)$$

Now suppose $M/2 < c < \delta(1)$. Again j does not defend against i in the possible set. In those situations in the possible set where i defends against j, j does not attack and i's payoff is

$$f_i = M - c - \delta(1) + M = 2M - c - \delta(1) < M \quad (4)$$

since

$$M = 2(M/2) < 2c < c + \delta(1).$$

In those situations where i does not defend, j attacks and i's payoff is

$$f_i = M - c + M - M = M - c < M. \quad (5)$$

From (2), (3), (4), and (5), then, we can see that no matter what the relative values of M, c, and $\delta(\cdot)$ are, the greatest payoff for i in this subset of his possible set is less than M, his greatest payoff in the first subset. Therefore there will be no good situations in the second subset.

The third and final subset of possible situations consists of situations in which $a_{ij} = 1$ and $a_{kj} = 1$ for some $k \neq i$. First, suppose that

$$M/4 > \delta(2) > \delta(1) > c. \quad (6)$$

Then in the possible set j defends against both k and i. Player j may attack either k or i without violating his commitment, and since $M/2 > c$ he will attack one or the other in the possible set, even if they both defend against him. Since $M/2 > \delta(1)$, there are no situations in the possible set where j attacks k and k does not defend (such situations are not acceptable to k). If $d_{ij} = 0$ and j attacks k, then, since k defends, j would be better off attacking i. Hence situations with $a_{jk} = 1$ and $d_{ij} = 0$ are not in the possible set. Then the only possible situations with $d_{ij} = 0$ have $a_{jk} = 0$ and hence $a_{ji} = 1$; so i's payoff is

$$f_i = M - c - M + {}^3\!/\!_8 M = {}^3\!/\!_8 M - c < M.$$

If $d_{ij} = 1$ and $d_{kj} = 1$, then j is indifferent between attacking k and attacking i. Situations where he attacks i, however, are not acceptable to k, since he is defending needlessly. If j attacks k, however, player i's payoff is:

$$f_i = M - c - \delta(1) + {}^3\!/_8\, M = {}^{11}\!/_8\, M - c - \delta(1).$$

This payoff will be larger than M iff

$$ {}^3\!/_8\, M > c + \delta(1) \qquad (7)$$

which is not inconsistent with (6). If

$$\delta(2) > M/4 \quad \text{and} \quad M/2 > \delta(1) > c \qquad (8)$$

then j does not defend. All other considerations remain the same, and player i's payoff in the possible situation where j attacks k is

$$f_i = M - c - \delta(1) + M/2 = {}^3\!/_2\, M - c - \delta(1)$$

which is greater than M iff

$$M/2 > c + \delta(1). \qquad (9)$$

If

$$\delta(1) > M/2, \qquad (10)$$

then $\delta(2) > M/4$ and in the possible set j does not defend. Player j will attack either k or i. Player k will not defend in the possible set, even if j attacks him. Hence attacking k is acceptable to j even if i does not defend. In such situations

$$f_i = M - c + M/2 = {}^3\!/_2\, M - c$$

which is greater than M iff

$$M/2 > c. \qquad (11)$$

Thus player i's good situations will be in the third subset of his possible set if either (6) and (7), or (8) and (9), or (10) and (11); otherwise they will be in the first subset. But if player i's good set is in his third subset, every other player's will be also, since (6)–(11) make no reference to i. Then there will be no equilibrium, because everyone will want to be an unattacked attacker, which is impossible. If, on the other hand, player i's good situations are in the first subset, then every other player's will be too. Each good set will have many members, but for every player the situation of peace will be in the good set. Thus peace will be an equilibrium. It will be in fact the only equilibrium, since in all situations in every player's good set he is not attacking.

Therefore, there will be an equilibrium with the Hammurabi commitment pattern if and only if neither (6) and (7), nor (8) and (9), nor (10) and (11), and the equilibrium situation will be peace.

How restrictive are the requirements of (6)–(11)? Consider a small example. Let $c=1$, $\delta(1)=3$, and $\delta(2)=5$. Then the Hammurabi commitment pattern will have an equilibrium iff $8 \geq M \geq 6$. Private vengeance is not a very effective system.

A more effective variant is the "pariah commitment pattern":

$$(\forall i)\ g_i^P(\cdot) = f_i \quad \text{if} \quad \exists j | a_{ij} = 1 \quad \text{and} \quad a_{jo} = 1$$
$$= 0 \quad \text{otherwise.}$$

Each player promises not to attack peaceable players, but makes no promise for any player who attacks anyone. In many respects this is a meddlesome commitment pattern; however, it will almost always have a peaceable equilibrium.

Once again we will proceed by considering three different subsets of player i's possible set. In the first subset $a_{io} = 1$. In these possible situations no one will attack i, and in the best of these situations i will not defend and so his payoff will be M. One of the possible situations with this payoff is peace.

In the second subset we have $a_{ij} = 1$ and $a_{jo} = 1$. Since $a_{jo} = 1$, $a_{kj} = 0$ for all $k \neq i$, in i's possible set.

If $M/2 > \delta(1)$, player j will defend against player i's attack. Since $M/2 > c$, it will be to player j's advantage to attack i, even if i defends, as long as no other player is attacking i. Since this would contradict our hypothesis of $a_{jo} = 1$ in the possible set, we know that at least one player will be attacking player i. If at least one player is attacking i, i's loss from the attack will be at least $M/2$, even if he defends. Since his gain from attacking j is only $M/2$, and there is a cost to attack, and possibly to defense, player i's payoffs in this subset will all be less than M.

If $\delta(1) > M/2 > c$, then j is not defending. Since $M/2 > c$, still, at least one player will attack i. Whatever defense strategy player i adopts, it cannot reduce his losses, compared with the strategy of no defense at all, by more than $M/2$. Since any defense strategy (other than no defense) costs at least $\delta(1)$, player i's payoffs are greatest when he has no defense. Then his loss will be M, just offsetting his gain, and his payoffs in this subset will always be less than M.

If $\delta(1) > c > M/2$, player j will still not defend. If player i does not defend, he will be attacked by at least one player and his payoff will be

$$f_i = M - c + M - M = M - c < M.$$

If he defends against $q_i \geq 1$ possible attackers (note that for acceptability to j given no other attackers, he must always defend against j), then his payoff cannot exceed

$$2M - c - \delta(q_i) \leq 2M - c - \delta(1) < M.$$

In the third subset of player i's possible set we have $a_{ij} = 1$ and $a_{ji} = 1$. Since both i and j are attacking, other players can attack them without violating their commitments.

First let us consider the situations (if any) in the third subset where neither i nor j defends against any attackers. Then

$$f_i = M - c + \frac{M}{|\Theta_j|} - M < M$$

since $|\Theta_j| \geq 1$.

Next consider the situations (again, if any) where both defend against all attackers. In these situations

$$\begin{aligned} f_i &= M - c + M(1/2)^{|\Theta_j|} \sum_{l=1}^{|\Theta_j|-1} (1/l) \binom{|\Theta_j|-1}{l-1} \\ &\quad - M[1-(1/2)^{|\Theta_i|}] - \delta(|\Theta_i|) \\ &= M - c + M\left\{(1/2)^{|\Theta_j|} \sum_{l=1}^{|\Theta_j|-1} (1/l) \binom{|\Theta_j|-1}{l-1} \right. \\ &\quad \left. + (1/2)^{|\Theta_i|} - 1\right\} - \delta(|\Theta_i|). \end{aligned}$$

Thus f_i is negatively related to both $|\Theta_j|$ and $|\Theta_i|$; hence f_i in these situations can never be greater than f_i when $|\Theta_j| = |\Theta_i| = 1$. But if $|\Theta_j| = |\Theta_i| = 1$, the term in curly brackets vanishes and we have $f_i = M - c - \delta(1) < M$. All these situations, moreover, will be better for i than situations where he defends against a proper nonempty subset of attackers; and there are never any possible situations where j defends against a proper nonempty subset of attackers (for the reasons given in our discussion of NEs). These situations are also clearly better for i than those situations in which j defends and i does not.

Thus the only remaining situations that might be good in the third subset are those where i defends (against all attackers) and j does not. In these situations

$$\begin{aligned} f_i &= M - c - \delta(|\Theta_i|) + M/|\Theta_j| - M[1-(1/2)^{|\Theta_i|}] \\ &= M - c - \delta(|\Theta_i|) + M\{1/|\Theta_j| + (1/2)^{|\Theta_i|} - 1\}. \end{aligned}$$

Since $|\textcircled{H}_i| \geq 1$ throughout the third subset, the expression in curly brackets will be nonpositive (which will make $f_i < M$) unless $|\textcircled{H}_j| = 1$. But suppose $|\textcircled{H}_j| = 1$. For such a situation to be acceptable to j, we need $M/2 < \delta(1)$; otherwise player j would be better off defending against i. But since $|\textcircled{H}_i| \geq 1$,

$$M(1/2)^{|\textcircled{H}_i|} \leq M/2$$

and

$$\delta(|\textcircled{H}_i|) \geq \delta(1);$$

so if $|\textcircled{H}_j| = 1$,

$$M(1/2)^{|\textcircled{H}_i|} < \delta(|\textcircled{H}_i|),$$

and

$$f_i = M - c - \delta(|\textcircled{H}_i|) + M(1/2)^{|\textcircled{H}_i|} < M - c < M.$$

Therefore, there are no good situations in the third subset of i's possible set.

Finally consider the fourth subset of the possible set—the situations where $a_{ij} = 1$ and $a_{jk} = 1$, $k \neq 0, i$. The arguments we used for the third subset will apply with equal force to all those situations in the fourth subset where $|\textcircled{H}_i| \geq 1$; none of them are good. Thus we need only examine situations in this subset where no one is attacking i. In all such situations, there is either some player $l \neq i$ who is not attacking anyone, or some player $l' \neq i$ for whom $|\textcircled{H}_{l'}| \geq 2$.

Suppose $l \neq i$ is not attacking anyone and i is not being attacked. For acceptability to l, we need $d_{il} = 1$ and $M/2 < c < \delta(1)$. Then

$$f_i \leq M - c - \delta(|\Delta_i|) + M \leq 2M - c - \delta(1) < M;$$

so these situations are not good.

Thus we must suppose that every player is attacking, and that at least one player is being attacked at least twice. Suppose, in such a situation, that some $l \neq i$ is not being attacked. Then l is not defending against anyone, and so anyone who attacks will gain M. But those who are involved in a multiple attack are gaining at most $M/2$. Thus situations where some $l \neq i$ is not being attacked are not acceptable to multiple attackers; they are not possible for i. Therefore we must suppose that every $l \neq i$ is being attacked at least once, and precisely one player is being attacked twice.

Even these situations are not possible for i if $M/2 > \delta(1)$. For if so, all players other than i and the player being double-attacked are defending only against the player attacking them. Either of the double-attackers could expect to gain $(3/4)M$ by attacking any singly-attacked player. Since they are gaining at most $M/2$ by attacking the double-attacked player, these situations are not acceptable to the double-attacking players; hence they are not possible for i.

If $M/2 < \delta(1)$, however, such situations are possible. For then no attacked player defends, since

$$M/4 < M/2 < \delta(1) < \delta(2).$$

The double-attackers gain $M/2$ and they would gain no more by attacking a singly attacked player. A singly attacking player gains M, and can only lose by changing his target of attack. Nor can he do any better by attacking i. A double-attacking player can gain $M > M/2$ by attacking i if i does not defend against him, but if i defends against both doubly-attacking players, neither can improve by attacking him. Since included among these possible situations are situations where j is not the double-attacked player, there are then possible situations where i's payoff is

$$f_i = M - c - \delta(2) + M = 2M - c - \delta(2).$$

This is greater than M iff $M > c + \delta(2)$ and possible iff $M/2 < \delta(1)$. Thus this sort of situation is good for i iff

$$2\delta(1) > M > c + \delta(2). \tag{12}$$

If (12) does not hold, then the first subset—where i does not attack—is good for i. Since the situations that are good when (12) holds are not symmetrical with respect to players, none will be good for all players, and there can be no equilibrium with the pariah commitment pattern when (12) holds. But when (12) does not hold, the situation of peace is the only equilibrium with the pariah pattern.

Comparing (12) with (6)–(11), we see that the range of values without an equilibrium is much smaller with the pariah commitment pattern than with the Hammurabi commitment pattern. In fact, if we let $c = 1$, $\delta(1) = 3$, and $\delta(2) = 5$, as we did with the Hammurabi pattern, we see that any value of M will have an equilibrium. In general, linearity of the defense function δ is sufficient to guarantee a peaceable pariah equilibrium.

III

Hobbes suggests that nation-states may be one means to a peaceable solution of the state-of-nature theft game. So does Nozick, who sees such states as an outgrowth of "protective associations." Let us consider, then, a family of commitment patterns that divides players into nation-states.

We call a representative commitment pattern in this family g^N. With each commitment pattern g^N is associated a different partition $\pi(g^N)$ of all players

$$\pi(g^N) = \{A_1, C_1, A_2, C_2, \ldots, A_p, C_p, \ldots, A_{\bar{p}(g^N)}, C_{\bar{p}(g^N)}\}$$

$$\bigcup_{p=1}^{\bar{p}(g^N)} [A_p \cup C_p] = I$$

$$A_p \cap C_q = \emptyset \qquad \forall p, q$$

$$A_p \cap A_q = C_p \cap C_q = \emptyset \qquad \forall p, q,\ p \neq q.$$

We will write $A_p \cup C_p \triangleq N_p$, and refer to N_p as the (set of players who make up the) p-th nation, A_p as the p-th army, and C_p as the p-th citizenry. Thus every commitment pattern in this family is associated with a different partition of players into nations, and within nations, into army and citizenry.

Given any partition $\pi(g^N)$, a "national" commitment pattern is:

$$\text{For } i \in C_p:\quad g_i^N(\cdot) = f_i(\cdot) \qquad \text{if } a_{ij} = 1 \quad \text{for any } j \in N_p \tag{13a}$$

$$\text{or if } a_{ij} = 1 \text{ and } \Sigma_{l \in N_p} \Sigma_{k \in N_q} a_{kl} = 0 \tag{13b}$$

$$\text{for any } q \neq p \text{ or for any } j \in N_q$$

$$= 0 \text{ otherwise.}$$

$$\text{For } i \in A_p,\quad g_i^N(\cdot) = f_i(\cdot) \qquad \text{if } a_{ij} = 1 \text{ and } \Sigma_{k \in N_p} a_{jk} = 0 \text{ for any } j \notin A_p \tag{13c}$$

$$\text{or if } i \notin F_p^A \tag{13d}$$

$$\text{or if } a_{ij} = 1 \text{ and } \Sigma_{k \in (F_p^C \cup F_p^A)} a_{jk} = 0 \text{ for any } j \in A_p \tag{13e}$$

where

$$F_p^C = \{k \in C_p \mid \Sigma_{l \in N_p} a_{kl} = 0\}$$

$$F_p^A = \{k \in A_p \mid a_{kj} = 0 \quad \text{for } j \in F_p^C$$

$$\text{and } a_{kj} = 0 \quad \text{for } j \in A_p \quad \text{if } \Sigma_{l \in F_p^C} a_{jl} = 0\}.$$

In (13a) each civilian promises to refrain from all attacking within his nation p and in (13b) he extends this promise to the nationals of any nation none of whose members are attacking any members of nation p. In (13c) members of the army promise not to attack anyone outside the army who is not attacking anyone in the nation; they promise, in (13d), to be upstanding members of the army, that is, members of F_p^A; and they promise in (13e), not to attack any army member who does not attack upstanding civilians or army members. Upstanding civilians—members of F_p^C—are defined as civilians who do not attack within the nation, and upstanding army members are army members who attack neither upstanding civilians nor army members who do not attack upstanding civilians.

To see what types of national commitment patterns will be associated with peaceable equilibria, we need to examine the good sets of players in both A_p and C_p for some representative nation p.

First, let $i \in C_p$, and consider the subset of i's possible set where $a_{io} = 1$. Clearly the best situations for i in this subset would be situations in which no one attacks i and i defends against no one. But are any such situations acceptable to all other players? Not attacking i is always acceptable for $j \in C_p$. Since $\Sigma_{k \in N_p} a_{ik} = 0$ in this subset, not attacking i is acceptable for $j \in A_p$. If no one else in N_p is attacking anyone in N_q, then not attacking i is acceptable for all $j \in N_q$, for all $q \neq p$. If no one in N_q attacks anyone in N_p, then not attacking anyone in N_q is acceptable for everyone in N_p. Thus there are situations—including the situation of peace—in the first subset of i's possible set, in which he is not attacked and does not defend. At these situations, of course, $f_i = M$.

The next subset of i's possible set that we wish to consider has $a_{ij} = 1$, $j \in N_p$ and relative international peace. By "relative international peace" we mean that nobody in N_p is attacking anyone outside it; hence no one outside is attacking anyone in N_p. Given international peace, $a_{jo} = 1$ for all $j \in C_p$, and thus it will not be acceptable for any member of A_p to attack any member of C_p except i. Members of A_p are not prevented by their commitments from attacking i, but will they? Since all other members of C_p will be upstanding, no members of A_p will attack any of them; since all members of A_p will be upstanding, there will be no intra-army attacking. Thus if $|A_p| \geq 1$ there will be at least one member of A_p attacking i as long as the gain from attacking is greater than c, the cost of attacking.

If $M/2 > \delta(1) > c$, then player j will defend against i's attack so that i's gain from attacking will be $M/2$. Since $M/2 > c$, at least one member of A_p will attack i, and i's loss will be at least $M/2$, even if he defends. Thus i's payoff in this subset will be less than $M - c$.

If $\delta(1) > M/2 > c$, then player j won't defend and i's gain from attack will be M. If player i defends against all those attacking him, he will lose at least $M/2$:

$$\begin{aligned} f_i &\leq M - c + M - M/2 - \delta(|\textcircled{H}_i|) \\ &= M - c + M/2 - \delta(|\textcircled{H}_i|) \leq M - c \end{aligned}$$

since

$$\delta(|\Theta_i|) \geq \delta(1) \geq M/2.$$

If player i does not defend against some player attacking him, his loss will be M, and clearly his payoff will be less than M.

If $\delta(1) > c > M/2$ and player i defends against every member of A_p, none will attack him, and his payoff will be

$$f_i = M - c + M - \delta(|A_p|) \leq 2M - c - \delta(1) < 2M - 2(M/2) = M.$$

If player i does not defend against some player in A_p, that player will attack him and his payoff will surely be less than M. Thus, as long as nation p is at international peace, no situations are better for i than those in which $a_{io} = 1$.

In the third subset of player i's possible set we have $a_{ij} = 1, j \in N_p$ and war between N_p and N_q. By war, we mean that there is some $k \in N_p$ attacking $k' \in N_q$ and $l \in N_q$ attacking $l' \in N_p$. Then anyone in N_q can attack anyone in N_p without violating commitments, and vice versa. Then the $|N_q| + |A_p|$ players in $N_q \cup A_p$ can all attack i; the players in N_q can also attack any other player in N_p; the players in A_p can also attack any other player in N_q. If $|A_p| > |N_q|$, then surely there will be a member of A_p to attack i and the same analysis as the second subset applies. Similarly, if $|N_q| \geq |N_p|$ there will be a member of N_q to attack i.

But if

$$|N_p| - 1 > |N_q| \geq |A_p|, \tag{14}$$

there is a situation in i's possible set where every member of A_p is attacking a member of N_q, and every member of N_q is attacking a member of N_p other than i and j. If $M/2 > \delta(1)$, all players being attacked defend. Then it would be better for any attacker in $A_p \cup N_q$ to switch to attacking i if i is not defending against him. Hence if i defends against all, he is not attacked and his payoff is

$$f_i = M - c - \delta(|A_p| + |N_q|) + \tfrac{1}{2}M$$

which is bigger than M iff

$$M/2 > c + \delta(|A_p| + |N_q|). \tag{15}$$

Note that (15) implies $M/2 > \delta(1)$.

If

$$M/2 < \delta(1) \tag{16}$$

then no attacked player defends. Since i need not defend either: $f_i =$

$2M - c > M$. So the first subset won't be good for i if (14) and either (15) or (16).

For those situations with more complicated international wars the same sort of reasoning holds. If N_p is at war with both N_q and N_r, but N_q and N_r are not at war with each other, $|N_q| + |N_r|$ replaces $|N_q|$ in (14) and (15):

$$|N_p| - 1 > |N_q| + |N_r| \geq |A_p| \tag{14a}$$

$$M/2 > c + \delta(|A_p| + |N_q| + |N_r|). \tag{15a}$$

If N_p is at war with both N_q and N_r and they are at war with each other, we have

$$|N_p| - 1 > \big|\, |N_q| - |N_r| \,\big| \geq |A_p| \tag{14b}$$

$$M/2 > c + \delta(|A_p| + |N_q| + |N_r|). \tag{15b}$$

If $a_{ij} = 1, j \in N_q$, we similarly have

$$|N_p| > |N_q| \tag{14c}$$

and

$$M/2 > c + \delta(|N_q|) \tag{15c}$$

with similar expressions for more complicated wars.

Thus, if $a_{io} = 1$ in the good set for all i, then (14abc) and either (15abc) or (16) cannot hold. Sufficient conditions for this result are:

(CS-1) There is only one nation

(CS-2) There are two nations with equal populations

(CS-3) $c + \delta(\min_{\substack{p,q \\ p \neq q}} (|A_p| + |N_q|)) > M/2 > \delta(1)$.

Now let us consider the good set for $i \in A_p$.

In the subset of i's possible set with $a_{io} = 1$, we have, as usual, the situation of peace, and other situations with $f_i = M$.

Next consider the subset with $a_{ij} = 1, j \in N_p$ and relative international peace. Then in the possible set $C_p = F_p^C$ and $A_p - \{i\} \subseteq F_p^A$; thus $j \in (F_p^C \cup F_p^A)$. Since then

$$\sum_{k \in (F_p^C \cup F_p^A)} a_{ik} = 1,$$

no other member of A_p is prevented by his commitment from attacking i. Nor is there any other player for any other member of A_p to attack. Thus as long as $|A_p| \geq 2$ we will be able to use the same sort of reasoning we used in the second subset of the possible set for $i \in C_p$, and $f_i < M$. If $|A_p| = 1$, of course, there will be no equilibrium: "Quis custodiet ipsos custodes?"

has an answer ("custodes ipsos") but "Quis custodiet ipsum custodem?" does not. A necessary condition for equilibrium to exist is:

$$|A_p| \geq 2 \quad \text{for all} \quad p. \tag{17}$$

Now let $a_{ij} = 1, j \in N_p$, and suppose there is war with N_q. By the same sort of reasoning as before, some of these situations will be good if

$$|N_p| - 1 > |N_q| \geq |A_p| - 1 \tag{14d}$$

and either

$$M/2 > c + \delta(|A_p| + |N_q| - 1) \tag{15d}$$

or

$$M/2 < \delta(1). \tag{16}$$

For simultaneous war with N_q and N_r who are not at war with each other, we have:

$$|N_p| - 1 > |N_q| + |N_r| \geq |A_p| - 1 \tag{14e}$$

$$M/2 > c + \delta(|A_p| + |N_q| + |N_r| - 1), \tag{15e}$$

and when N_q and N_r are at war with each other:

$$|N_p| - 1 > ||N_q| - |N_r|| \geq |A_p| - 1 \tag{14f}$$

and (15e).

When $a_{ij} = 1, j \in N_q$ and war only between N_p and N_q, we have (14c) and (15c), just as with $i \in C_p$.

Thus we see that the three conditions we set forth above for well-behaved good sets for $i \in C_p$ are also sufficient for well-behaved good sets for $i \in A_p$ as well, provided (17). Thus if

$$|A_p| \geq 2 \quad \text{for all} \quad p \tag{17}$$

and either

(S-1) There is only one nation; or
(S-2) There are two nations with equal populations; or
(S-3) $c + \delta(\min_{\substack{p,q \\ p \neq q}} (|A_p| + |N_q|)) > M/2 > \delta(1)$; or
(S-4) $N_p = A_p$ for all p

there will be a peaceable equilibrium with a national commitment pattern. Thus there is a national commitment pattern that will be associated with an equilibrium for every M, c, $\delta(1)$.

Our results, particularly (S-2) and (S-3), are considerably more encouraging to the formation of large numbers of nations, even in the same geographic area, than Hobbes's, Nozick's or Schotter's.

IV

We have seen three types of commitment patterns—Hammurabi, pariah, and national—that are sometimes associated with peaceable equilibria. Thus we have made great progress on our first question: why isn't everybody a criminal? We have made no progress on the second question: why are some people criminals? The peaceable equilibria we have found have no crime whatsoever—a rather poor description of the real world. Is there some way, then, we can modify the commitment patterns to produce equilibria with some crime, but not the war of all against all?

Working in the realm of pure strategies, we have not been able to obtain any encouraging results. The most natural way to introduce crime would seem to be to modify the commitment patterns so that a small number of amoral "rascals" are making no commitments whatsoever. We would hope to find that if the number of rascals is small enough there will be equilibria with some crime but without *bellum omnium contra omnes.* Unfortunately, however, we find that for each of our three original commitment patterns, if there is even one rascal the only equilibrium situation is *bellum omnium contra omnes.*

Consider first the family of "rascal-fied" Hammurabi commitment patterns:

$$\text{For} \quad i \in R \quad g_i^{RH}(\cdot) \equiv 0$$

$$\text{For} \quad i \notin R \quad g_i^{RH}(\cdot) = f_i(\cdot) \quad \text{if } \exists j | a_{ij} = 1 \quad \text{and} \quad a_{ji} = 0$$

$$= 0 \quad \text{otherwise.}$$

Goodness for nonrascals can be dealt with quickly. Symmetry among nonrascals means that no situation where rascals are attacking some but not all nonrascals can be agreed upon. If rascals are attacking all nonrascals, then we have *bellum omnium contra omnes*, which we are attempting to avoid. Thus we need situations with $a_{io} = 1$, for all $i \in \bar{R}$ (the set of nonrascals), and $a_{ji} = 0$, for all $j \in R$, $i \in \bar{R}$. But by our previous discussion of the Hammurabi pattern, we know that such situations will be good for $i \in \bar{R}$ only if $M/2 > \delta(1)$, which we must therefore assume to be the case.

On this basis let us consider goodness for $i \in R$. First consider the subset of i's possible set where $a_{io} = 1$. Then in this subset $a_{ji} = 0$ for $j \in \bar{R}$. If, as is possible, the other $|R| - 1$ members of R are attacking each other, one on one, then there will be no one to attack i. But since $M/2 > \delta(1)$, all players being attacked will defend; hence to avoid attack player i must defend against all other rascals:

$$f_i = \max(0, M - \delta(|R| - 1)). \tag{18}$$

The next subset has $a_{ij} = 1, j \in R$, and $a_{kj} = 0$ for $k \neq i$. Then again $a_{ki} = 0$ for $k \in \bar{R}$. Player j is attacking either R or $\bar{R}$. If j attacking in $\bar{R}$ is good for i, then agreement with $\bar{R}$ and hence equilibrium is impossible. So suppose j attacking in R. Aside from i, there are $|R| - 1$ other players in R. If none attacks i or j and none double attacks, then there are only $|R| - 2$ targets for attack in R. Thus it will be better for i if one of the other rascals attacks in $\bar{R}$; this frees him from counter attack and gives him payoff:

$$f_i = \max(M/2 - c, {}^3\!/\!{}_2 M - c - \delta(|R| - 1))$$

which is always greater than the payoff of nonattack in (18). Thus it will always be good for $i \in R$ for some rascal to attack in $\bar{R}$; agreement with R is impossible, save in *bellum omnium contra omnes*.

Now consider the rascal-fied pariah commitment pattern:

$$\text{For} \quad i \in R \;\; g_i^{RP}(\cdot) \equiv 0$$

$$\begin{aligned}\text{For} \quad i \in \bar{R} \;\; g_i^{RP}(\cdot) &= f_i(\cdot) \quad \text{if } \exists j \,|\, a_{ij} = 1 \quad \text{and } a_{jo} = 1.\\ &= 0 \quad \text{otherwise.}\end{aligned}$$

Since rascals will always attack, it will always be acceptable for some nonrascal to attack a rascal. But then it will be acceptable for any other nonrascal to attack the nonrascal who is attacking a rascal—and so we proceed in domino fashion until all players are attacking. *Bellum omnium contra omnes* is thus the only NE with the rascal-fied pariah commitment pattern.

Finally, consider the rascal-fied national commitment pattern, and for simplicity suppose there is only one nation:

$$\text{For } i \in R \quad g_i^{RN}(\cdot) \equiv 0.$$

$$\begin{aligned}\text{For } i \in C \quad g_i^{RN}(\cdot) &= f_i(\cdot) \qquad \text{if } \exists j \,|\, a_{ij} = 1\\ &= 0 \quad \text{otherwise.}\end{aligned}$$

$$\begin{aligned}\text{For } i \in A \quad g_i^{RN}(\cdot) = f_i(\cdot) \qquad & \text{if } \exists j \,|\, a_{ij} = 1 \quad \text{and } \textstyle\sum_{k \in N} a_{jk} = 0\\ & \text{for } j \notin A\\ & \text{or if } i \notin F^A\\ & \text{or if } \exists j \,|\, a_{ij} = 1 \quad \text{and } \textstyle\sum_{k \in F^c \cup F^A} a_{jk} = 0\\ & \text{for } j \in A,\\ = 0 \quad & \text{otherwise.}\end{aligned}$$

In situations acceptable to the rascals, they will be attacking somebody and hence, in situations acceptable to the army, the army will be attacking the rascals. In situations good for civilians, rascals will be attacking each other or the army, and in particular, since army members will be attacking some rascals, some rascals will attack army members. In situations good for army members, though, no rascals will attack army members—they will attack civilians instead. Thus no agreement is possible.

V

Thus our three commitment patterns for the state-of-nature theft game provide no explanation for the existence of crime in a civilized world. Perhaps there are other commitment patterns that might perform more effectively; this approach, however, does not seem particularly promising. Enriching players' strategy sets by including purely punitive variables that let a player do harm without gaining anything himself and by allowing interplayer payments could be one fruitful alternative; modern criminal justice systems are operated by individuals who are paid to threaten to harm people and derive no benefit from the harming. Or we could create enough economic interdependence to allow enforcement by boycott, as prescribed by the Brehon code. Eliminating symmetry among players might also help.

The most parsimonious approach, though, is simply to allow mixed strategies in the basic state-of-nature theft game. Such an approach will also explain the high degree of randomness that seems apparent in criminal behavior.

Let us illustrate with an example in the two-player state-of-nature theft game. In the two-player game, all three of the pure strategy commitment patterns we studied in detail are identical. To be concrete, let

$$M = 10$$
$$c = 2$$
$$\delta(1) = 3$$

and let each player $i = 1, 2$ have four pure strategies:

1. Attack the other player and defend against him.
2. Don't attack, but defend.
3. Attack but don't defend.
4. Don't attack and don't defend.

A mixed strategy for player 1 will be a probability vector (x_j), $j = 1, \ldots, 4$

$$\sum_{j=1}^{4} x_j = 1$$

$$x_j \geq 0,$$

where x_j represents the probability that player 1 will choose strategy j. Similarly, (y_j) will represent a mixed strategy for player 2.

The pure strategy payoff bi-matrix for this game is

		Player 2			
		1	2	3	4
Player 1	1	5, 5	2, 10	3, 10	0, 15
	2	10, 2	7, 7	13, 2	10, 7
	3	10, 3	2, 13	8, 8	0, 18
	4	15, 0	8, 10	18, 0	10, 10

and thus the payoff functions are

$$\begin{aligned} f_1(x,y) = {} & 5x_1y_1 + 10x_1y_2 + 10x_1y_3 + 15x_1y_4 \\ & + 2x_2y_1 + 7x_2y_2 + 2x_2y_3 + 7x_2y_4 \\ & + 3x_3y_1 + 13x_3y_2 + 8x_3y_3 + 18x_3y_4 \\ & \qquad + 10x_4y_2 \qquad\qquad + 10x_4y_4 \end{aligned}$$

$$\begin{aligned} f_2(x,y) = {} & 5x_1y_1 + 2x_1y_2 + 3x_1y_3 \\ & + 10x_2y_1 + 7x_2y_2 + 13x_2y_3 + 10x_2y_4 \\ & + 10x_3y_1 + 2x_3y_2 + 8x_3y_3 \\ & + 15x_4y_1 + 8x_4y_2 + 18x_4y_3 + 10x_4y_4 \\ = {} & 5x_1y_1 + 2x_1y_2 + 3x_1y_3 \\ & \qquad - 3x_2y_2 + 3x_3y_3 + 10x_2 \\ & + 10x_3y_1 + 2x_3y_2 + 8x_3y_3 \\ & + 5x_4y_1 - 2x_4y_2 + 8x_4y_3 + 10x_4, \end{aligned}$$

where use has been made of the equality

$$y_4 = 1 - \sum_{j=1}^{3} y_j.$$

Consider the following family of commitment patterns:

$$\begin{aligned} g_1(x,y) &= f_1(x,y) \quad \text{if} \quad x_1 + x_3 > \alpha \quad \text{and} \quad y_1 + y_3 \le \beta \\ &= 0 \quad \text{otherwise} \end{aligned}$$

$$\begin{aligned} g_2(x,y) &= f_2(x,y) \quad \text{if} \quad y_1 + y_3 > \beta \quad \text{and} \quad x_1 + x_3 \le \alpha \\ &= 0 \quad \text{otherwise,} \end{aligned}$$

where α, $\beta < .5$. This commitment pattern is like the naked trade pattern, except that the subjects of the promises are probabilities of attack, not quantities of goods. We will show that there is a civilized but not crime-free equilibrium with this commitment pattern.

First we will need to find the situations that are acceptable to player 1. In doing so, we will need to consider the partial derivatives of player 1's payoff with respect to his strategies, and denote them specially:

$$\begin{aligned} \partial f_1/\partial x_1 &= 5y_1 + 10y_2 + 10y_3 + 15y_4 \\ &= 5y_1 + 10(y_2 + y_3) + 15(1 - y_1 - y_2 - y_3) \\ &= 15 - 10y_1 - 5(y_2 + y_3) \triangleq Q_1(y) \end{aligned}$$

$$\begin{aligned} \partial f_1/\partial x_2 &= 2y_1 + 7y_2 + 2y_3 + 7(1 - y_1 - y_2 - y_3) \\ &= 7 - 5(y_1 + y_3) \triangleq Q_2(y) \end{aligned}$$

$$\begin{aligned} \partial f_1/\partial x_3 &= 3y_1 + 13y_2 + 8y_3 + 18(1 - y_1 - y_2 - y_3) \\ &= 18 - 15y_1 - 5y_2 - 10y_3 \triangleq Q_3(y) \end{aligned}$$

$$\partial f_1/\partial x_4 = 10y_2 + 10 - 10y_4 = 10(y_1 + y_3) \triangleq Q_4(y).$$

It is easy to see that $Q_j(y) > 0$ for any $j \neq 4$ and $Q_4(y) \ge 0$.

$$\begin{aligned} Q_1(y) - Q_2(y) &= 15 - 10y_1 - 5(y_2 + y_3) - 7 + 5(y_1 + y_3) \\ &= 8 - 5y_1 - 5y_2 + 5y_3 > 0 \end{aligned}$$

$$\begin{aligned} Q_1(y) - Q_4(y) &= 15 - 10y_1 - 5(y_2 + y_3) - 10 + 10(y_1 + y_3) \\ &= 5 - 5y_2 + 5y_3 \ge 0 \end{aligned}$$

$$\begin{aligned} Q_3(y) - Q_2(y) &= 18 - 15y_1 - 5y_2 - 10y_3 - 7 + 5(y_1 + y_3) \\ &= 11 - 10y_1 - 5y_2 - 5y_3 > 0 \end{aligned}$$

$$\begin{aligned} Q_3(y) - Q_4(y) &= 18 - 15y_1 - 5y_2 - 10y_3 - 10 + 10(y_1 + y_3) \\ &= 8 - 5y_1 - 5y_2 > 0. \end{aligned}$$

Thus

$$\begin{aligned} &Q_1(y) > Q_2(y) \\ &Q_1(y) \ge Q_4(y) \end{aligned}$$

$$Q_3(y) > Q_2(y)$$
$$Q_3(y) > Q_4(y)$$

always.

There are two major parts to player 1's acceptable set, and the first part has several subparts:

Case 1. If $y_1 + y_3 > \beta$, then clearly $x_2 = x_4 = 0$ in acceptable situations for player 1.

Case 1a. If $Q_1(y) > Q_3(y)$, then $x_1 = 1$, $x_3 = 0$.

In this subcase we have:

$$\begin{aligned} Q_1(y) = 15 - 10y_1 - 5(y_2 + y_3) > Q_3(y) &= 18 - 15y_1 - 5y_2 - 10y_3 \\ 5y_1 - 5y_3 &> 3 \\ y_1 - y_3 &> .6. \end{aligned}$$

Case 1b. If $y_1 - y_3 = .6$, then $Q_1(y) = Q_3(y)$ and $x_1 + x_3 = 1$ in player 1's acceptable set.

Case 1c. If $y_1 - y_3 < .6$, then $Q_1(y) < Q_3(y)$ and $x_1 = 0$, $x_3 = 1$.

Case 2. If $y_1 + y_3 \leq \beta$, then no situation with $x_1 + x_3 > \alpha$ will be acceptable to player 1. Acceptable situations are those that include solutions to

$$\max_x f_1(x, y)$$

$$\text{s.t.} \quad \sum x_j = 1$$

$$x_1 + x_3 \leq \alpha.$$

First-order conditions include

$$\partial\mathcal{L}/\partial x_1 = Q_1(y) + \lambda_1 + \lambda_2 \leq 0$$

$$\partial\mathcal{L}/\partial x_2 = Q_2(y) + \lambda_1 \leq 0$$

$$\partial\mathcal{L}/\partial x_3 = Q_3(y) + \lambda_1 + \lambda_2 \leq 0$$

$$\partial\mathcal{L}/\partial x_4 = Q_4(y) + \lambda_1 \leq 0$$

where λ_1 refers to the first constraint and λ_2 to the second. Since for all y, $Q_1(y)$ and $Q_3(y)$ are greater than $Q_2(y)$ and $Q_4(y)$, λ_2 will always be negative and hence:

$$x_1 + x_3 = \alpha.$$

Now suppose $Q_2(y) \geq Q_4(y)$. Then

$$7-5(y_1+y_3) \geq 10-10(y_1+y_3)$$
$$y_1+y_3 \geq .6.$$

But

$$y_1+y_3 \leq \beta < .5$$

in this case. So we need $Q_2(y) < Q_4(y)$.

Similarly suppose $Q_1(y) \geq Q_3(y)$. Then $y_1 - y_3 \geq .6$. But $y_3 \geq 0$ implies $y_1 \geq .6$, which also contradicts the hypothesis of this case.

Then we must have $Q_2(y) < Q_4(y)$ and $Q_1(y) < Q_3(y)$.
Thus acceptable situations for player 1 will have

$$x_3 = \alpha,\ x_4 = 1-\alpha,\ x_1 = x_2 = 0.$$

Now let us find what situations are good for player 2. Player 2's possible set is player 1's acceptable set; thus good situations for player 2 are merely those situations in player 1's acceptable set where player 2's payoff is greatest.

In *case 1-a* of player 1's possible set, $x_1 = 1$, $x_2 = x_3 = x_4 = 0$, $y_1 + y_3 > \beta$, $y_1 - y_3 > .6$ and player 2's payoff is $f_2(x,y) = 5y_1 + 2y_2 + 3y_3$. This payoff is greatest when $y_1 = 1$, and its value then is 5.

For *case 1-b* we have $x_1 + x_3 = 1$, $y_1 + y_3 \geq \beta$, $y_1 - y_3 = .6$ and $x_2 = x_4 = 0$. The payoff to player 2 is

$$\begin{aligned} f_2(x,y) &= 5x_1y_1 + 2x_1y_2 + 3x_1y_3 + 10x_3y_1 + 2x_3y_2 + 8x_3y_3 \\ &= 5x_1y_1 + 2x_1y_2 + 3x_1(y_1 - .6) + 10(1-x_1)y_1 \\ &\quad + 2(1-x_1)y_2 + 8(1-x_1)(y_1 - .6) \\ &= -4.8 - 10x_1y_1 + 3x_1 + 18y_1 + 2y_2, \end{aligned}$$

and so player 2's greatest payoff is at the situation $y_1 = .6$, $y_2 = .4$, $x_3 = 1$, $x_1 = y_3 = 0$, and its value is 6.8.

For *case 1-c*, we have $x_3 = 1$, $y_1 + y_3 \geq \beta$, $y_1 - y_3 < .6$ and $x_1 = x_2 = x_4 = 0$. Player 2's payoff in these situations is always less than his payoff in the best situation of case 1-b; it approaches that value as y_1 approaches .6.

Finally, for *case 2*, we have $y_1 + y_3 \leq \beta$, $x_3 = \alpha$, $x_4 = 1 - \alpha$, $x_1 = x_2 = 0$. So player 2's payoff in these situations is:

$$\begin{aligned} f_2(x,y) &= 10\alpha y_1 + 2\alpha y_2 + 8\alpha y_3 \\ &\quad + 5(1-\alpha)y_1 - 2(1-\alpha)y_2 + 8(1-\alpha)y_3 + 10(1-\alpha) \\ &= 10(1-\alpha) + 5y_1(1+\alpha) + 2y_2(2\alpha - 1) + 8y_3. \end{aligned}$$

Since $\alpha < .6$, y_3 has a greater coefficient than either y_1, or y_2. Hence

$y_3 = \beta$, $y_1 = 0$ in the best situations for player 2 in this part of player 1's acceptable set. Since $\alpha < .5$, the coefficient of y_2 is negative: $y_2 = 0$, and so $y_4 = 1 - \beta$. Player 2's payoff is

$$10(1-\alpha)+4.8 > 6.8 \quad \text{if } \alpha < .8$$

and so the situation

$$x_3 = \alpha,\ x_4 = 1-\alpha,\ y_3 = \beta,\ y_4 = 1-\beta,\ x_1 = x_2 = y_1 = y_2 = 0$$

is good for player 2 as long as $\alpha < .5$.

By similar reasoning, this same situation is good for player 1 as long as $\beta < .5$. Thus we have found a set of equilibria, one associated with every pair (α, β), $\alpha, \beta < .5$. One of these equilibria ($\alpha = \beta = 0$) is associated with complete peace, and in none is there all out war. Since α need not equal β, there is no requirement for symmetry: one player can be a criminal and the other a saint. Neither wastes resources defending, the probability of no attack at all is always at least .25, and the expected number of attacks is always less than 1.5.

Crime picks random targets at random times, and criminals may have backgrounds no different from those of law-abiding citizens. But when there is agreement on commitment pattern parameters, we will see stable statistical relationships.

The mixed strategy theft game, then, can answer both of our basic questions about crime, and should be the starting point for more detailed analyses.

B ▪ Games Without Free Disposal

"Man proposes but God disposes."
THOMAS À KEMPIS

Our theorems about commitment equilibrium have all rested on the axiom of "free disposal of utility"—that one can always make oneself thoroughly miserable and hence that any commitment pattern $g \leq f$ is always worthy of consideration. In this appendix we will show that eliminating this axiom causes only minor perturbations in the theory of commitment equilibria.

I

Let us assume that for each player i only those commitments in an arbitrary set H_i are feasible. We will require that H_i include the null commitment if it includes no other, but if it includes at least one other commitment it need not even include the null commitment. We denote by $\langle I, S, f, H\rangle^{**}$ the game with this arbitrarily restricted set of strategic moves; note that if H_i is the only null commitment for all i

$$\langle I, S, f, H\rangle^{**} = \langle I, S, f\rangle$$

and if H_i is all commitments $g \leq f$

$$\langle I, S, f, H\rangle^{**} = \langle I, S, f\rangle^{*}.$$

Thus we are dealing with a generalization that encompasses both games without strategic moves and games with unrestricted strategic moves.

For each $s \in S$ and $i \in I$ denote by $O(i, s, H_i)$ the set of allowable commitments that will make s acceptable to i:

$$O(i, s, H_i) = \{g_i \in H_i | (f_i - g_i)(s) \geq (f_i - g_i)(s_{-i}, \hat{s}_i), \quad \forall \hat{s}_i \in S_i\}.$$

Let $g^*_{si}(\cdot)$ denote a commitment in $O(i, s, H_i)$ that maximizes player i's net payoff at s:

$$(f_i - g^*_{si})(s) \geq (f_i - g_i)(s) \quad \text{for all } g_i \in O(i, s, H_i)$$

and let $f_i^*(s)$ denote that maximal net payoff if $O(i, s, H_i)$ is nonempty

$$f_i^*(s) = (f_i - g_{si}^*)(s)$$

while, if $O(i, s, H_i)$ is empty, let $f_i^*(s) = -1$. Let $G(i,s)$ be the set of all $g_{si}^*(\cdot)$'s. It turns out that the modified payoff function f^* will play a role very similar to that played by f in free-disposal games. This similarity will allow us to show that all free-disposal equilibria with feasible commitment patterns are also equilibria in restricted games.

We proceed by a series of lemmas, several of which mimic and generalize our free-disposal results.

First, though, we need to generalize our definition of commitment equilibrium in the obvious way:

(g, s) is a commitment equilibrium iff

(a) $g_i \in H_i$ for all i
(b) $s \in N(g)$
(c) (g, s) is not beaten by any (g', s') where $g_i' \in H_i$ for all i.

Lemma B-1. If (g, s) is an equilibrium, then $g_i \in O(i, s, H_i)$ for all i.

Proof. Suppose $g_i \notin O(i, s, H_i)$ for some i. Then either $g_i \notin H_i$ or $s \notin A(i, g)$. If $g_i \notin H_i$, then by (a) in the generalized definition, (g, s) is not an equilibrium. If $s \notin A(i, g)$, then $s \notin N(g)$ and by (b) in the generalized definition, (g, s) is not an equilibrium. ■

Lemma B-2. If (g, s) is an equilibrium, then $g_i \in G(i, s)$ for all i.

Proof. Suppose $g_i \notin G(i, s)$ for some i. Then since by Lemma B-1, $g_i \in O(i, s, H_i)$, there is a $g_{si}^* \in O(i, s, H_i)$ with

$$(f_i - g_{si}^*)(s) > (f_i - g_i)(s). \tag{1}$$

Consider the commitment pattern $\hat{g}$ given by

$$\hat{g}_j = g_j$$

$$\hat{g}_i = g_{si}^*.$$

For $j \neq i$, $A(j, \hat{g}) = A(j, g)$ and since by definition of an equilibrium $s \in A(j, g)$, $s \in A(j, \hat{g})$. By definition of $O(\cdot)$, $s \in A(i, \hat{g})$. Hence $s \in N(\hat{g})$ and from (1)

$$(f_i - \hat{g}_i)(s) > (f_i - g_i)(s).$$

Thus $(\hat{g}, s)$ beats (g, s) through i. Since $\hat{g}_i \in H_i$ (from definition of $O(\cdot)$) and $\hat{g}_j \in H_j$ for all $j \neq i$, (g, s) is not an equilibrium. ■

Corollary (Minimum Real Suffering). If (g, s) is a commitment equilibrium,

$$(f - g)(s) = f^*(s).$$

Lemma B-3. (Possible Points). Let $(f_i - g_i)(s) = f_i^*(s)$. Then (g, s) is beaten through i iff there is an $s' \in P(i, g)$ such that $f_i^*(s') > f_i^*(s)$.

Proof. Sufficiency. Suppose $f_i^*(s') > f_i^*(s)$ for some $s' \in P(i, g)$. Construct g' in the following manner:

$$g_j' = g_j \quad \text{for } j \neq i$$
$$g_i' = g^*_{s'i}.$$

Since $s' \in P(i, g)$ and $A(j, g) = A(j, g')$ for $j \neq i$, $s' \in A(j, g')$ for all $j \neq i$. Since by definition $g_i' = g^*_{s'i} \in O(i, s', H_i)$, $s' \in A(i, g')$. Thus $s' \in N(g')$. But

$$(f_i - g^*_{s'i})(s') = (f_i - g_i')(s') = f_i^*(s') > f_i^*(s) = (f_i - g_i)(s)$$

and so (g, s) is beaten through i by (g', s').

Necessity. Suppose $(\hat{g}, \hat{s})$ beats (g, s) through i. Either $\hat{s} \in P(i, g)$ or not. Suppose not. Then for some j $\hat{s} \notin A(j, g)$. Beating through i requires $A(j, g) = A(j, \hat{g})$. Thus $\hat{s} \notin N(\hat{g})$ which is a contradiction. Thus $\hat{s} \in P(i, g)$. Since $\hat{s} \in N(\hat{g})$ by the hypothesis of beating, $\hat{s} \in A(i, \hat{g})$ and thus

$$\hat{g}_i \in O(i, \hat{s}, H_i).$$

If $f_i^*(s) \geq f_i^*(s')$ for all $s' \in P(i, g)$

$$(f_i - \hat{g}_i)(\hat{s}) \leq f_i^*(\hat{s}) \leq f_i^*(s) = (f_i - g_i)(s)$$

which means that $(\hat{g}, \hat{s})$ does not beat (g, s). Thus (g, s) is beaten through i only if there is an $s' \in P(i, g)$ with

$$f_i^*(s') > f_i(s).$$

■

Define "extended goodness" as the analogue of free-disposal goodness, but with comparisons using f^* instead of f:

$$B^*(i, g) = \{s \in P(i, g) | (\forall s' \in P(i, g)) f_i^*(s) \geq f_i^*(s')\}.$$

Then we have an extended goodness result:

Lemma B-4. (Goodness). (g, s) is an equilibrium iff $s \in \bigcap_i B^*(i, g)$.

Proof. Sufficiency. Suppose $s \in \bigcap_i B^*(i, g)$. Then

$$s \in \bigcap_i P(i,g) = \bigcap_i \bigcap_{j\neq i} A(j,g) = \bigcap_i A(i,g) = N(g)$$

and by Lemma B-3, (g, s) is not beaten.

Necessity. Suppose that for some i, $s \notin B^*(i,g)$. Then either $s \notin P(i,g)$ or $s \in P(i,g)$. If $s \notin P(i,g)$, then there is some $j \neq i$ with $s \notin A(j,g)$ and thus $s \notin N(g)$ and (g,s) is not an equilibrium. If $s \in P(i,g)$, then there is some $s' \in P(i,g)$ with $f_i^*(s') > f_i^*(s)$; hence by Lemma B-3 (g,s) is beaten through i and is not an equilibrium. ■

Theorem B-1. (Extension). If (g,s) is an equilibrium of $\langle I, S, f\rangle^*$ and $g_i \in H_i$ for all i, then (g,s) is an equilibrium of $\langle I, S, f, H\rangle^{**}$.

Proof. Since (g,s) is an equilibrium of $\langle I, S, f\rangle^*$,

$$g(s) = 0 \tag{2}$$

by the No Real Suffering Theorem. Moreover, $s \in N(g)$ and hence $s \in A(i,g)$ for all i. Since $g_i \in H_i$ for all i by hypothesis, this means that $g_i \in O(i, s, H_i)$ for all i. From (2), then,

$$f(s) = f^*(s).$$

Thus for all i and all $s' \in P(i,g)$

$$f_i^*(s) = f_i(s) \geq f_i(s') \geq f_i^*(s')$$

where the first inequality follows from goodness in $\langle I, S, f\rangle^*$ and the second from the nonnegativity of commitments. Thus $s \in B^*(i,g)$ for all i and by Lemma B-4, (g,s) is an equilibrium of $\langle I, S, f, H\rangle^{**}$. ■

In general, the converse of the Extension Theorem is not true because we have no means of preserving under f^* the ordering of situations under f. This is because we have placed no limits whatsoever on the commitment restrictions H. When we limit H to one of two broad classes—and I can think of no plausible type of H that does not fall into these two classes—we can achieve considerably stronger results.

II

Therefore let us consider as the first class those commitment restrictions without "situation-interdependence." By this we mean that each $g_i(s)$ is restricted to lie in a set $H_i(s)$ no matter what values the other parts of the player's commitment take. We assume without loss of generality that every $H_i(s)$ includes zero—otherwise the payoff function could be reduced by the amount of the smallest feasible commitment—and, to facilitate argument, that it includes some maximum value $h_i(s)$.

Restrictions without situation-interdependence lead to particularly tractable forms for g^* and f^*. To be specific suppose that $O(i, s, H_i)$ is nonempty and contains some feasible commitment g_i. If $g_i(s) \neq 0$, consider $\hat{g}_i(\cdot)$ where

$$\hat{g}_i(s) = 0$$

$$\hat{g}_i(s') = g_i(s')$$

for $s' \neq s$. Since $s \in A(i, g)$, clearly $s \in A(i, \hat{g})$ and since $\hat{g}_i \in H_i$, $\hat{g}_i \in O(i, s, H_i)$. Thus $g^*_{is}(s) = 0$ and $f_i^*(s) = f_i(s)$ if $O(i, s, H_i)$ is nonempty.

How can we tell whether $O(i, s, H_i)$ is nonempty? It will be nonempty if there is no feasible commitment that will make s acceptable to i, and there will be no such commitment unless the commitment where we subtract as much as possible from each situation $(\hat{s}_i, s_{-i})$, $\hat{s}_i \neq s_i$, and as little as possible from s makes s acceptable. If this commitment does not "do the trick," no feasible commitment will. Thus $O(i, s, H_i)$ will be nonempty iff:

$$f_i(s) \geq (f_i - h_i)(\hat{s}_i, s_{-i}) \qquad \text{for all } \hat{s}_i \in S_i.$$

We denote by $R(i, H_i)$ the set of situations where this inequality holds for i (they are "reachable") and by $R(H)$ the situations that are reachable by all players:

$$R(H) = \bigcap_i R(i, H_i).$$

We can then summarize the f^* matrix:

$$\begin{aligned} f_i^*(s) &= f_i(s) \quad \text{if} \quad s \in R(i, H_i) \\ &= -1 \quad \text{otherwise.} \end{aligned} \tag{3}$$

Thus we have:

Lemma B-5. If (g, s) is an equilibrium of the game $\langle I, S, f, H\rangle^{**}$ where H is not situation-interdependent, then $s \in R(H)$.

Proof. Suppose $s \notin R(i, H_i)$ for some i. Then for every feasible g, $s \notin A(i, g)$. Then $s \notin N(g)$ and so (g, s) is not an equilibrium. ■

Lemma B-6. (No Real Suffering). If (g, s) is an equilibrium of the game $\langle I, S, f, H\rangle^{**}$ where H is not situation-interdependent, then

$$g(s) = 0.$$

Proof. From the Minimum Real Suffering Corollary to Lemma B-2, $f(s) - g(s) = f^*(s)$. From (3) and Lemma B-5, $f^*(s) = f(s)$. Hence $g(s) = 0$. ■

Theorem B-2. (Individual Rationality). If (g,s) is an equilibrium of the game $\langle I, S, f, H\rangle^{**}$ where H is not situation-interdependent, then

$$f_i(s) \geq \max_{\hat{s}_i \in S_i} \min_{\hat{s}_{-i} \in S_{-i}} f_i(\hat{s}_i, \hat{s}_{-i}) \qquad \text{for all } i.$$

Proof. By arguments identical to those in chapter 5, but using Lemma B-3 instead of Theorem 2, we obtain

$$f_i^*(s) \geq \max_{\hat{s}_i \in S_i} \min_{\hat{s}_{-i} \in S_{-i}} f_i^*(\hat{s}_i, \hat{s}_{-i}). \tag{4}$$

Now consider the situation (or situations) s^* which we define as:

$$s^* = (s_i^*, s_{-i}^*) = \arg \max_{\hat{s}_i \in S_i} \min_{\hat{s}_{-i} \in S_{-i}} f_i(\hat{s}_i, \hat{s}_{-i}).$$

By definition of a maximum

$$f_i(s^*) \geq f_i(\hat{s}_i, s_{-i}^*) \qquad \text{for all} \quad \hat{s}_i \in S_i$$

and hence $s^* \in A(i,0)$. Since $0 \in H_i$, $s^* \in R(i, H)$. From (3), then

$$f_i^*(s^*) = f_i(s^*)$$

or

$$\max_{\hat{s}_i \in S_i} \min_{\hat{s}_{-i} \in S_{-i}} f_i^*(\hat{s}_i, \hat{s}_{-i}) = \max_{\hat{s}_i \in S_i} \min_{\hat{s}_{-i} \in S_{-i}} f_i(\hat{s}_i, \hat{s}_{-i}).$$

and from Lemma B-6

$$f_i^*(s) = f_i(s).$$

Substituting in (4), we have

$$f_i(s) \geq \max_{\hat{s}_i \in S_i} \min_{\hat{s}_{-i} \in S_{-i}} f_i(\hat{s}_i, \hat{s}_{-i}).$$

■

Theorem B-3. (Extension—Partial Converse). Let H lack situation-interdependence, let (g, s) be an equilibrium of $\langle I, S, f, H\rangle^{**}$, and let $\bar{R}(i, H_i) = S - R(i, H_i)$ for all i. If for all i there is no $s' \in [\bar{R}(i, H_i) \cap P(i, g)]$ for which

$$f_i(s') > f_i(s)$$

then (g, s) is an equilibrium of $\langle I, S, f\rangle^*$.

Proof. From (3),

$$\begin{aligned} B^*(i,g) &= \{\hat{s} \in P(i,g) \mid f_i^*(\hat{s}) \geq f_i^*(\tilde{s}) \quad \text{for all} \quad \tilde{s} \in P(i,g)\} \\ &= \{\hat{s} \in [P(i,g) \cap R(i, H_i)] \mid f_i(\hat{s}) \geq f_i(\tilde{s}) \\ &\qquad \text{for all} \quad \tilde{s} \in [P(i,g) \cap R(i, H_i)]\}. \end{aligned}$$

By definition

$$B(i,g) = \{\hat{s} \in P(i,g) \mid f_i(\hat{s}) \geq f_i(\tilde{s}) \quad \text{for all} \quad \tilde{s} \in P(i,g)\}.$$

Thus $B(i,g)$ will differ from $B^*(i,g)$ iff there is an $\tilde{s} \in [P(i,g) \cap \bar{R}(i,H_i)]$ which provides a greater payoff to i than any situation in $B^*(i,g)$. Since (g,s) is an equilibrium of $\langle I, S, f, H\rangle^{**}$, $s \in B^*(i,g)$ for all i. By hypothesis, then, there is no $\tilde{s} \in [P(i,g) \cap \bar{R}(i, H_i)]$ which provides a greater payoff to i than any situation in $B^*(i,g)$. Thus for all i, $B^*(i,g) = B(i,g)$. Since $s \in \bigcap_i B^*(i,g)$, $s \in \bigcap_i B(i,g)$, and by goodness (g,s) is an equilibrium of $\langle I, S, f\rangle^*$. ■

Corollary. If $R(H) = S$ and (g,s) is an equilibrium of $\langle I, S, f, H\rangle^{**}$, then (g,s) is an equilibrium of $\langle I, S, f\rangle^*$.

III

It is difficult to think of plausible situation-interdependent ways to restrain commitments. The only common situation-interdependent constraint, as far as we know, is that which arises in mixed strategy games when commitments can be made only in pure strategies. The commitment on every mixed strategy situation, then, is constrained to be exactly a weighted average of the commitments on pure strategies. Rather strong results can be achieved for games of this type.

We will need some different notation. Let $\langle I, S, f\rangle$ denote a pure strategy game. Its mixed strategy extension is $\langle I, P, F\rangle$ where

$$P_i = \{p_i = (p_i(s_i^1), p_i(s_i^2), \ldots, p_i(s_i^{m_i})) \mid p_i(s_i^k) \geq 0$$
$$\text{for all } k \quad \text{and } \textstyle\sum_{k=1}^{mi} p_i(s_i^k) = 1\}$$

$$m_i = |S_i|$$

$$P = \mathop{\mathsf{X}}_{i=1}^{n} P_i$$

$$p \in P$$

$$F_i(p) = \sum_{s \in S} \left[\prod_{j=1}^{n} p_j(s_j)\right] f_i(s)$$

$$F(p) = (F_1(p), F_2(p), \ldots, F_n(p)).$$

Even though situations are the product of mixed strategies, commitments can only be made in pure strategies: i.e., g must be subtracted from f. If a commitment g is made in pure strategies, payoffs to mixed strategies are given by:

$$(F_i - G_i)(p) = \sum_{s \in S} \left[\prod_{j=1}^{n} p_j(s_j) \right] (f_i - g_i)(s)$$

so

$$G_i(p) = \sum_{s \in S} \left[\prod_{j=1}^{n} p_j(s_j) \right] g_i(s). \tag{5}$$

If we take H_i to be the constraint on $G_i(\cdot)$ that there be some $g_i(\cdot)$ that satisfies (5), then $\langle I, P, F, H \rangle^{**}$ is a constrained commitment game of the type that has been the subject of this appendix.

We are interested, then, in the circumstances under which (G,p) will be an equilibrium of $\langle I, P, F, H \rangle^{**}$. Through (5), though, every pure strategy commitment pattern g determines uniquely a mixed strategy commitment pattern G. Thus it will not be a serious abuse of notation to speak of (g,p) as an equilibrium of $\langle I, P, F, H \rangle^{**}$ if (G,p) is an equilibrium and G is derived from g by (5). Such notation is considerably more convenient.

We will proceed by several lemmas to show that equilibria in these mixed strategy games are merely probability combinations of pure strategy equilibria.

Lemma B-7. If (g,p) is an equilibrium of $\langle I, P, F, H \rangle^{**}$ and $s \notin A(i,g)$ in $\langle I, S, f - g \rangle$ for some i, then $\Pi_{j=1}^{n} p_j(s_j) \triangleq p(s) = 0$.

Proof. Suppose $s \notin A(i,g)$. Then there is some $\hat{s}_i \in S_i$ such that

$$(f_i - g_i)(\hat{s}_i, s_{-i}) > (f_i - g_i)(s).$$

If $p_i(s_i) = 0$, then $p(s) = 0$ and there is nothing more to prove. So suppose $p_i(s_i) > 0$. Then define $\hat{p}_i(\cdot)$ in the following manner:

$$\hat{p}_i(s_i) = 0$$

$$\hat{p}_i(\hat{s}_i) = p_i(\hat{s}_i) + p_i(s_i)$$

$$\hat{p}_i(\tilde{s}_i) = p_i(\tilde{s}_i) \quad \text{otherwise}$$

Then

$$\begin{aligned}(F_i - G_i)(\hat{p}_i, p_{-i}) = (F_i - G_i)(p) - \prod_{j \neq i} p_j(s_j)[&p_i(s_i)(f_i - g_i)(s) \\ &+ p_i(\hat{s}_i)(f_i - g_i)(\hat{s}_i, s_{-i}) \\ &- (p_i(\hat{s}_i) + p_i(s_i))(f_i - g_i)(\hat{s}_i, s_{-i})] \\ = (F_i - G_i)(p) + p(s)[(f_i - g_i)&(\hat{s}_i, s_{-i}) - (f_i - g_i)(s)]\end{aligned}$$

which is greater than $(F_i - G_i)(p)$ unless $p(s) = 0$. Thus unless $p(s) = 0$, p will not be acceptable to i in $\langle I, P, F - G \rangle$ and hence (g,p) will not be an equilibrium. ∎

Lemma B-8. If (g,p) is an equilibrium of $\langle I, P, F, H\rangle^{**}$ and $s \in B(i,g)$ (in $\langle I, S, f\rangle^{*}$), then

$$F_i(p) \leq f_i(s).$$

Proof. We first show that $p(\hat{s}) > 0$ only if $\hat{s} \in P(i,g)$. For suppose $s' \notin P(i,g)$. Then $s' \notin A(i,g)$ for some i and hence by Lemma B-7, $p(s') = 0$.

Thus $F(p)$ is a weighted average of $f_i(\hat{s})$ for $\hat{s} \in P(i,g)$. But by definition of goodness

$$f_i(s) \geq f_i(\hat{s}) \quad \text{for all } \hat{s} \in P(i,g).$$

Thus $f_i(s)$ is greater than any weighted average of $f_i(\hat{s})$. ■

Lemma B-9. If (g,p) is an equilibrium of $\langle I, P, F, H\rangle^{**}$ and $s \in B(i,g)$, then

$$(F_i - G_i)(p) \geq f_i(s).$$

Proof. Suppose $(F_i - G_i)(p) < f_i(s)$, $s \in B(i,g)$. We will construct a $(\hat{g},\hat{p})$ that beats (g,p) through i. Construct $\hat{p}$ as

$$\hat{p}_j(s_j) = 1 \qquad \text{for all } j.$$

Construct $\hat{g}$ as

$$\begin{aligned} \hat{g}_j &= g_j && \text{for all } j \neq i \\ \hat{g}_i(s) &= 0 \\ \hat{g}_i(\tilde{s}) &= f_i(\tilde{s}) && \text{for all } \tilde{s} \neq s. \end{aligned}$$

It is easy to see that

$$(F_i - \hat{G}_i)(\hat{p}) = f_i(s) > (F_i - G_i)(p);$$

thus we need only show that $\hat{p} \in N(\hat{G})$.

Since

$$(F_i - \hat{G}_i)(\hat{p}) = f_i(s) \geq (F_i - \hat{G}_i)(\tilde{p}_i, \hat{p}_{-i}) = \tilde{p}_i(s) f_i(s) \quad \text{for all } \tilde{p}_i$$

we know that $\hat{p} \in A(i, \hat{G})$.

For $j \neq i$, it follows from $s \in B(i,g)$ that $s \in P(i,g)$ and $s \in A(j,g)$; that is

$$(f_j - g_j)(s) \geq (f_j - g_j)(\tilde{s}_j, s_{-j}), \quad \forall \tilde{s}_j \in S_j.$$

Then

$$\begin{aligned} (F_j - \hat{G}_j)(\hat{p}) = (f_j - g_j)(s) &\geq (F_j - \hat{G}_j)(\tilde{p}_j, \hat{p}_{-j}) \\ &= \sum_{\tilde{s}_j \in S_j} \tilde{p}_j(\tilde{s}_j)(f_j - g_j)(\tilde{s}_j, s_{-j}) \end{aligned}$$

and hence $\hat{p} \in A(j, \hat{G})$. Thus $\hat{p} \in N(\hat{G})$ and $(\hat{g},\hat{p})$ beats (g,p) through i. ■

Lemma B-10. If (g, p) is an equilibrium of $\langle I, P, F, H\rangle^{**}$ and $s \in B(i, g)$, then

$$f_i(s) = F_i(p) \quad \text{and} \quad G_i(p) = 0.$$

Proof. From Lemmas B-8 and B-9, if (g, p) is an equilibrium and $s \in B(i, g)$,

$$(F_i - G_i)(p) \geq f_i(s) \geq F_i(p).$$

Thus

$$G_i(p) = 0 \quad \text{and} \quad f_i(s) = F_i(p).$$

■

Theorem B-4. If (g, p) is an equilibrium of $\langle I, P, F, H\rangle^{**}$ and $p(s) > 0$, then (g, s) is an equilibrium of $\langle I, S, f\rangle^{*}$, and $(F - G)(p) = F(p) = f(s)$.

Proof. Since (g, p) is an equilibrium and $p(s) > 0$, it follows from Lemma B-7 that $s \in A(j, g)$ for all j and $s \in P(i, g)$ for all i.

Suppose, then, that for some i, $s \notin B(i, g)$. Since $P(i, g)$ is not empty, it contains some $\hat{s}$ which is good:

$$\hat{s} \in B(i, g), \; f_i(\hat{s}) > f_i(s).$$

By Lemma B-10

$$f_i(\hat{s}) = F_i(p). \tag{6}$$

By Lemma B-7, $p(\tilde{s}) > 0$ only if $\tilde{s} \in N(g)$; thus

$$F_i(p) = p(\hat{s}) f_i(\hat{s}) + p(s) f_i(s) + \sum_{\substack{\tilde{s} \in N(g) \\ \tilde{s} \neq s \\ \tilde{s} \neq \hat{s}}} p(\tilde{s}) \, f_i(\tilde{s}).$$

Since $p(s) > 0$, $p(\hat{s}) + \Sigma p(\tilde{s}) < 1$. Since $\tilde{s} \in N(g)$, $\tilde{s} \in P(i, g)$ and $f_i(\hat{s}) \geq f_i(\tilde{s})$, since $\hat{s}$ is good, and $f_i(\hat{s}) > f_i(s)$.

Thus $F_i(p) > f_i(\hat{s})$ which contradicts (6).

Thus we must conclude that $s \in B(i, g)$ for all i and hence (g, s) is an equilibrium of $\langle I, S, f\rangle^{*}$. Since $s \in B(i, g)$, for all i, Lemma B-10 requires

$$f(s) = F(p) \quad \text{and} \quad G(p) = 0.$$

■

Theorem B-5. If (g, s) is an equilibrium of $\langle I, S, f\rangle^{*}$ and p is given by

$$p_i(s) = 1 \quad \textit{for all } i$$

then (g, p) is an equilibrium of $\langle I, P, F, H\rangle^{**}$.

Proof. Suppose (g, s) is an equilibrium of $\langle I, S, f\rangle^*$. We must show:

(a) $p \in N(G)$ and
(b) (g, p) is not beaten.

Ad (a). We must show $p \in A(i, G)$ for all i. Suppose $p \notin A(i, G)$ for some i. Then there must be some $\hat{s}_i \in S_i$ such that increasing $p(\hat{s}_i, s_{-i})$ and correspondingly decreasing $p(s)$ increases $(F_i - G_i)(\cdot)$. But this can be the case only if

$$(f_i - g_i)(\hat{s}_i, s_{-i}) > (f_i - g_i)(s)$$

i.e., only if $s \notin A(i, g)$. But if $s \notin A(i, g)$, $s \notin N(g)$, and (g, s) is not an equilibrium. Since this contradicts our hypothesis, we have shown that $p \in N(g)$.

Ad (b). Suppose $(\hat{g}, \hat{p})$ beats (g, p) through player i. Then

$$(F_i - \hat{G}_i)(\hat{p}) > (F_i - G_i)(p) = f_i(s)$$

so that

$$F_i(\hat{p}) > f_i(s).$$

Then there must be some $\hat{s}$ for which $f_i(\hat{s}) > f_i(s)$ and $\hat{p}(\hat{s}) > 0$. Since $f_i(\hat{s}) > f_i(s)$, and $s \in B(i, g)$, $\hat{s} \notin P(i, g)$; thus there must be some $j \neq i$ for whom $\hat{s} \in A(j, g)$. Since $\hat{g}_j = g_j$ by definition of beating

$$\hat{s} \notin A(j, \hat{g})$$

and so there is some $\tilde{s}_j \in S_j$ for which

$$(f_j - \hat{g}_j)(\tilde{s}_j, \hat{s}_{-j}) > (f_j - \hat{g}_j)(\hat{s}).$$

Since $\hat{p}(\hat{s}) > 0$, $\hat{p}_j(\hat{s}_j) > 0$. Consider $\tilde{p}_j(\cdot)$ defined by

$$\begin{aligned} \tilde{p}_j(\tilde{s}_j) &= \hat{p}_j(\tilde{s}_j) + \hat{p}_j(\hat{s}_j) \\ \tilde{p}_j(\hat{s}_j) &= 0 \\ \tilde{p}_j(\bar{s}_j) &= \hat{p}_j(\bar{s}_j) \qquad \text{otherwise} \end{aligned}$$

Then

$$\begin{aligned} (F_j - \hat{G}_j)(\tilde{p}_j, \hat{p}_{-j}) &= (F_j - \hat{G}_j)(\hat{p}) + \prod_{k \neq j} \hat{p}_k(\hat{s}_k) \times \\ &\qquad [\hat{p}_j(\hat{s}_j)(f_j - \hat{g}_j)(\tilde{s}_j, \hat{s}_{-j}) - \hat{p}_j(\hat{s}_j)(f_j - \hat{g}_j)(\hat{s})] \\ &= (F_j - \hat{G}_j)(\hat{p}) + \hat{p}(\hat{s})[(f_j - \hat{g}_j)(\tilde{s}_j, \hat{s}_{-j}) - (f_j - \hat{g}_j)(\hat{s})] \\ &> (F_j - \hat{G}_j)(\hat{p}), \end{aligned}$$

so that $\hat{p} \notin A(j, \hat{G})$. Hence $\hat{p} \notin N(\hat{G})$ and (g, p) is not beaten. ∎

Thus we see from Theorems B-4 and B-5 that the pure-strategy game $\langle I, S, f\rangle^*$ tells us practically everything we need to know about the constrained mixed-strategy extension $\langle I, P, F, H\rangle^{**}$. All equilibria in the pure-strategy game are equilibria in the mixed, and the only equilibria in the mixed game that are not equilibria in the pure are probability combinations of equilibria in the pure. Payoffs are always the same, and when a pure commitment pattern has only one situation in equilibrium with it, the correspondence is perfect.

IV

We have seen that the axiom of free disposal of utility is not unduly restrictive. Equilibria from free-disposal games carry over easily into constrained-disposal games, and constrained-disposal games have equilibria unrelated to free-disposal equilibria only in fairly rare circumstances. Moreover, for every constrained-disposal game $\langle I, S, f, H\rangle^{**}$ there is a free-disposal game $\langle I, S, f^*\rangle^*$ that behaves the same way.

Since plausible constraints on commitments are hard to come by, free-disposal presents no serious problem.

C ▪ Newcomb's Problem

"Timeo Danäos et dona ferentes"
Virgil, *Aeneid*

Suppose that a superior being has appeared on Earth, with all the appropriate science-fiction trappings, and claimed to be able to predict flawlessly what human beings will do. Its claim has been tested on a fabulously large number of occasions, and never been found to be false.

One day it approaches you and puts two boxes in front of you. In box 1 it puts $1,000. You cannot see what it put in box 2, but this is what it tells you: "You may take either box 2 alone and keep its contents, or take both boxes and keep their contents. But remember this: if I predicted that you would take box 2 only I put $1 million in it; if I predicted that you would take both boxes, box 2 is empty. So long now." Then it leaves.

You sit and ponder. In a while, two wise and trusted friends stop by. You explain the situation and ask their advice. The first says, "Maximize your expected utility. Taking both boxes almost certainly results in getting $1,000. Taking only box 2 almost certainly yields $1 million. Therefore, take only box 2." The second friend says, "Taking both boxes is a sure thing. Whatever the predictor did (and it's done now), you're $1,000 better off if you take both boxes. If it put $1 million in box 2, taking both boxes gives you $1,001,000 but taking box 2 only gives you only $1 million. If it didn't put anything in box 2, taking both boxes gives you $1,000 but taking box 2 only gives you nothing. So take both."

The first friend replies: "Thousands of people just like you have gone through this experiment. Everyone who took only what was in box 2 ended up with $1 million. Everyone who listened to the sure-thing argument and took both boxes ended up with $1,000. All of them were no more predictable and no smarter than you."

The second friend replies: "The predictor has already made its prediction, placed the $1 million in the box or not, and left—all this happened an hour ago. Box 1 is transparent. You and I both see $1,000 sitting there. You do not know what is in box 2, but you do know that what is there now is exactly the same thing that was there an hour ago. If the money is already there, it will stay there whatever you choose. It is not going to disappear. If it is not already in the box, your choosing only box 2 will not make it suddenly appear. So why should you pass up the $1,000 which you plainly see?"

I

This is Newcomb's problem. It was first brought to public attention by Nozick (1970), and has been the subject of a rising level of discussion since then. The apparent conflict between the expected utility maxim and the sure-thing maxim has intrigued philosophers, and supporters of neither side have claimed a clear-cut victory. Snow (1976) and Horgan (1981) have argued for the expected utility maxim (take box 2 only), while Nozick, in his original discussion, tentatively supported the sure-thing maxim (take both boxes). Gibbard and Harper (1978), Lewis (1979), Cartwright (1979), and Skryms (1980) have also argued for the sure-thing maxim.

Taking both boxes is what one would do if the rest of the world satisfied secularity, as it usually does in such circumstances. It is only because the predictor's fantastic past record raises questions about whether secularity still holds that one can entertain the single-box solution. After all, the argument for that solution is that the predictor cares what we do, and therefore has arranged or will arrange matters so that if we take both boxes box 2 will be empty.

II

A game-theoretic analysis can make all these points quite clear, and illuminate the matter far better than a discussion in decision-theoretic terms. Newcomb's problem is largely a game of strategy, and should not be treated, as philosophers have been wont to treat it, as a game against nature. As a game, Newcomb's problem is quite easy to deal with, and we will not even need to consider commitments (other than Mother Nature's).

The game tree for Newcomb's problem is presented in figure 11. Mother Nature moves first, and as usual we will assume that we know her commitment (on this last assumption, more later). Mother Nature's decision is whether or not the predictor has abnormal powers. If the predictor does not have abnormal powers (vertex x_2), then it moves next, decides whether or not to put $1 million in box 2, and after it acts you take either both boxes or box 2 only. If the predictor has abnormal powers (vertex x_1) you act first and then the predictor decides how much to put in box 2. When you move,

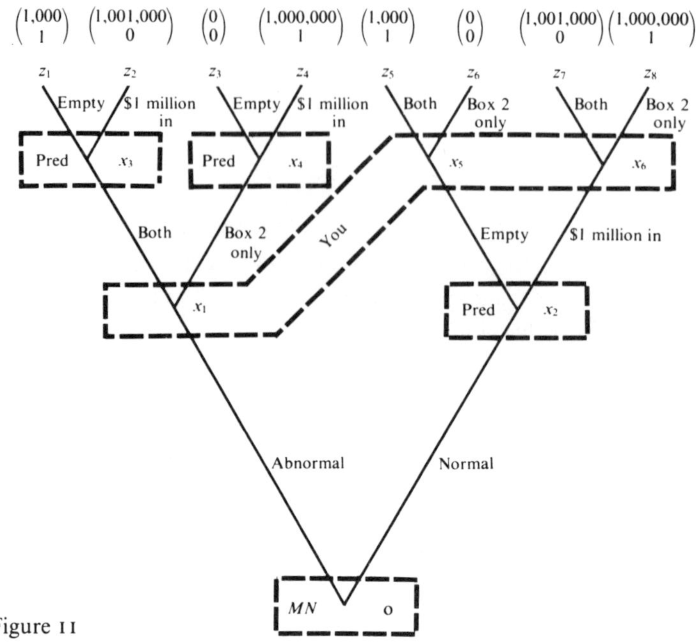

Figure 11

you do not know what Mother Nature and the predictor have done; thus all your vertices (x_1, x_5, and x_6) are in the same information set. Your payoffs (the top numbers in figure 11) are those given by the Newcomb story assuming you are risk neutral; the predictor's are derived from the assumption, which seems to be implicit in the Newcomb story, that it is merely trying to display technical virtuosity. Thus the predictor's payoff is one at those endpoints (z_1, z_4, z_5, and z_8) where it appears to have predicted correctly, and zero otherwise.

We will take a behavioral strategy for Mother Nature to be a probability p that the predictor has abnormal powers, a behavioral strategy for you to be a probability q of taking both boxes, and a behavioral strategy for the predictor to be a triplet (t_2, t_3, t_4) where t_i is the probability of leaving box 2 empty at the information set identical to vertex i. Thus the payoff functions for you and the predictor, $f^y(\cdot)$ and $f^p(\cdot)$ respectively, are:

$$f^y(p,q,t) = 1000\,pqt_3 + 1{,}001{,}000\,pq(1-t_3) + 1{,}000{,}000\,p(1-q)(1-t_4) + 1000\,(1-p)\,qt_2$$

$$+ 1{,}001{,}000(1-p)(1-t_2)q$$
$$+ 1{,}000{,}000(1-p)(1-q)(1-t_2)$$

$$f^P(p,q,t) = pqt_3 + p(1-q)(1-t_4) + (1-p)qt_2 + (1-p)(1-q)(1-t_2).$$

The perfect Nash equilibria of this game are:

Type 1: $p<.001,\ q=1,\ t_2=1,\ t_3=1,\ t_4=0$
Type 2: $p>.001,\ q=0,\ t_2=0,\ t_3=1,\ t_4=0$
Type 3: $p=.001,\ q<\frac{1}{2},\ t_2=0,\ t_3=1,\ t_4=0$
Type 4: $p=.001,\ q=\frac{1}{2},\ t_2\leq 1,\ t_3=1,\ t_4=0$
Type 5: $p=.001,\ q>\frac{1}{2},\ t_2=1,\ t_3=1,\ t_4=0$

Thus when there is a significant chance that Mother Nature has given the predictor abnormal powers (type 2), the predictor is rational to put $1 million in box 2 as long as it does not see that you will take both boxes, and you are rational to take only box 2. When the chance that Mother Nature has given the predictor abnormal powers is insignificant (type 1), then the predictor will be rational to leave box 2 empty and you will be rational to take both boxes. When p is exactly .001, a variety of situations are possible.

III

Thus the key question is what is the probability that Mother Nature has given the predictor abnormal powers. Whether the sure-thing maxim or the expected utility maxim holds sway over decision theory is entirely irrelevant. The question that matters is extra-rational, as we termed it in chapter 5, and answerable only in the realm of science and epistemology.

Our analysis of rationality can provide some assistance, though, in answering this question, if only by indicating blind alleys. In particular, it shows that the predictor's record of making correct predictions shows almost nothing about the value of p. From the perfect Nash equilibria we can see that as long as $p \neq .001$ the predictor will always be right. Even if $p = .001$ (an event of zero probability in some sense), the predictor will be right at least 50% of the time and possibly all the time. I myself could compile a perfect record as a predictor like this.

References

Ackermann, R.J.

1960 "Simplicity and the acceptability of scientific theories," Ph.D. dissertation, Michigan State University.

Arrow, Kenneth J.

1951 "Alternative approaches to the theory of choice in risk-taking situations," *Econometrica*, 19, 404–438.

1973 "The theory of discrimination," pp. 13–33 in Orley Ashenfelter and Albert Rees, eds., *Discrimination in Labor Markets*, Princeton, Princeton University Press.

1978 "The future and the present in economic life," *Economic Inquiry*, 16, 157–169.

______, and Frank Hahn

1971 *General Competitive Analysis*, Amsterdam, North Holland.

Aumann, Robert J.

1961 "The core of a cooperative game without side payments," *Transactions of the American Mathematical Society*, 98, pp. 539–552.

1964 "Markets with a continuum of traders," *Econometrica*, 32, 39–50.

______, and Michael Maschler

1964 "The bargaining set for cooperative games," pp. 443–447 in Dresher, Shapley, and Tucker.

______, and Lloyd S. Shapley

1974 *Values of Non-Atomic Games*, Princeton, Princeton University Press.

______, and Mordecai Kurz

1977 "Power and taxes," *Econometrica*, 45, 1137–1161.

Azariadis, Costas

1981 "Self-fulfilling prophecies," *Journal of Economic Theory*, 25, 380–396.

Barro, Robert J., and Herschel I. Grossman

1971 "A general disequilibrium model of income and employment," *American Economic Review*, 61, 82–93.

Becker, Gary

1968 "Crime and punishment: An economic approach," *Journal of Political Economy*, 76, 169–217.

Benassy, J-P

1975 "Neokeynesian disequilibrium in a monetary economy," *Review of Economic Studies*, 42, 502–523.

Blackwell, David and M.A. Girshick

1954 *Theory of Games and Statistical Decisions*, New York, Wiley.

Boehm, Volker, and P. Lévine
1976 "Temporary equilibrium with quantity rationing," CORE Discussion Paper 7614, Louvain, Belgium.

Borel, Émile
1924 "À propos d'un traité de probabilités," *Revue Philosophique*, 98, 321–336; reprinted in *Pratique et Philosophie des Probabilités* by Borel, 1939, Paris, Gauthier-Villars; translated by Smokler in Kyburg and Smokler (1964), 44–60.

Boyd, Richard
1973 "Underdetermination and a causal theory of evidence," *Noûs*, 7, 1–12.

Braithwaite, Richard B.
1955 *Scientific Explanation: A Study of the Function of Theory, Probability, and Law in Science*, Cambridge, Cambridge University Press.

Cartwright, Nancy
1979 "Causal laws and effective strategies," *Noûs*, 8, 419–437.

Clower, R.W.
1965 "The Keynesian counterrevolution: a theoretical appraisal," in F.H. Hahn and F. Brechling, eds., *The Theory of Interest Rates*, London, Macmillan.

Debreu, Gerard
1962 "New concepts and techniques for equilibrium analysis," *International Economic Review*, 3, 257–273.

———, and H. Scarf
1963 "A limit theorem on the core of an economy," *International Economic Review*, 4, 235–246.

Doeringer, Peter B., and Michael Piore
1971 *Internal Labor Markets and Manpower Analysis*, Lexington, Mass., D.C. Health.

Drazen, Allan
1980 "Recent developments in macroeconomics disequilibrium theory," *Econometrica*, 48, 283–306.

Dresher, Melvin, Lloyd Shapley, and A.W. Tucker, eds.
1964 *Advances in Game Theory*, Princeton, Princeton University Press.

Drèze, Jacques H.
1960 "Les probabilités subjectives ont-elles une signification subjective," *Economie Appliqué*, 13, 55–70.
1961 "Les fondements logiques de l'utilité cardinale et de la probabilité subjective," pp. 73–87 in *La Décision*, Paris, Centre National de la Recherche Scientifique.
1971 "Individual decision making under partially controllable uncertainty," Ph.D. dissertation, Columbia University, New York.
1972 "Econometrics and decision theory," *Econometrica*, 40, 1–17.
1975 "Existence of an equilibrium under price rigidity and quantity rationing," *International Economic Review*, 16, 301–320.

Edgeworth, Francis Ysidro
1881 *Mathematical Psychics*, London, C. Kegan Paul.

Fisher, Franklin
1976 "The stability of general equilibrium: results and problems," pp. 3–29 in Michael

Artis and Robert Nobay, eds., *Essays in Economic Analysis*, Cambridge, Cambridge University Press.

Freeman, Richard B.

1976 *Black Elite: The New Market for Highly Educated Black Americans*, New York, McGraw-Hill.

Gibbard, Allan

1973 "Manipulation of voting schemes: a general result," *Econometrica*, 41, 587–602.

1977 "Manipulation of schemes that mix voting with chance," *Econometrica*, 45, 665–681.

1978 "Straightforwardness of games with lotteries as outcomes," *Econometrica*, 46, 595–614.

———, and William Harper

1978 "Counterfactuals and two kinds of expected utility," pp. 155 et seq. in C.A. Hooker, J.J. Leach, and E.F. McClennen, eds., *Foundation and Applications of Decision Theory*, vol. 1, Boston, Reidel.

Gillies, D.B.

1953 "*Some theorems on n-person games*," Ph.D. dissertation, Princeton University, Princeton.

Glicksberg, I.L.

1952 "A further generalization of the Kakutani fixed point theorem, with application to Nash equilibrium points," *Proceedings of the American Mathematical Society*, 3, 170–172.

Goodman, Nelson

1958 "The test of simplicity," *Science*, 78, 1064–1069.

Hildenbrand, Werner

1970 "On economies with many agents," *Journal of Economic Theory*, 2, 161–188.

1974 *Core and Equilibria of a Large Economy*, Princeton, Princeton University Press.

Hobbes, Thomas

1651 *Leviathan: or the Matter, Form, and Power of a Commonwealth, Ecclesiastical and Civil*, London.

Horgan, Terence

1981 "Counterfactuals and Newcomb's problem," *Journal of Philosophy*, 78, 331–355.

Ito, Takatoshi

1980 "Methods of estimation for multi-market disequilibrium models," *Econometrica*, 48, 97–125.

Jourdain, Philip E.B.

1918 *The Philosophy of Mr B*rtr*nd R*ss*ll*, London, G. Allen & Unwin.

Kemeny, John G.

1955 "Two measures of simplicity," *Philosophical Review*, 57.

Keynes, John Maynard

1921 *A Treatise on Probability*, London & New York, Macmillan. Reprinted for the Royal Economic Society, 1973, New York, St. Martin's Press.

1936 *The General Theory of Employment, Interest and Money*, New York, Harcourt Brace.

1937 "The General Theory of Employment," *Quarterly Journal of Economics*, 51, 209–223.

Knight, Frank H.

1921 *Risk, Uncertainty and Profit*, New York, Houghton Mifflin.

Kuhn, H.W.

1953 "Extensive games and the problem of information," pp. 193–216, in Kuhn and Tucker.

Kuhn, Howard W. and A.W. Tucker, eds.

1953 *Contributions to the Theory of Games II*, vol. 28 in *Annals of Mathematics Studies*, Princeton, Princeton University Press.

Kyburg, Henry E., Jr.

1961 *Probability and the Logic of Rational Belief*. Middletown, Connecticut, Wesleyan University Press.

Kyburg, Henry E., Jr. and H.G. Smokler, eds.

1964 *Studies in Subjective Probability*, New York, Wiley.

Kydland, Finn E.

1977 "Equilibrium solutions in dynamic dominant-player models," *Journal of Economic Theory*, 15, 307–324.

———, and Edward C. Prescott

1977 "Rules rather than discretion: the inconsistency of optimal plans," *Journal of Political Economy*, 85, 473–491.

Leijonhufvud, Axel

1968 *On Keynesian Economics and the Economics of Keynes: A Study in Monetary Theory*, London, New York, and Toronto, Oxford University Press.

1976 "Schools, revolution and research programmes in economic theory," pp. 65–108 in Spiro Latsis, ed., *Method and Appraisal in Economics*, Cambridge, Cambridge University Press.

Lewis, David

1979 "Prisoners' dilemma is a Newcomb problem," *Philosophy and Public Affairs*, 8, 235–240.

Lucas, William F.

1968 "A game with no solution," *Bulletin of the American Mathematical Society*, 7, 237–239.

Luce, R. Duncan

1955 "Ψ-stability: a new equilibrium concept for n-person games," pp. 32–44 in *Mathematical Models of Human Behavior*, Stamford, Dunlap and Associates.

———, and Howard Raiffa

1957 *Games and Decisions: Introduction and Critical Survey*, New York, Wiley.

Malinvaud, Edmond

1977 *The Theory of Unemployment Reconsidered*, Oxford, Basil Blackwell.

Nash, John F.

1950 "Equilibrium points in n-person games," *Proceedings of the National Academy of Sciences of the USA*, 36, 48–49.

1951 "Non-cooperative games," *Annals of Mathematics*, 54, 286–295.

von Neumann, John

1928 "Zur theorie der gesellschaftsspiele," *Mathematische Annalen*, 100, 295–320. Translated by Sonya Bergmann, "On the theory of games of strategy," pp. 13–42 in Tucker and Luce, 1959.

1953 "Communication on the Borel notes," *Econometrica*, 21, pp. 124–125.

______, and Oskar Morgenstern

1944 *Theory of Games and Economic Behavior*, Princeton, Princeton University Press.

Nikaidô, Hukukane and Kazuo Isoda

1955 "Note on noncooperative convex games," *Pacific Journal of Mathematics*, 5, 807–815.

Nishino, H.

1970 "Kohan-Keisai no Core to Sono Kyokugunteiri" (The cores of exchange economies and the limit theorems), pp. 131–168 in M. Suzuki, ed., *Kyoso-shaksi no Game no Riror* (*Theory of Games in Competitive Society*), Tokyo, Keiso-shobo.

Nozick, Robert

1970 "Newcomb's problem and two principles of choice," in N. Rescher, ed., *Essays in Honor of Carl G. Hempel*, Dordrecht, Holland, D. Reidel.

1974 *Anarchy, State, and Utopia*, New York, Basic.

Owen, Guillermo

1968 *Game Theory*, Philadelphia, Saunders.

Poincaré, Henri

1908 *Science et Méthode*, Paris. Translated by Francis Maitland, 1914, New York, Dover.

Putnam, Hilary

1975 *Mind, Language and Reality*, New York, Cambridge University Press.

Reichenbach, Hans

1968 *The Philosophy of Space and Time*, New York, Dover.

Rudner, Richard S.

1961 "An introduction to simplicity," *Philosophy of Science*, 28.

1966 *Philosophy of Social Science*, Englewood Cliffs, N.J., Prentice-Hall.

Samuelson, Paul

1958 "An exact consumption-loan model of interest with or without the social contrivance of money," *Journal of Political Economy*, 66, 467–482.

Satterthwaite, Mark A.

1975 "Strategy-proofness and Arrow's conditions: Existence and correspondence theorems for voting procedures and social welfare functions," *Journal of Economic Theory*, 10, 185–217.

Schelling, Thomas C.

1960 *The Strategy of Conflict*, Cambridge, Harvard University Press.

Schotter, Andrew

1981 *The Economic Theory of Social Institutions*, Cambridge, Cambridge University Press.

Selten, Reinhard

1975 "Reexamination of the perfectness concept for equilibrium points in extensive games," *International Journal of Game Theory*, 4, 25–55.

Shackle, G.L.S.

1949 *Expectation in Economics*, Cambridge, Cambridge University Press.

Shapley, Lloyd S.

1953 "A value for n-person games," pp. 307–318 in Kuhn and Tucker.

Shubik, Martin

1959 "Edgeworth market games," in Tucker and Luce.

1968 "Game Theory: Economic Applications," pp. 69–73 in vol. 6, *International Encyclopedia of the Social Sciences*, New York, Macmillan.

1975 "The general equilibrium model is incomplete and not adequate for the reconciliation of micro and macroeconomic theory," *Kyklos*, 28, 545–573.

Skryms, Brian

1980 *Causal Necessity*, New Haven, Yale University Press.

Snow, Paul

1976 "Newcomb's problem and the dominance principle," Framingham, Massachusetts, unpublished manuscript.

Sober, Elliott

1975 *Simplicity*, Oxford, Clarendon Press.

Thorburn, W.M.

1918 "The myth of Occam's Razor," *Mind*, 27, n.s., 345–353.

Tucker, A.W., and R. Duncan Luce

1959 *Contributions to the Theory of Games IV*, vol. 40 in *Annals of Mathematics Studies*, Princeton, Princeton University Press.

Ville, Jean

1938 "Note sur la théorie générale des jeux où intervient l'habilité des jouers," in "Applications aux jeux de hasard," by Émile Borel and Jean Ville, Tome IV, Fascicule II in Borel, *Traité du Calcul des Probabilités et de ses applications*, Paris, Gauthier-Villars.

Vorob'ev, Nikolai Nikolaevich

1977 *Game-theory*. Translated and supplemented by S. Kotz, New York and Berlin, Springer-Verlag.

Weitzman, M.L.

1982 "Increasing returns and the foundations of unemployment theory," *Economic Journal*, 92, 787–804.

Supplementary Bibliography

Barnett, Victor

1973 *Comparative Statistical Inference*, New York, Wiley.

Bernoulli, Jacques

1713 *Ars Conjectandi, opus posthumum*, Basileae. No English translation. German translation: *Wahrsheinlichkeitsrechnung*, 2 vol., 1899.

Black, Max

1968 "Probability," pp. 465–479 in *Encyclopedia of Philosophy*, P. Edwards, ed., vol. 6, London, Collier-MacMillan.

Carnap, Rudolf

1950 *Logical Foundations of Probability*, Chicago, University of Chicago Press. 2d ed., 1962.

Cournot, A.

1843 *Exposition de la Théorie des Chances et des Probabilités*, Paris, L. Hachette.

DeCanio, S.J.

1979 "Rational expectations and learning from experience," *Quarterly Journal of Economics*, 93, 47–57.

de Finetti, Bruno

1937 "La prévision: ses lois logiques, ses sources subjectives," *Annales de l'Institut Henri Poincaré*, 7, 1–68; translated by Kyburg in Kyburg and Smokler (1964), 93–158.

1968 "Probability: Interpretations," pp. 496–505 in *International Encyclopedia of the Social Sciences*, vol. 12, New York, Macmillan.

Derksen, A.A.

1978 "Why probabilities are not assigned to propositions," *Mind*, 87, 250–256.

Ellis, R. Leslie

1843 "On the foundations of the theory of probability," *Transactions, Cambridge Philosophical Society*, 8.

Friedman, Benjamin M.

1979 "Optimal expectations and the extreme information assumptions of 'rational expectations' macro-models," *Journal of Monetary Economics*, 5, 23–41.

Jeffreys, Harold

1939 *Theory of Probability*, Oxford, Clarendon Press.

Kantor, Brian

1979 "Rational expectations and economic thought," *Journal of Economic Literature*, 17, 1422–1441.

Kolmogorov, A.N.

1933 *Grundbergriffe der Wahrscheinlichkeitrechnung*, Berlin, J. Springer. Translated by Nathan Morrison, *Foundations of the Theory of Probability*, New York, Chelsea Publishing Co., 1950.

Leamer, Edward E.

1978 *Specification Searches: Ad Hoc Inference with Nonexperimental Data*, New York, Wiley.

Lewis, Geoffrey

1981 "The Phillips curve and Bayesian learning," *Journal of Economic Theory*, 24, 240–264.

von Mises, Richard

1957 *Probability, Statistics and Truth*, 2d Eng. ed. London, George Allen & Unwin.

Muth, John F.

1961 "Rational expectations and the theory of price movements," *Econometrica*, 29, 315–335.

Pascal, Blaise

1950 *Pensées*, translated by H.F. Stewart, New York, Pantheon.

Port-Royal Logic

1662 *La Loguique, où l'Art de Penser, contenant, outre les regles communes, plusieurs observations nouvelles, propres à former le jugement*, Paris. Translated by T.S. Baynes, London, 1851. Often attributed to A. Arnauld and P. Nicole.

Ramsey, Frank P.

1931 *The Foundations of Mathematics and Other Logical Essays*, London, Routledge and Kegan Paul.

Reichenbach, Hans

1949 *Theory of Probability*, Berkeley, University of California Press.

Russell, Bertrand

1948 *Human Knowledge: Its Scope and Limits*, London, George Allen & Unwin.

Sargent, Thomas J. and Neil Wallace

1975 "'Rational expectations,' the optimal monetary instrument and the optimal money supply rule," *Journal of Political Economy*, 83, 241–254.

Savage, Leonard J.

1954 *The Foundations of Statistics*, New York, Wiley. 2d ed., 1962.

Suppes, Patrick

1968 "Decision Theory," pp. 310–313 in *Encyclopedia of Philosophy*, P. Edwards, ed., vol. 2, London, Collier-Macmillan.

Taylor, John B.

1975 "Monetary policy during transition to rational expectations," *Journal of Political Economy*, 83, 1009–1021.

Venn, John

1866 *The Logic of Chance*, London and Cambridge, Macmillan.

Index